Emotional Presence i

MW00719314

Emotional Presence in Psychoanalysis provides a detailed look at the intricacies of attaining emotional presence in psychoanalytic work. John Madonna and a distinguished group of contributors draw on both the relational and modern psychoanalytic schools of thought to examine a variety of different problems commonly experienced in achieving emotional resonance between analyst and patient, setting out ways in which such difficulties may be overcome in psychoanalytic treatment, practical clinical settings, and in training contexts.

A focused review of relevant comparative literature is followed by chapters featuring individual clinical case studies, each illustrating particularly challenging aspects. The uniqueness of this book lies not simply in the espousal of the commonly accepted importance of emotional resonance between analyst and patient; rather it is in the way in which emotional presence is registered by both participants, requiring a working through, which at times can be not only difficult but dangerous. Such efforts involve a theory which enables the lens to understanding, an effective methodology which guides intervention. The book also calls for the art of the analyst to construct with patients meanings which heal, and possess the heart to persist in commitment despite the odds. *Emotional Presence in Psychoanalysis* is about patients who suffer, struggle, resist, and prevail. It offers distinctive, transparently told accounts of analysts who engage with patients, navigating through states of confusion, hatred, and more controversial feelings of love.

Emotional Presence in Psychoanalysis features highly compelling material written in an accessible and easily understood style. It will be a valuable resource for psychoanalysts and psychoanalytic psychotherapists, psychologists, and clinical social workers as well as teachers, trainers, and students seeking to understand the power and potential of the analytic process and the resistances to it.

John Madonna is a licensed psychologist, training analyst, faculty member, and teacher at the Boston Graduate School of Psychoanalysis. He has written and presented papers on the treatment of children, adolescents, and adults. He is co-author of two books: *The Play Therapy Treatment of Sexually Abused Children* and *Treating Police Stress*.

"A rich anthology of writings by some of the most interesting thinkers in psychoanalysis today, *Emotional Presence in Psychoanalysis* beautifully conveys the therapeutic value of a consistent, focused attention by the analyst on the turbulent feelings of love and hate generated in both patient and analyst in the psychoanalytic session. It makes a powerful argument that the therapist's ability to acknowledge and tolerate all feelings frees the patient to resolve resistances to feeling, thinking, remembering, and saying everything, and it is this freedom that is ultimately curative."

–**Lucy Holmes**, Center for Modern Psychoanalytic Studies,
New York Graduate School of Psychoanalysis, author of
Wrestling with Destiny: The Promise of Psychoanalysis

"Particularly in reading the chapter Darkness of Night, dealing with the issue of emotional transparency between analyst and patient during times of the analyst's illness and potential demise, I was moved by Dr. Madonna's own descriptions of the loss of his father and his analyst and how those losses affected him. Beautifully written and fascinating."

–**Carl Fulwiler, MD, Ph.D.**, Professor of Psychiatry, University of
Massachusetts Medical School

"In this rich and insightful book, Dr. Madonna and his colleagues courageously share honest and often vulnerable descriptions of the psychoanalytic process. We are invited to learn from their wisdom and reflect upon the extent of our true emotional presence in relationships. As a clinician who enters in the therapeutic relationship with a cognitive-behavioral 'theoretical compass,' I was challenged at times to step out of my well-trodden path onto an unfamiliar territory. This was a journey well worth taking, and I highly recommend this book to everyone who is interested in exploration of and growth through healing relationships."

–**Monika Kolodziej, Ph.D.**, Clinical Psychologist

Emotional Presence in Psychoanalysis

Theory and clinical applications

Edited by
John Madonna

Routledge
Taylor & Francis Group

LONDON AND NEW YORK

First published 2017
by Routledge
2 Park Square, Milton Park, Abingdon, Oxon OX14 4RN

and by Routledge
711 Third Avenue, New York, NY 10017

Routledge is an imprint of the Taylor & Francis Group, an informa business

© 2017 selection and editorial matter, John Madonna; individual chapters, the contributors

The right of the editor to be identified as the author of the editorial material, and of the authors for their individual chapters, has been asserted in accordance with sections 77 and 78 of the Copyright, Designs and Patents Act 1988.

All rights reserved. No part of this book may be reprinted or reproduced or utilised in any form or by any electronic, mechanical, or other means, now known or hereafter invented, including photocopying and recording, or in any information storage or retrieval system, without permission in writing from the publishers.

Trademark notice: Product or corporate names may be trademarks or registered trademarks, and are used only for identification and explanation without intent to infringe.

British Library Cataloguing in Publication Data
A catalogue record for this book is available from the British Library

Library of Congress Cataloging in Publication Data
Names: Madonna, John M., editor.
Title: Emotional presence in psychoanalysis : theory and clinical applications / edited by John Madonna.
Description: Abingdon, Oxon ; New York, NY : Routledge, 2016. | Includes bibliographical references and index.
Identifiers: LCCN 2016001398 | ISBN 9781138889323 (hardback : alk. paper) | ISBN 9781138889330 (pbk. : alk. paper)
Subjects: LCSH: Psychotherapist and patient. | Transference (Psychology) | Psychoanalysis. | Psychotherapy.
Classification: LCC RC480.8 .E496 2016 | DDC 616.89/17--dc23
LC record available at http://lccn.loc.gov/2016001398

ISBN: 978-1-138-88932-3 (hbk)
ISBN: 978-1-138-88933-0 (pbk)
ISBN: 978-1-315-71295-6 (ebk)

Typeset in Times New Roman
by Taylor & Francis Books

Contents

Preface

Chapter 1 defines and sites the historical precedence for utility of emotional presence in psychoanalytic treatment. This eventuates into a consideration of three contemporary schools, the interpersonal, intersubjective, and modern analytic, and how each comes to understand and utilize, in effectively therapeutic ways, the emotional interplay in the analytic dyad. Chapter 2 is an early discussion by four theorists, who were master clinicians, describing how they grappled with the issue of attaining emotional presence in order to enter the psychic worlds of the seriously disordered patients with whom they worked.

In Part II of this book, Chapters 3 through 8, the authors present clinical cases in which they are tested by resistance, their own and those of their patients, in their efforts to establish resonance of feeling and the healing which is inherent.

The chapters of Part III are devoted to discussion of the intricacies of and challenges to facilitative emotional connection between supervisor and supervisee, university professor and students, as well as the analyst-instructor and analysand-student in training institutes. The final chapter examines the complexity of maintaining synchronicity of feeling and therapeutic purpose when the analyst is in a state of physical decline and psychological stress.

Acknowledgements

I would first like to express my gratitude to the patients whose stories are represented here. The poignancy of their struggles and courage in pursuing a better life is nothing short of heroic.

I would like to thank those who generously contributed to this work: Dr. June Bernstein, Dr. Danielle Egan, Dr. Daniel Gilhooley, Dr. Adrian Jarreau, Dr. Theodore Laquercia, and Dr. Jane Snyder. The depth of their clinical insight and talent in conveying that, combined with the keen capacity for realizing the power of emotional presence in the analytic encounter, is remarkably portrayed.

Thanks is given to *Modern Psychoanalysis*, the journal of the Center of Modern Psychoanalytic Studies, who gave permission to reuse the article material which forms the basis of Chapters 2–3 and 5–9, as well as *The Candidate* journal for kind permission to reprint the article upon which Chapter 10 is based.

A special thanks to Kate Hawes (Publisher), Kristen Buchanan (Senior Editorial Assistant), and Sue Wickenden (Editorial Assistant) at Routledge for their acceptance and support of this work. I would like to also express my gratitude to Charles Bath (Editorial Assistant) whose editorial expertise and diligence brought this work down the home stretch to completion. A special thanks also to Emily Boyd for her special effort in the final phase of editing this work.

I am indebted to the psychoanalysts and many supervisors and teachers at the Boston Graduate School for Psychoanalytic Studies who have analysed, supervised, and educated me. Most particularly, June Bernstein, Phyllis Meadow, and Ted Laquercia. I am grateful as well to Lynn Perlman and Faye Newsome for their guidance at various points over the years. Also, I am fortunate for and so appreciative of my many other colleagues and students who continue to inspire me.

Thanks also to Amy Cohen-Rose (Librarian) who was always responsive to my requests and invariably helpful. Thank you to Jennifer Jackson and Kara Mckeon, who were of great assistance in transcribing and editing this book.

I wish to acknowledge my appreciation to my Staten Island cousins who on our South Carolina excursions always made me laugh, even during some of the more difficult times in the writing of this work. A special thanks as well to the Higgins family in whose coastal Maine homes I was always met with affection and support.

Finally, I owe a great debt of gratitude to my wife Karen, children Mat, Kara, Jeff, Kathryn, and Iris, my sister Diane, as well as my many grandchildren who keep me grounded in the emotional importance of our lives together.

Contributors

June Bernstein, Ph.D., is Director of Public Information at the Center for Modern Psychoanalytic Studies, Dean of Students at the Boston Graduate School of Psychoanalysis, and co-editor of the journal, *Modern Psychoanalysis*. She is a faculty member, training analyst, and supervisor at both schools and practices in New York City and Boston. She has published numerous articles pertaining to the practice of psychoanalysis as well as the training of its practitioners.

Danielle Egan, Ph.D., is the Coordinator of Gender and Sexuality Studies at St. Lawrence University. She is the recipient of the Louis and Francis Maslow Award at St. Lawrence University, a Bok Fellow for Teaching Excellence at Harvard University, and the Donald White Teaching Excellence Award at Boston College. Dr. Egan is the author and co-author of books on sexualization, including *Dancing for Dollars: The Relationships between Exotic Dancers and their Regulars; Theorizing the Sexual Child in Modernity*; and *Sexual: A Critical Appraisal of Girls and Sexualization*. She is also the author of 30 professional articles on gender and sexuality. She is currently an analyst in training at the Boston Graduate School of Psychoanalysis.

Dan Gilhooley, Psya.D., is a licensed psychoanalyst in private practice in New York City and Bellport, New York. He is a faculty member at the Center for Modern Psychoanalytic Studies and a graduate of that institute, the Boston Graduate School of Psychoanalysis, and the C. Z. Meadow Institute. In 2007, Dr. Gilhooley was a research fellow in the psychoanalytic research program jointly sponsored by the Anna Freud Centre and the Yale Child Study. A visual artist with 18 one-person exhibitions, he was elected to the National Academy of Design in 1991. In 1995, he received a Gradiva Award for Art Advancing Psychoanalysis from the National Association for the Advancement of Psychoanalysis.

Adrian Jarreau, PsyA-FFPA, practices psychoanalysis in Seattle. He is a graduate of the Northwestern Psychoanalytic Society, where he is on the faculty and serves on the Board of Directors as Treasurer and on the Education Committee as Chair of Admissions.

Theodore Laquercia, Ph.D., is a faculty member, training analyst, and professor emeritus at the Boston Graduate School of Psychoanalysis and the Center for Modern Psychoanalytic Studies in Manhattan, New York. Dr. Laquercia is the past president at the Boston Graduate School of Psychoanalysis and the current president of the Society for Modern Analysts. He is the author of a number of professional articles.

John Madonna, Editor, Ed.D., is a licensed psychologist and certified psychoanalyst in private practice in Brookline and Worcester, Massachusetts. He is a faculty member and training analyst at the Boston Graduate School of Psychoanalysis. He has written and presented papers on the psychological treatment of children and adults and is the co-author of two books: *The Play Therapy Treatment of Sexually Abused Children* and *Treating Police Stress*. Dr. Madonna is also the founder and executive director of Chandler Psychological Services, which provides psychological services to numerous police and public safety agencies and religious organizations.

Jane Snyder, Ph.D., is a licensed psychologist and certified psychoanalyst and is the president of the Boston Graduate School of Psychoanalysis. She is a faculty member and training analyst and conducts a private practice in Brookline, Massachusetts. She has written and presented many papers on a variety of topics related to psychoanalytic treatment, and research including most recently an article entitled "Toward the better use of psychoanalytic concepts: A model illustrated using the concept of enactment" in the *International Journal of Psychoanalysis* and the *Journal of Analytic Psychology*.

Part 1

Chapter 1

Introduction: emotional presence in psychoanalysis

Theory and clinical applications

John Madonna

We know now that it is not understanding ascribed from without by a distant voice that cures the broken human spirit. It is the resonating presence of the other, without provocation, allowing and allowed. Reflecting and mirroring like the good mother, the analyst sharing the primordial dawning of experience, at times in soundless rhythms, beyond words. Then, the eventual coming forth of the longings, fears, the furies, the person separate and suffering in the encounter. And then the light of knowing, which grows within, in the mutual presence which enables advance in psychic development. But this journey can be long, at times perilous. The patient resists out of desperate fear and a need for stasis, and then a dreaded mix of powerful feelings to hate and destroy, to love and preserve—and so recoils, a shattered mind. In less serious, but still profound instances, the individual proceeds through life emotionally and interactionally impaired.

Emotional presence is the ability to sense, feel, and then think the experience of the patient. This occurs as a result of the processes of projection, projective identification, the analyst's objective counter transference, as well as the analyst's innate inclination for empathy. Also crucial is the ability and determination to see through the resistances which are prevalent, appreciate and believe in the patient's potential for health. It is fundamental for starting anew, the chance again to relive, and so reformulate, the beginnings of human psychic experience. Though the urge to do so has a pull which is built in, it is so strongly resisted not just because of the feelings which cannot be managed, but because the urge for endings which lies beneath them is so compelling. The desire for eternal sleep, as Shakespeare (1603) said, which is the "consummation devoutly to be wished for" (p. 626), takes hold in the face of inordinate challenge. Freud's (1920) theory of death drive is based on this.

So the efforts of the analyst to make and maintain presence need to be both wisely fashioned, and at times heroic. An analyst is present according to the capacity for attentiveness to the patient, in the tolerance of the patient's various dynamics, and in the skill of his understanding. With more integrated patients, interpretation may be employed aimed at the reasonable ego in an attempt to address the "afflicted ego" of the patient (Geltner, 2013, p. 161). In more serious cases emotional communication is more productive in addressing transferential conflict and challenge. In the broadest sense presence is whatever the patient needs to be held in treatment and to move toward eventual relatedness. That might mean little contact or much contact, intellectual or emotional resonance as the circumstance requires.

Beyond his primary method of analysis of transference and resistance, Freud (1913) emphasized the broader context of the analytic relationship in which encouragement and education was also used to support and reinforce the patient's progress. Freud's presence as a benignly interested authority figure is well documented and reflects his capacity for empathy (Gay, 1988). Certainly his emphasis on the immediacy and salience of encounter was inherent in his thinking about transference itself:

> Freud came to feel that the displacement of forbidden impulses and fantasies onto the person of the analyst is essential in helping the patient to experience and work through the issues as lived and deeply felt realities rather than intellectual abstractions and memories.
>
> (Mitchell & Black, 1995, p. 231)

Even in the classical tradition the classical analyst needs to be able to be present and remain so in order to receive the transference and not, as Josef Breuer did, flee from it. In being present the analyst, as an interested authority, comes to understand and can help the patient through interpretation (i.e. making the unconscious conscious) to realize the origins of the transference.

The analyst as a separate figure was apparent in the concept of the superego which Freud developed later. "Repression is instituted and maintained not just because the forbidden impulses are dangerous (the ego's concern) but because the child thinks they are wrong, evil, bad (the superego's concern)" (p. 238). When the analyst interprets the transference the curative effect is not just related to the lifting of repression but the availability of the analyst as a separate but interested entity in the present. This lessens the projective-introjective repetition which keeps the grip of the superego tight (p. 239). As the patient introjects the mediating aspects of the analyst, the patient's internal attitudes toward self and others become more realistic and less punitive.

In this regard Sandor Ferenzci did much to weaken the power of the superego by carrying the notion of the analyst's presence to an extreme, engaging in at least two known instances of sexual encounter with female patients (Stanton, 1991). The impropriety of such behavior notwithstanding he innovated a method of mutual analysis which was to be the harbinger of transparency which characterized the later interpersonal and intersubjective schools of analytic thought. This set the stage for the focus on countertransference as the site for intervention.

The analyst as a separate parenting presence is emphasized by contemporary object relations theorists, Freudian ego analysts, and self-psychologists. They "all agree that what is curative in the analytic relationship is the analyst's offering some form of basic parental responsiveness that was missed early on" (Mitchell & Black, 1995, p. 240). There are two trends to this thinking according to Mitchell and Black. They cite Strachey's belief that "normal analyzing is not an absence but a presence that provides missing parental responsiveness" (p. 240). They also cite Pine (1985) who says that "the very activities of reliable attendance, careful listening, thoughtful interpreting are usually similar enough to attentive parenting to reanimate the stalled developmental process" (p. 240), which elevates transference dynamics for interpretative action.

Another trend of thought asserts that the analyst must be even more active in intervening, "has to do something different from ordinary interpreting, to create, in the analytic situation real experience that evokes the specific missed provision of childhood … to be more available … to respond to their needs in a more individualized way" (p. 240). Winnicott's altering of the environment and highly personalized intervention (Little, 1985) and Kohut's (1984) mirroring of patients with specific kinds of self-deficits are examples. The interpersonal tradition advocated honesty in the authentic here and now encounter. And it was in the working of the countertransferential field that these theorists made a tremendous impact. "Fromm felt that the analyst's frank and honest reactions were just what the patient needed to know about and understand … (through) judicious and constructive disclosure" (Mitchell & Black, 1995, pp. 244–245).

In line with this "Sullivan regarded the basic unit of the mind as an inter-actional field rather than as a bounded individual" (Mitchell & Black, 1995, p. 244). The Kleinian notion of projective identification, and the counter-transference play that results, "regards the analyst's experience as the site where the patient's dynamics are to be discovered and recognized … a key device for gaining access to the repetitive self object configurations of the patient's internal mold" (p. 245). Working through the transference and countertransference neurosis is considered to be the fundamental core of the analytic work (p. 245). Neo Freudians (i.e. Chused, 1989; Jacobs, 1991) as well as some self-psychologists (i.e. Kohut, 1984; Stolorow, Branschaft, & Atwood, 1987) and others (i.e. Aron, 1991; Bleckner, 1992; Hoffman, 1983) also espouse the view of the utility of the analyst's versatile presence in the countertransference process in enabling the patient to gain therapeutic comfort with him/herself and for the eventual giving up of the transferential repetition.

The patient gaining comfort with the self is an important aspect of cure and while Pine (1990) asserts interpretation in the transference as central, the process of change he says also occurs "in the context of intense and intimate relationship where things matter for the patient, both verbal interventions and relational factors" (p. 255). This is not always easily achieved.

The difficulty associated with being present in the face of early pathology is well documented by practitioners in the Modern School of Psychoanalysis (Bernstein, 1992, 2013; Holmes, 2013; Liegner, 1995; Margolis, 1994; Spotnitz,

1985). Less concerned about the use of interpretation as primary, Hymen Spotnitz (1985) set the standard for establishing therapeutic presence with those individuals suffering severe narcissistic injury, merging across the fluid ego boundaries which characterize the preoedipal psyche. By measured responses to the patient's contact function (i.e. the manner by which the patient makes verbal or non-verbal contact with the analyst), the analyst provides an interactional environment which is not overly stimulating. It is an environment which respects the narcissistic defense constructed to prevent hostile destructive impulses from being enacted toward the objects in the patient's mind, as well as in the patient's actual world. Spotnitz asserted that by innovative processes of joining (i.e. allowing, accepting, and agreeing with what the patient presents in terms of non-verbal and verbal communication) and reflecting (i.e. echoing, reiterating, mirroring communications) of the patient's resistance to verbally focused relationship, verbal communication could eventually occur. Processes of joining and reflecting give the necessary and reassuring impression that the analyst is like the patient. This can at times, however, as Spotnitz (1969, p. 40) says, lead to a "torrent of threats, insults and verbal abuse" toward the analyst, as the inherent hostility embedded in the joining and reflection is expressed back and results in increases of intensity.

The extent to which the analyst is able to receive and tolerate the patient's expression of such feelings, often murderous, sustained by a persistent caring interest in the patient's mental health, will result in a growing realization by the patient that his words do not injure or destroy. The narcissistic defense then becomes unnecessary. In the caldron of numerous such exchanges, and increased tolerance for them, the patient comes to be able to differentiate those which had their origins during the preoedipal phase of development when self and object impressions were merged and confused, and more clearly defined later stages. Object relatedness occurs after that early hostility and rage, having found suitable expression, frees the individual to be able to experience more affectionate feelings.

Echoing Spotnitz, Meadow (2005) affirms the need for the analyst to conduct analysis "with the conviction that there is an innate urge to destroy" (p. 5). She says that this inclination must be recognized in every case with the aim of providing appropriate discharge in language. Detecting the presence of such feeling and intention can at times, however, be like searching for a rare coin. Much depends upon the analyst's capacity to listen well. "The analyst will get to know the patient by how he himself thinks, and more importantly, feels about the patient he is with" (p. 6). Careful attention to and toleration of one's induced feelings coupled with "object and ego oriented questions, explanations which facilitate communication … echoing … overvaluing and undervaluing … ego syntonic and later ego dystonic joining" helps to resolve the resistance to communication (p. 119).

Though it seems a straightforward enough process, Spotnitz (1985) warns of the complexity of such an undertaking. The difficulty lies in the need to receive and hold "the induced feelings deeply and undefensively" (p. 164), and to simultaneously analyze the residue of one's own pathology stirred as it may be by the patient's inductions. The perils associated with objective countertransference reactions are, according to Spotnitz, formidable in and of themselves; "The realistically induced feelings account more for failures in the treatment of schizophrenics than subjective reactions" (p. 163). This may be due to the variability and intensity of such inductions which can surprise the analyst with their occurrence, overwhelming defenses as well as composure. Insofar as the analyst may have some familiarity with his own subjective countertransference inclinations, he may be somewhat more able to recognize and deal with those. However, the subjective propensities of the analyst may in some cases become so infused by the patient's inductions as to reach a level of intensity which is nevertheless debilitating. To be present to the patient, the analyst needs to be acutely present to himself.

Spotnitz urged the analyst to allow the negativity associated with the objective induction(s) to grow within and not resist it by attempting to respond "therapeutically" in ways which are premature and hence pre-emptive. More specifically Spotnitz concludes that "the main source of countertransference resistance ... is the therapist's need to defend himself against the rage and anxiety induced by the patient's hostile impulses" (p. 170). Despite the pressure on the analyst "selectivity and timing of interventions is crucial" (p. 165).

In keeping with Spotnitz, Meadow (2005) stated that, in an effort to reach a level of emotional awareness, the analyst's definitive awareness of self is crucial to the course and outcome of treatment. She asserted that a certain courage is required to face the "primitive residues in one's own personality," as these, stirred by the inductions of the patient, collide producing "uncomfortable thoughts and feelings" that can propel us away from truly being in contact with the patient's intra-psychic experience (p. 74). Self-analysis, as well as consultation with a supervisor/colleague, can aid in the persistent holding of the induction(s), and can inform analytic intuitive awareness of the patient's inner world, and ultimately enable the analyst to construct emotional communications which foster and reinforce a sense of presence.

That said, owing to how strong the inductions can be with the consequent countertransference affects, the difficulty on the part of the analyst in recognizing, metabolizing, and utilizing these can be enormous. The prevalence of discussion regarding countertransference resistance behavior in psychoanalytic literature attests to this. Spotnitz (1985) provides a list of such behaviors which is, however, by no means complete:

> Stopping a session early or late; having difficulty keeping quiet; finding oneself unexpectedly thinking about a patient between sessions; focusing one's mind to go in a particular direction; expressing feelings when one has no intention of doing so; unwillingness to communicate emotion;

forgetting an appointment or name of a patient; impatience at feeling out of touch with a patient; behaving in a way to prevent the patient from saying something one does not want to hear; responding in a hostile tone of voice to the patient's hostility; striving to appear more knowledgeable than the patient; impatience over the patient's unclear communication or failure to provide analytic material; clinging rigidly to one technique; states of anxiety before or after, as well as during the session which do not appear to be connected in any way with the patient; accepting the validity of the patient's feeling that he is incurable; joining the patient in undisciplined discharge reactions; various feelings of anxiety or disturbance that interfere with analytic activity; cloudy understanding or misunderstanding of some information that the patient is communicating over and over again.

(p. 170)

Though the treatment destructive potential of such countertransference resistance behavior is ubiquitous, there may be instances when such behavior can be as useful. This supposes that irreparable damage has not been done to either patient or analyst and that the experience has yielded valuable information about the patient, analyst, and the process. Indeed, in some cases significant countertransference resistance is inevitable given the seriousness of the pathology. Though the intensity may signify that the resistance is there in force, so too is the heightened opportunity to address it. Caught in and navigating through states of countertransference resistance provides opportunity for a primal type of resonance. The fear provoked in the analyst associated with doing so, however, can be profound and at times paralyzing.

A case discussed by Vaccaro (2008) exemplifies how acute the challenge can sometimes be and how difficult it is to establish and maintain therapeutic emotional presence. This analyst struggled with embryonic states of silence presented by a chronically schizophrenic woman. The sparse verbalization in response to object oriented questions was so lacking in spontaneity and affect that the analyst "had fantasies of not surviving – not being able to breath. There was 'no mirror'" (p. 147). The analyst's countertransference was heavy with feelings of loss, anger, incompetence, and a sense of having been eradicated ... the fear and the urge to leave was pronounced and preoccupying:

The patient's blank, self-contained stillness, lack of attachment, and lack of interest were too frustrating. Silences induced hostility and helplessness in me. I did not know what was expected or how to provide avenues for contact ... I felt that I was only left with myself – my own history, thoughts, feelings and images. I experienced subjective countertransference in memories of my own isolation in early childhood ... yearning for contact ... an inability to initiate or respond.

(p. 147)

Having the fortitude to, nevertheless, stay in the moment she achieved an awareness of the difficulties in her own early psychic evolution, and sustaining that, Vaccaro experienced an "eerie calm." She was then able to refocus upon the patient and become more interested in her. She was able to engage in increasing levels of "nonverbal mirroring ... twitching, blinking, bobbing and turning" as the patient did. By so doing, she was "providing a bodily likeness ... a twin image" (p. 148). Through this creative intervention, Vaccaro attained a level of synchronous, reflected presence with the patient. As a consequence of the effectiveness of this, the patient eventually became more verbal and interactive, able to express her desire for contact and her dissatisfaction without the need for absolute silence or psychomotor agitation (pp. 154–155).

Sheftel (2011) reminds us of another, albeit subtle, aspect of therapeutic presence, infrequently cited but which characterized Spotnitz's demeanor with patients. She referred to this as his attitude. By attitude, meaning the ability "to tolerate, sustain and control the most difficult induced countertransference state, in itself, a powerful emotional communication to the patient" (p. 37). Attitude, Sheftel says was "embedded in all of Spotnitz's clinical techniques that relate the patient's need for ego insulation and protection" (p. 38). In addition to those techniques familiar to modern analysts, "contact function, joining, mirroring, emotional communication and creating the emotional climate the patient needs" (p. 35), attitude encompasses even more. It is also reflected in:

> intangible unconscious communications that flow from patient to analyst and analyst to patient. It may have to do with the analyst's tone of voice, general demeanor, particular choice of words and how they are uttered, or in the way analyst and patient greet each other, as well as all aspects of the patient/analyst interaction.
>
> (p. 38)

I would add that this attitude is made possible by what Meadow (2005) refers to as the analyst's capacity to care about the emotional health of the patient. She says:

> it is only the loving feeling experienced toward the patient that makes it possible to put up with the long periods of negative reactions as the patient uses his primitive defenses to cope ... love allows the analyst to use negative feelings in his interchanges with patients.
>
> (p. 61)

Love is inherent, I believe, in providing the patient a calm holding environment in the face of disengaged silence or more overt provocation. It is expressed via the analyst's abiding interest in the patient's contact, and by the capacity to stay with it. Much depends on the sensitivity and skill of the analyst in striking the right enough balance. "Love combined with assertiveness should shape our interventions" (p. 61). It is with love, which inspires the analyst's determination and commitment to go into the dark places with our patients, that the analyst is enabled to come also to hate the right way, at the right time, in the right measure. And so we achieve what Winnicott (1949) and later Liegner (1980) referred to as a hate that cures. It is a hate that creates and affirms a sense of felt contact between analyst and patient; it defines and facilitates the progressive relational enhancing communication that heals.

The importance of the therapeutic value of emotional presence is illustrated in the case of a seriously anxious and depressed man who was referred by a colleague for treatment after having been hospitalized for a "breakdown." This man, the fourth child of six, experienced himself as having been ignored by his mother who seemed to have preferred his five sisters. His father was benign but passive, remote and only marginally engaged. A key remembrance of this patient was of being sent away at about the age of three to live with his mother's sister while his mother gave birth to her sixth child. He was not brought home for several weeks; when he did return he had lost his ability to speak, the trauma of separation having apparently rendered him speechless. It was only after a long time following his return that he was again able to talk.

It was no accident that later in life the progression of women to whom he was attracted "never looked quite right" to him, and inevitably were disappointments. They were only of true erotic interest "if their asses were exposed." He was driven to repeat sadistically demeaning enactments both with the ordinary women he dated, as well as with the numerous prostitutes whom he engaged. After many years of this behavior, a failed marriage, and the dissolution of an important relationship with another woman who was special to him, he slipped into a state of depression and acute and unremitting anxiety which necessitated treatment.

This man chose to remain in treatment with me, after not having done so with others prior because of the emotional contact I made with him during the first interview. I had simply commented that it sounded like he had been through hell. In his sessions this patient's sensitivity to contact and its absence was apparent in very basic ways. Often he called in between times. If I did not answer, or if I "did not sound right," or did not seem to him to have the "right attitude" (i.e. be attentive enough), he would invariably act out in sexually perverse and risky ways. This would also occur if my vacations appeared to him to be too long. Later in treatment being present was a function of my being able to tolerate his sadism toward me in the transference. For example, he would make such statements as "I am paying you. If I want to give it to you up the ass, you should bend over and take it." He was able eventually to work through this eroticized transferential hostility and understand its source.

Ultimately, therapeutic presence with this man was defined in terms of my being able to express my understanding of his frantically experienced loss of the maternal object, and as a consequence the impairment of his object relatedness. This had eventuated into desperate excursions into a deviant world of dangerous sexual behavior, intense self-loathing, and ultimately the feared loss of his own mental processes. The obstacles to my capacity at times to express my understanding of his situation was the activation of my own sadistic impulses toward a person I experienced at early junctures as hostile and ungrateful. As I reflect on this case now, I must say that I did not initially feel the sustaining love in the way that Spotnitz and Meadow spoke of it. In the beginning I was motivated by scientific interest, combined to some extent with a need for a sense of professional/technical facility. Yet in my attempt to be present to him, I was willing to expand the boundaries of contact beyond that of scheduled sessions by always taking his calls, which seemed helpful to him. The regard and the love came much later in the form of an evolving sense of admiration for how heroic this man was in struggling with his impulses, and how persistent and determined he was to get well. The bond between us strengthened because of the many emotional storms we had weathered together over a long time. This stirred a sense of empathy in me.

Introducing a theory of intersubjectivity, the self-psychologist Robert Stolorow, with colleagues, (1978) emphasized the central importance of empathy in psychoanalytic treatment:

> Psychoanalytic treatment requires a capacity on the analyst's part to empathically understand the subjective meanings implicit in his patient's expressions. Probably the single most important source of such empathy resides in the therapist's ability to identify with his patient and find analogues in his own life of the experiences which are presented to him …
>
> (p. 250)

In the interwoven world of psychic experience empathy is the means of understanding, truly knowing the other. De-emphasis of the unconscious, with emphasis on the interpretation of the social experience of the other, is what provides the foundation for healing.

Greenberg and Mitchell (1983), reflecting Harry Stack Sullivan's (1962) theory of interpersonal field, inaugurated a relational theory which emphasized the salience of object relations over drive theory models. Later retaining the concept of drive, Greenberg (1993, 2001) "described the relational approach to clinical technique as eschewing belief in any single correct technique and as promoting flexibility in technique that is unique to each analytic dyad" (Schwartz, 2012, p. 413). The innovative shift from analysand to analyst's contribution to transference is guided by empathy and derived from an appreciation of the intersubjective field. "The analsand may then reasonably, seek solutions to his problems in the analyst's behavior rather than himself" (p. 413). In this regard Harold Searles' (1965) capacity to experience and identify the unresolved subjective countertransference process in himself and comment on them to his patients was a truly creative and prescient leap. So too Gill (1982) and Gill and Hoffman (1982) advocated for active levels of scrutiny of both patient and analyst in the here and now. Hoffman believed:

> that by allowing the analsand occasional access to the analyst's personal thoughts and feelings, greater depth could be achieved in the ultimate aim of understanding the patient, and trust in the analyst strengthened. By demonstrating that the rituals of analysis (e.g., anonymity) could be questioned, the analyst was also modeling the analsand's potential to question his self-definitions.
>
> (Schwartz, 2012, p. 418)

While Bollas (2001) also believed in judicious self-disclosure, he emphasizes remaining in the background and allowing intersubjective presence at the unconscious level, "by surrendering himself to his own unconscious (the analyst) is deeply present and an intersubjective participant, communicating through the textures of silence, echoed words, affective affinities, questions and interpretations" (p. 102). It is through this subliminal process that the analyst becomes known and can be used optimally by the patient. Like Bollas, Ogden's (2005) intersubjectivity is in the unconscious transaction. He speaks of the analytic third which is the relationship shared/created in the analysis and eventuating from transference-countertransference experience. Reverie and dreaming emerge out of the analytic thirdness, gleaned and metaphorically elaborated, which enables both patient and analyst to come alive in the analytic moment.

In keeping with the relational and intersubjective orientations, Lewis Aron (2001) thoughtfully explicates the issue of mutuality in psychoanalysis. He asserts that "transference is not simply a distortion that emerges or unfolds from within the patient, independent of the actual behavior and personality of the analyst." Rather, he says, the analyst has, and should have an interpersonal impact on the process (p. 13). In this, "self-revelation is not an option for the analyst, it is an inevitability ... one cannot not communicate and all communications have report or content, aspects and command or relational aspects" (pp. 228–229). He says the analyst is never neutral and always self-disclosing. And by so doing is revealing himself in the co-construction of the experience with the patient (p. 229).

The value of self-disclosure lies in its confirmation of the patient's sense of reality, the analyst's honesty, genuineness, humanness, as well as that the analyst too has transference, explicates the impact of the analysand upon the analyst and others, and can resolve resistances and impasses (p. 231). Disclosure, according to Aron, includes the analyst's sharing of emotional states, for example letting the patient know when he is feeling sad or annoyed, and forthrightly so, though with clinical discretion: "there are times when analysts need to confront patients directly, whether or not patients are asking for this feedback" (p. 246).

Aron is guided by the belief that:

> one way of thinking about the quality of our expertise is that it is part of our function as analyst to allow ourselves to be and (through our own training analysis) to prepare ourselves to be emotionally vulnerable to our patients.
>
> (p. 248)

Lawrence Brown (2011) explores intersubjectivity from a Freudian, Kleinian, and Bionian perspective. Accordingly he asserts that intersubjectivity "is a process of unconscious communication, receptivity and meaning making within each member of the dyad to bring idiosyncratic significance to the shared emotional field that interacts with an analogous function in the partner" (p. 7). This communication between both participants "travels along many pathways including linguistic, pictographic, extraneous experiences (random thoughts, unbidden tunes), bodily sensations, and other yet to be understood channels that ... may be called telepathic" (p. 7).

According to Brown (2011) this process of "mutual affective attunement and regulation which is a means of working on the shared emotional field" leads to the "co-construction" of a meaning narrative (p. 42), an "approximation of a truth" about the patient's life which is uncleansed of the analyst's personality, such that the "analyst's voice echoes in that narrative" (p. 44). Guided, focused, and oscillating processes of projection and projective identification are also crystallized in states of reverie, day and night dreaming. The participants come to know each other in becoming the narrative, the analytic third, "the unfolding emotional truth" they create (pp. 78–79).

Maroda (2009) provides an example of unabashed advocacy for direct transparency and authenticity of the analyst's emotional response: "I am convinced that affective disclosures at the patient's behest are at the heart of the therapeutic moment" (p. 183). This position is also motivated by Maroda's belief in self-revelation as a necessary foil to the analyst's propensity for countertransference dominance that is the insipient and ubiquitous reenactment of the analyst's past and pathology at the expense of the patient (Maroda, 1999).

Guided by these convictions Maroda will, for example, answer "sincere" questions put to her by her patients, short of those of an erotic nature. She has found that when she does so, her patients "will typically respond candidly to my inquiries about what prompted the question and relate any fantasies they may have had about the issue or my answer" (p. 186). Nor is she hesitant to apologize if she has upset a patient.

Though in her beliefs and style she is interpersonal, her commitment to emotional communication is similar to that of the Modern Analytic School: "If I experience an intense, and repetitive, emotional reaction to a particular patient, I am inclined to reveal that feeling when the patient provides an opportune moment," including such feelings as anger and disgust (p. 186). In addition to verbal disclosure, she believes that the judicious use of touch can be therapeutic in the reassurance, reorientation, and affirmation that it provides. She adds:

> I have also found that my facial expressions or voice tone are not as likely to be intrusive as a verbalization of feeling can be. The patient is free to note what I am feeling, or not to note it, as he wishes. Very often the patient goes on talking even if my eyes are filled with tears, or he may begin to cry. Affective communication does not require words, either in the sending or receiving, and therefore can be accomplished without impinging on the patient's narrative flow and without risk of over stimulation that can result from a verbal self-disclosure.
>
> (p. 187)

Where Maroda diverges somewhat from modern analysts with regard to emotional communication is that while she is inclined to express anger and disgust, it is more often than not in the expressed belief in the patient's better angels. For example, she is apt to say "I am angry with you because I know you are capable of better." A modern analyst might take this tack, but would also be open, depending on the situation and guided by the patient's inductions, to saying simply "You really are a despicable person," and allowing the patient's fuller emotional reaction without the preemptory need to repair.

Maroda, uncomfortable, as she indicates, with her own sadism, would be apt to apologize for certain expressions of anger, as she did with one patient who had continually rejected her efforts to be affirming of the patient's capacity to make her life better. Maroda said in anger, "Well, I guess you could just hang around and do nothing, since you are so convinced that nothing will do any good, and just wait around to become the world's oldest virgin" (p. 133). What is of significance here is Maroda's inclination to encounter the patient emotionally, to experience and express her anger, sadism, and remorse, not to interpret it away, to in effect be vulnerable and present. It is an intervention, a way of being in the treatment, which is original and powerful.

It is an orientation which Aron (2001) had articulated in his discussion of relational theory. Aron proposes the analyst's:

> inevitable personal participation in the analytic project ... the patient's experience and understanding of the analyst as well as the analyst's experience and understanding of the patient are constructions based both on their individual histories and characteristic organizational patterns and in their perceptions of the participation of the other ...
>
> (p. 229)

In keeping with the modern analyst Phyllis Meadow's (1987) belief in the myth of the impersonal analyst, Aron stated that "the analyst is never neutral or anonymous but is always disclosing and indeed suggesting something about and co-constructing his or her relationship with the patient" (pp. 228–229).

Cognizant that self-disclosure can have the potential to complicate the treatment by burdening the patient with the analyst's problems, divert the attention from the patient's concerns to the analyst's needs, Aron, nevertheless, sites the benefits:

> Self-disclosures may confirm the patient's sense of reality. They may help to establish the therapist's honesty and genuineness. They may show that the therapist is not so different from the patient, that the therapist, too, is human and has transferences. Self-disclosures clarify the nature of the patient's impact on the therapist and on people in general. Self-disclosures may help to break through treatment impasses and clarify deeply entrenched resistances.
>
> (p. 231)

Aron does seem to follow Searles' (1975) practice of only revealing what is evoked in the session, rather than from the analyst's life outside. Doing so can be anxiety provoking for the analyst given that he exposes himself to the scrutiny and more poignant affective encounter of the patient in the effort to co-construct the analytic experience which they share.

It is the intersubjective, relational, and modern psychoanalytic orientations that all share in their allowance for the range of feelings possible in an analytic encounter. In so doing they promise, though not at times without complexities and dangers, a wider depth of analytic experience, continued opportunities for the enhanced emotional presence that advances treatment. Patients are often instrumental in helping to achieve this. Depending on the level of maturational development, the form their efforts take will vary.

I am, for example, reminded of the young woman, M, then in her mid-thirties, who entered treatment many years ago out of a plaguing concern that there was "no meaning in the world, no point to existence." She had the urge to kill herself which frightened her. An accomplished academic, with an advanced degree in graphic arts, she had many positions but considered herself insufficient in her profession. The weight of this condemnation precluded any real joy she might otherwise have taken in her work. She was well versed in the visual arts, literature, and film. I often marveled at the easy facility with which she made reference to these. Yet despite her intellectual capacity, M's voice was that of a much younger person; she spoke with the colloquialisms and slang of that era's adolescents. The discrepancy was startling.

M had few friends and was estranged from her parents. She was one of seven children and her siblings were scattered throughout the country. M complained of a childhood in which her mother was depressed and her father, who though a successful academic, was eccentric, emotionally labile, and given at times to physically abusive outbursts. M stated that though she felt little emotional connection to her parents or siblings, she periodically visited her divorced parents who lived in separate cities far away. She did this out of a sense of obligation and guilt rather than true desire.

Sensitive and easily hurt, when she suspected potential rejection, M would disappear often impulsively leaving relationships and jobs. Her journeys alone would take her to distant places and sometimes into dangerous circumstances. This pattern of leaving began as a young teenager when she once bought a ticket to another country, in order, she said, to visit the museums there. Cut off from awareness and understanding of her affective life, when questioned about this, she denied that she might have been angry or that she was responding as a result of any other feeling.

As I was concerned that this repetition might be reenacted with me, I discussed openly its possibility; I asked when she thought she might be dumping me, that is, what circumstances might prompt such behavior. M assured me that it would not happen. She said that she liked me and wanted to get well. I, nevertheless, remained unconvinced and often boldly raised the issue.

I mention M because invariably during sessions she would ask me questions: Had I seen this or that movie? Did I like a particular artist? Did I believe in the philosophy of so and so? I was hesitant at first to answer. But becoming more and more aware of her history, feeling of alienation, and the oddly compelling little girl quality of her voice and language, I chose to do so. My responses were short and prudent, usually followed by my queries as to why she wanted to know. What emerged were further revelations by M of her problematic family history. This included her father's alcohol abuse and the details of his lapses into violence, her parents' divorce, the rejection by her older narcissistic sister, and that she was suffering from a rare form of cancer that could be fatal—and that the family "never talked about any of this." There seemed to be whole segments of family experience that were, according to her, missing and what she did remember was devoid of feeling.

The tone and repetitiveness of her questioning seemed to create, or replicate, the parent-child dyad in a state of comfortable and pleasant rumination. It was as though she was attempting both to test my tolerance for her and to try to connect with me. Supporting this impression she had also begun to ask if I were bored with her, found her uninteresting. She asked frequently if I were angry with her. When I asked why she thought she was asking these questions, she simply said that she "wanted to know." There seemed no apparent awareness that her questions were connected in any way to the origins of her early family life or psychic development. There were also many apologies for her imagined and actual infractions (i.e. showing up late for sessions and on occasion not showing up at all). My principal feeling in response to this was curiosity, which I conveyed to her followed by the question about whether she was trying to keep me inconsequential so she could more easily disappear, as she had done on so many other occasions in the past.

I think it was my willingness to answer her questions first before attempting to analyze what was prompting them that enabled M to reveal the depth of her lack of a sense of connectedness, permanence, and value, and attach that to the circumstances of her life experience. She began after some months to do this with tears. By being willing to answer, I was able to respond to her need to attach, by means which were tenable for her. It was a decision to simply follow her lead, to be responsively present in the way she defined it which had, I believe, profound ramification in terms of her ability to stay in treatment, not flee and begin to do the work of analysis at a more effective level.

Another case also illustrates the importance of being emotionally present through processes of joining and mutuality, in the manner necessary for the patient, despite the apprehension which was immediately provoked in me. F, a man of about 40, requested treatment as a result of his dread that the world was about to come to a cataclysmic end. He was a huge man, with a shock of thick unkempt red hair and penetrating eyes. This combined with the avidness of his delusion of pending catastrophe provoked a sense of fear in me. I wondered about the potential for violence. I found myself breathing in a slow and measured pace (to calm myself), becoming extremely interested (and over thinking/theorizing as a way to feel empowered and protected), and as I often do, praying (to assure myself that I was not alone). This helped and I was able to listen and focus.

Highly intelligent and well read, this man could not tolerate the pronouncement of a fundamentalist segment of his Catholic religion which advanced the theology of doom for those who did not embrace their views. While on the one hand he was appropriately skeptical and outraged that the Church allowed, even supported, this faction, his obsessional inclinations caused him to doubt himself and become locked in rumination and worry.

F was caught and painfully vacillated in his dilemma of truth or fiction, belief or disbelief, faith or heresy. He seemed comforted by my recognition of the truly tormented state he seemed to be in, as well as my willingness to also answer his questions. "Do you think it is wrong for people to prey upon the fears of others?" he would ask. "Absolutely," I responded. He urged, "Why does the Church allow this?" Perceiving his underlying disinclination for those in authority, I said "Perhaps to promote membership and consolidate power." Such answers appeared to assuage F's fears, particularly since he knew that I was familiar with and accepting of Catholic theology and could, nevertheless, be critical of the practices of "the men who ran the Church." His own cynicism felt justified by such responses, though not heretical so.

"Do you think I am a misanthrope?" "Yes," I said with conviction. "There would be something wrong with you if you were not." And so I readily joined him, perceiving early the intensity of this man's suffering, the tenuousness of his sense of well-being, and the need for confirmation of his perceptions and feelings. Attempts to interpret early in the treatment the driving force of his obsessional conflict would have, I believe, simply made him more uncomfortable. Increasingly assured that I understood, accepted, and was with him, he began to talk about the heart aching sense of loss of a loving but deceased mother, the rejection he experienced from an indifferent father, several narcissistically self-absorbed sisters, and two engaged but competitive, at times harsh, brothers. With few friends and a skeptical view of humanity F had turned to religion where, however, his hope was to be disappointed.

Aware that his sarcasm and inclination to be acerbic also reflected a capacity for humor, I became emboldened to employ a somewhat joking style with F at times. For example, I elaborated an outrageous revenge fantasy in which he could "settle the score" with his family. I told him he should start wearing more expensive clothes, buy an impressive new car and let slip to various family members that he was planning to leave the remainder of his unspent and considerable inheritance to his newly acquired 24-year-old girlfriend. His laughter signaled a break in his somberness. I think it was that such ideas gave him, at least in fantasy, one outlet for the pent up rage which he felt. I believe that he experienced me in such moments as a comrade in his attempt to alleviate his despair.

Accepted as emotionally "tuned in" with him, I was also able to challenge F with regard to his fascination with misery generally and inclination in particular to be overly focused on unlikely cataclysmic events, rather on the more immediate family tragedy which caused him such formerly unexpressed hurt feelings. When he was able to adjust his focus appropriately on the pathos of this, he became much less delusionally troubled by end-of-the-world fears. The calibrated answering of questions as well as the use of intentional humor provided both a confirmation of his distress and an outlet for this man's aggression. It enabled him to moderate a painful ambivalence. That is, the pull between cynicism on the one hand and being a true believer on the other, to be uncritically loving or justifiably angry, even hateful. The mediating effects of this treatment relied upon an interventional attitude which affirmed and justified both dimensions of F's experience. He was able to move toward a position which enabled him to be a critical believer in both his religious orientation and his life—to love and hate in appropriate measure, thus relaxing somewhat the need for a self-punishing cataclysmic end-of-the-world compulsion.

What follows in the chapters of this book are clinical accounts that provide an inside look at how analysts struggle to make and maintain emotional presence in the face of their own resistances, as well as those of the patients they treat. These are complex and perilous journeys guided by a humbling awareness of the awesome and beguiling power of the forces which drive intrapsychic pathology and its interpersonal manifestations. Ultimately these are stories of faith in the patient's innate capacity for psychic health, the power of the mutually constructed effort, and a belief that attaining the right emotional presence enables all else which is therapeutic.

References

Aron, L. (1991). The patient's experience of the analyst's subjectivity. *Psychoanalytic Dialogues*, 1, 29–51.

Aron, L. (2001). *A meeting of minds: Mutuality in psychoanalysis*. Hillsdale, NJ: The Analytic Press.

Bernstein, A. (1992). Beyond countertransference: The love that cures. *Modern Psychoanalysis*, 17, 15–31.

Bernstein, J. (2013). An approach to the management of treatment impasses. *Modern Psychoanalysis*, 38, 3–24.

Bleckner, M. (1992). Working in the countertransference. *Psychoanalytic Dialogues*, 2, 161–180.

Bollas, C. (2001). Freudian intersubjectivity: Commentary on paper by Julie Gerhardt and Annie Sweetnam. *Psychoanalytic Dialogues*, 11, 93–105.

Brown, L. J. (2011). *Intersubjective processes and the unconscious*. London: Routledge.

Chused, J. (1989). The evocative power of enactments. *Journal of the American Psychoanalytic Society*, 39, 615–639.

Freud, S. (1913). *On beginning treatment* (Standard Edition), 12. London: Hogarth Press.

Freud, S. (1920). *Beyond the pleasure principle* (Standard Edition), 18, 7–66. London: Hogarth Press.

Gay, P. (1988). *Freud, A life for our time*. New York: W.W. Norton & Company.

Geltner, P. (2013). *Emotional communication: Countertransference analysis and the use of feeling in psychoanalytic technique*. New York: Routledge.

Gill, M. M. (1982). *Analysis of transference (Vol. 1), Theory and technique*. Madison, CT: International University Press.

Gill, M. M., & Hoffman, I. Z. (1982). *Analysis of transference (Vol. 2), Studies of nine audio-recorded psychoanalytic sessions*. Madison, CT: International University Press.

Greenberg, J. R. (1993). *Oedipus and beyond: A clinical theory*. Cambridge, MA: Harvard University Press.

Greenberg, J. R. (2001). The analyst's participation: A new look. *Journal of the American Psychoanalytic Association*, 49, 359–381.

Greenberg, J. R., & Mitchell, S. A. (1983). *Object relations in psychoanalytic theory*. Cambridge, MA: Harvard University Press.

Hoffman, I. (1983). The patient as interpreter of the analyst's experience. *Contemporary Psychoanalysis*, 19, 389–422.

Holmes, L. (2013). *Wrestling with destiny: The promise of psychoanalysis*. New York: Routledge.

Jacobs, T. (1991). *The use of the self*. New York: International Universities Press.

Kohut, H. (1984). *How does analysis cure*. Chicago, IL: University of Chicago Press.

Liegner, E. (1980). The hate that cures: The psychological reversibility of schizophrenia. *Modern Psychoanalysis*, 5, 5–95.

Liegner, E. (1995). The anaclitic countertransference in resistance resolution. *Modern Psychoanalysis*, 20, 153–164.

Little, M. (1985). Winnicott working in areas where psychotic anxieties predominate – a personal record. *Free Associations*, 3, 9–42.

Margolis, B. (1994). Narcissistic countertransference: Further considerations. *Modern Psychoanalysis*, 19, 149–159.

Maroda, K. J. (1999). *Seduction, surrender and transformation*. Hillsdale, NJ: The Analytic Press.

Maroda, K. J. (2009). *The power of countertransference: Innovations in analytic technique*. New York: Routledge, Taylor & Francis Group.

Meadow, P. (1987). The myth of the impersonal analyst. *Modern Psychoanalysis*, 12, 131–150.

Meadow, P. (2005). *The new psychoanalysis*. Lanham, MD: Rowman & Littlefield Publishers, Inc.

Mitchell, S., & Black, M. (1995). *Freud and beyond: A history of modern psychoanalytic thought*. New York: Basic Books.

Ogden, T. H. (2005). *The art of psychoanalysis*. New York: Routledge.

Pine, F. (1985). *Developmental theory and clinical process*. New Haven, CT: Yale University Press.

Pine, F. (1990). *Drive, ego, object and self: A synthesis for clinical work*. Phoenix, Arizona: Basic Books.

Schwartz, H. P. (2012). Intersubjectivity and dialecticism. *The International Journal of Psychoanalysis*, 93, 401–425.

Searles, H. (1965). *Collected papers on schizophrenia and related subjects*. New York: International University Press.

Searles, H. (1975). The patient as therapist to his analyst. In P. Giovacchini (Ed.), *Tactics and techniques of psychoanalytic therapy* (pp. 95–151). New York: Aronson.

Shakespeare, W. (1603). The tragedy of Hamlet, Prince of Denmark. In G. B. Harrison (Ed.), *Shakespeare: Major plays and the sonnets*. New York: Harcourt, Brace & World, Inc.

Sheftel, S. (2011). Turning points in modern psychoanalysis. *Modern Psychoanalysis*, 36, 29–41.

Spotnitz, H. (1969). *Modern psychoanalysis of the schizophrenic patient: Theory of the technique*. New York: Grune and Stratton.

Spotnitz, H. (1985). *Modern psychoanalysis of the schizophrenic patient: Theory of the technique*. New York: Human Sciences Press.

Stanton, M. (1991). *Sandor Ferenczi: Reconsidering active intervention*. Northvale, NJ: Jason Aronson.

Stolorow, R. D., Atwood, G. E., & Ross, J. M. (1978). The representational world in psychoanalytic therapy. *International Review of Psychoanalysis*, 5, 247–256.

Stolorow, R. D., Branschaft, B., & Atwood, G. (1987). *Psychoanalytic treatment: An intersubjecctive approach*. Hillsdale, NJ: Analytic Press.

Sullivan, H. S. (1962). *Schizophrenia as a human process*. New York: Norton.

Vaccaro, A. (2008). Working through silence with a schizophrenic woman. *Modern Psychoanalysis*, 32, 142–156.

Winnicott, D. W. (1949). Hate in the countertransference. *International Journal of Psychoanalysis*, 30, 69–74.

Chapter 2

Countertransference issues in treatment of borderline and narcissistic personality disorders

A retrospective on the contributions of Gerald Adler, Peter L. Giovacchini, Harold Searles, and Phyllis W. Meadow

John Madonna

What follows are the summarized proceedings from a 1990 psychoanalytic conference conducted at Clark University in Worcester, Massachusetts. It was Freud's venue for presenting, at the invitation of G. Stanley Hall, his Introductory Lectures. The title of that 1990 conference was On Becoming the Patient: Countertransference Issues in the Treatment of Borderline and Narcissistic Personality Disorders. These proceedings, which I organized and moderated, constituted my first thinking about the primary importance of emotional presence in psychoanalytic work.

The four master clinicians, Gerald Adler, Peter L. Giovacchini, Harold Searles, and Phyllis W. Meadow, represented somewhat separate theoretical orientations with regard to their views on intervention, object relations, intersubjective and modern analytic. Yet each relied on the significance of receptivity to the emotional inductions of the difficult patients that they treated. The felt understanding that resulted enabled them to actually become the patient, or some important aspect of the patient. Interventions became possible which were emotionally resonate and non interpretive, more in the way of authentic encounters which led to progressive communications and had the potential to move treatment forward.

In the morning, Dr. Adler presented, then Dr. Giovacchini. Discussion followed.

Gerald Adler—core borderline issues and challenges of treatment: the salience of emotional communication

Dr. Adler began his presentation by defining countertransference. He cited the historical perspective that countertransference referred to the unconscious issues of the analyst, which were generally seen to be pathological. However, Adler indicated that he thought of countertransference as:

all of the responses which we have toward a patient, conscious as well as unconscious, and not just the pathological. Some of the most creative feelings and fantasies we have are those we have in response to a patient and they tell us a lot both about ourselves and our patients.

Adler then began a definition of the borderline patient, discussing the various aspects of that condition: impulsivity, the intensity of that relationship with the therapist, and neediness, profound rage, self-destructive behavior, identity disturbances and a propensity for bringing out the worst in the analyst.

A core issue for borderline patients is the aloneness that results because borderline patients cannot count on internal resources "to soothe, comfort or hold themselves." What is missing is evocative memory; the ability, when under stress, to remember "the caring, holding, soothing relationships of the past." Under stress of separation in life or treatment, such people lose whatever capacity they have to soothe, comfort or hold themselves. They become needy, panicky and desperate. They lose touch with this inner soothing-holding feeling of the analyst.

A second core issue is the "need-fear dilemma." Borderline patients desire to be close to others, but are profoundly afraid of deteriorating into a psychotic state. They dread that this will happen if they lose separation between self and other, both in the world and in their mind. This condition is manifest in the treatment situation with the patient's desperate neediness and profound, devouring hunger for contact with the analyst, which rapidly oscillates with erratic disappearances from the treatment situation and other distancing behaviors. Maintaining a holding environment becomes a difficult challenge for the analyst.

A third core issue is the primitive guilt that results from the patient's profound rage, often projected outward onto others and specifically onto the analyst. It is a rage-guilt that has an all-or-nothing quality, and indeed is often murderous in intensity to oneself and is projected onto the therapist who is seen as hating the patient. Helping the patient to mediate the intensity of this experience without becoming treatment destructive becomes an important challenge for the analyst, as is also the need for the analyst to maintain within himself the projected feelings in the situation until they can be therapeutically understood and interpreted. Ultimately in the course of successful treatment and especially when the aloneness issues have been worked out, borderline patients often advance to being narcissistic characters. These narcissistic personalities take two forms. First are the "bleeding heart narcissistic personalities." These individuals are easily injured. Both they and the analyst are perceived as worthless, the analyst especially, if he misses the exact intervention or errs slightly in the interaction. The second type is the "self-sufficient personality" who strives for total autonomous function. To need is to be dependent, and so there is a defense against experiencing that dependency state, which carries with it considerable envy and rage. These feeling states are intolerable. Often these two personality types fluctuate.

Having defined the borderline personality state with its core issues, Adler went on to discuss the countertransference issues in the treatment of this disorder. Aloneness becomes an important experience for both patient and analyst. Often the therapist may not have a formulation for the component of aloneness, that is, may not be tuned in to the intensity and extensiveness of that experience for the patient, does not have an awareness of the patient's lack of evocative memory for the analyst. The patient becomes more and more needy in the treatment relationship. As the patient destroys internal aspects of self or projects badness onto the analyst, the patient begins to lose touch with the analyst as a sustaining, holding person. The patient will ask for more and more, while simultaneously becoming more provocative via the process of the projective identification. It is easy to misunderstand this condition, to misread the evocative memory problems, and feel the patient is demonstrating, in a manipulative way, unresolved hatred. The analyst may then move to set stringent limits upon the patient's behavior. Needless to say, the analyst during these phases does not have the feeling of being in a working alliance with the patient, but rather under attack and alone. And this situation becomes even more challenging when the need-fear dilemma is calculated in. One moment the patient will be there, "hungry, greedy in a devouring state" for contact and the next moment the patient will be fleeing the treatment. Induced feelings in the therapist may include a sense that he is being respected, and perhaps envied, having an important therapeutic effect, and the next moment being discarded and abjectly rejected.

The experience of primitive guilt on the part of the patient works against the therapeutic process. There are moments in the treatments when progress is being made, and it is apparent to both the patient and the analyst. The patient may reverse the progress as a consequence of this primitive and pervasive sense of guilt. It is a form of self-punishment, often a result of the patient's envy and hatred. The occurrence can be experienced as quite provocative by the therapist and can result in various difficult countertransference feelings in the therapist.

Melanie Klein first described projective identification. The patient who engages in projective identification is able to get rid of a part of himself, which is intolerable, and is also able to preserve a part of himself that he fears will be destroyed if it remains within the psyche. Once this part of the self is deposited in the psyche of the analyst, it needs to be managed and controlled by the patient. The patient provokes in the analyst responses, which confirm the projection. The projective identification process is possible because "each of us is a sitting duck" in the sense that we all have to a greater or lesser degree split-off parts, which correspond to what the patient is attempting to project. There is a resonance. Projective identification can be a creative, remediative experience. If the therapist can contain, and understand empathetically the aspect of the patient that is being projected, he can ultimately form empathetic feeling-relevant interpretations. The challenge is that the analyst must be keenly attuned to his feeling states and have the comfort to contain and interpret feelings which belong to the patient and are experienced within the analyst.

One model of cure is repeated projective identification by the patient, containment by the analyst despite the provocative or discomforting nature of the projection, and the understanding of the projection by the analyst, interpretation and reinternalization of the modified projection by the patient.

A case was described in which a patient who had originally shown interest in an interpretation refused to discuss the matter further. In subsequent sessions when Adler attempted to refer back to the issues associated with the interpretation the patient rejoined, "You want to hear shrink talk." Adler become furious with this devaluation and decided to express emotion. "This is infuriating," he said. "You missed the point. The point is, you missed the point." Adler then pounded on the chair and continued,

> I try to get you to understand something and here you go and give me this shrink talk stuff and you destroy everything I am trying to do to help you. I talk and talk and there is no way to get anything across to you. I talk and I talk and it is worthless and I am furious.

Adler recognized that he had much control over the expression of his emotions in this situation and cautioned that this type of intervention was to be made only when appropriate, only when the patient is well known, and was not an intervention he encouraged everyone to make. The result proved therapeutic for the patient who told Adler that what he said was exactly what she and her mother had said for years. With the patient's help, Adler realized that he was enacting the role of the patient and the patient's mother, and to the extent that he was feeling helpless and devalued, was experiencing the feelings of the patient herself. It is of interest that it was the process of specific and appropriate emotional communication by the analyst that enabled the patient to arrive at her own insightful interpretation of an aspect of her behavior, which in turn furthered the analyst's understanding of his patient's repetition. Cure comes not only from repeated episodes of containment and interpretation by the analyst, enabling the taking back of the modified projection, but also from the ability on the part of the analyst to specifically and appropriately express feeling. It seems that in the experience and the expression of the induced feeling, Adler succeeded in truly becoming the patient, and by doing so, freed the patient to take the lead in her own treatment.

Peter L. Giovacchini—countertransference reactions with borderline patients: the power of visual imagery

Dr. Giovacchini discussed countertransference reactions in the treatment of borderline patients with five issues in mind: 1) the forcing of various repetition compulsions instituted in the early infantile relationship of the patient and the parental object; 2) the issue of the psychoanalytic paradox, that is, the infantile environment and analytic session having certain phenomological similarities, and the patient's difficulty separating personal therapeutic interaction from past traumatic occurrences in life; 3) formal elements of analysis; 4) personal factors of the analyst's character, specifically the analyst's professional ego ideal as it is threatened, thus constituting an existential anxiety; 5) and finally the situations in which the patient does not allow the development of any self-observing functions as is often the case in psychotic transference situations.

Before discussing these five areas, Giovacchini stated that he, like Adler, had a global notion of countertransference. He referred to countertransference as "every action, feeling, thought that the therapist had directed toward the patient, in a hierarchy from unconscious to conscious," and he further indicated that "the more unconscious the relationship the more transference and countertransference processing."

Giovacchini defined countertransference as of two types: idiosyncratic and homogenous. Idiosyncratic is the countertransference reaction in the analyst due to certain features of the analyst's background. The homogenous countertransferences are the expected reactions within the analyst. For example, if a patient pulled out a gun during a session, the expected reaction in any analyst would be anxiety. If there were no anxiety, there might be an idiosyncratic countertransference reaction being experienced by the analyst. He referred to one idiosyncratic countertransference reaction that he had at one time, a feeling of dread with regard to setting up a schedule with a woman who had applied to him for treatment. Upon self-examination, he realized that the woman was a "dead ringer for his mother. Who would want his own mother on the couch?"

In explicating the ways in which patients force various repetition compulsions representative of the early infantile relationships onto the analyst, Giovacchini indicated that often there is some countertransference confusion which signals the advent of such a process. This is unavoidable, and in fact, a trap of sorts. Giovacchini illustrated this with an example of a therapeutic failure, a case of a 25-year-old woman who had a history of sexual and other sorts of physical abuse. A woman who lives on the streets. She had to quit college because she collapsed and required hospitalization. When she applied for treatment to Giovacchini, it was with the query about why he would be interested in treating her. She presented herself as an impossible case, but he found her a challenge. There were many valuable aspects of her personality. She began treatment by expressing her anger. Giovacchini soothed her inner agitation. She kept stressing her need for help and pleading for Giovacchini to do something. Everything he did was valueless. He was not empathetic, not helpful. Giovacchini began to be irritated with the situation. He felt that a confrontation would be counterproductive.

The patient took whatever he said as an attack. Whether he said something or did not say something, she was provoked. She felt that he was not helping her, and that she was feeling abandoned and left the treatment in that state. Everything that occurred during sessions was traumatic for her as she forced the repetition into the relationship, and there was nothing he felt that he could do about it. He was helpless, as every one of her previous therapists had been. The treatment ended in the same way, as did all previous treatments, with the therapeutic figure unable to feel effective and with the patient feeling attacked, in pain and with a sense of abandonment.

In discussing the issue of the intrusion of the infantile conflict in the therapeutic environment, Giovacchini cited the patient's inability to form and hold a mental representation. "Adler had referred to this as the failure of evocative memory." Giovacchini presented a case of a patient who demonstrated this ego defect in the form of a need to plan every event in life. During the very first session, the patient inquired as to when Giovacchini would be away. As the treatment progressed, the patient often complained about impending absences, having to know where he was going to be at all times. The patient had given Giovacchini a statuette, which he kept. It symbolized the patient, "Giacommeti—like with no arms, no mouth." He felt as though he were constantly on call and began to become aware of the countertransference reaction of irritation. He found the sense of constantly being on call an irksome thing, his freedom and autonomy threatened. The patient had psychotic episodes, creating a sense of urgency, and once arrived in the office and assembled a row of steak knives on the floor. She asked Giovacchini to put the knives in his file.

His irritation intensified. On one occasion, he had to be away overnight. He did not feel the need to tell her, as he would not be missing a session. But she perceived that he would be absent and asked him where he was going. He replied, "What difference does it make?" and she responded, "You just do not understand." "Oh, what difference does it make?" he persisted. "Do you expect me to be here seven days a week, 24 hours a day?" and the patient responded, "Of course." At this point Giovacchini understood the patient's need for constancy and was better able to achieve a more accepting state.

Giovacchini liked the statuette, which the patient had given him, and knowing this, the patient would break the statue whenever she got angry; Giovacchini would glue it back together again. On an occasion before treatment ended, the patient grabbed the statue and was about to break it. Giovacchini did not react as he usually did, which was to show some concern. The patient asked about this. He said that it was "all right, he did not need the statuette anymore." During the treatment he had been unable to hold a mental representation of the patient and used the statue as an aid to doing so. The analyst no longer needed the object for that purpose. He had, in effect, acquired an ego defect similar to the patient's and resolved it and enabled the patient to do so ultimately as well. Perhaps it was with his understanding of the patient's need for constancy, the recognition of which arrived as a result of Giovacchini's emotional communication to the patient. In an irksome state he asked the question, "Do you expect me to be here seven days a week, 24 hours a day?" prompted by an important feeling which led to a developmental advance.

Giovacchini also presented the case of a young man who threatened the professional ego ideal of the analyst. The young man had accomplished nothing in his life, yet he was an authority on everything. It seemed as though he had the objective of converting Giovacchini from psychoanalysis to astrology. Although the patient was cooperative in the usual sense, Giovacchini was aware of a countertransference reaction that he could not stand this young man. Giovacchini asked the patient one day if he could tape the session. The young man had agreed, perhaps flattered that those listening to the tape would learn a great deal from him. At the seminar in which this tape was presented, everyone who listened was furious at the apparent arrogance of the patient: a homogenous countertransference reaction. Upon exploration it was apparent that the patient was "clothing a psychosis in reality terms." Instead of paranoid delusions, for example, he had extremely rational ways of relating to the world, attitudes which were essentially psychotic. The seeming rationality, this reality-oriented way of presenting an essentially psychotic self, had the effect of driving the hearers crazy. The underlying psychosis ultimately became apparent in a session in which he was furious with Giovacchini for not pre-venting him from sleeping with a certain type of woman. Upon inquiry, his distress was related to his notion that he was from an illustrious family and had been betraying his lineage. He also belonged to a prestigious country club and might be kicked out if people knew of this. At a deeper level he explained simply that he was the messiah and if others heard of this, he would lose his godlike status. This was the nuclear encapsulated delusion.

Giovacchini presented another situation in which the ego identity of the analyst was threatened. This was the case of the patient who sought to replace the rational scientific attitude, that is, Giovacchini's group of concepts, his modus operandi, with his, the patient's, own delusional-oriented megalomania. This patient, a psychotherapist, denigrated psychoanalysis. He had a better system of studying and impacting human behavior. He was a handsome man with an expensive car. He frequently complained that he was not getting better as a result of the analysis and he would rather be at his martial arts training. One day, Giovacchini complimented the man on his nice car. The man subse-quently became furious and accused Giovacchini of unprofessional behavior, or being hostile and sarcastic. The patient associated to his relationship with a professional in another part of the country and accused Giovacchini of hating him, that is, the other professional. Giovacchini responded with a transference interpretation. The next day, however, he had a fantasy of the tape-recorder being stopped by the patient whenever he, Giovacchini, was speaking. Giovacchini studied his fantasy as the patient accused him of having a reverse Oedipus conflict, which is, suffering from an old man's envy at the possibilities and potential of a young man. Giovacchini did remember that he was feeling sarcastic and irritated in the previous session. He allowed himself to free associate. The patient had a prominent mother and a peddler father. The mother ignored the existence of the father who was used only as a provider of money. Giovacchini realized that this man as a boy had identified with the introjection of his father's nonexistent image. He was overcompensating for the self-deprecating introject by giving himself an exalted image. Giovacchini's visual fantasy of the tape-recorder being stopped whenever Giovacchini spoke was the way in which Giovacchini experienced the projection of the father. Giovacchini offered a unique contribution here in understanding countertransference induction and one way in which it may occur, in this instance through a visual image, a specific fantasy production. The poignancy of the image was profound. It helped Giovacchini realize that this was not an Oedipal situation, but an existential one. The attendant intense existential anxiety related to the simultaneous momentary obliteration of the analyst's own professional identity through the insertion of an important projection on the part of the patient. For Giovacchini, one path to becoming the patient had been receptivity to the experience of an important guiding visual image.

Panel discussion following the presentations of Gerald Adler and Peter L. Giovacchini

DR. MADONNA: We would like to now invite members of the panel to raise any questions or comments they might have regarding what has been heard thus far this morning from Dr. Adler and Dr. Giovacchini.

DR. SEARLES: As to the question that was just raised about holding the patient, I share Peter Giovacchini's reaction. I have always thought that hell hath no fury like a woman scorned, and that is how a woman must feel as a male therapist presumes to believe that he can hold her without getting carried away by sexual passion. It seems to me an enormous insult to the more adult aspect of the woman patient so I regard it as great folly.

When I was listening to Dr. Adler's presentation, I heard many things that I found illuminating and valuable and that I do not hear anybody else saying, especially about the borderline patients being unable to count upon, to rely upon the holding introjects within them. That is an enormously useful concept.

When Dr. Madonna was making his introductory remarks he asked to what extent must the analyst become the patient. Well one thought I had about that was that one could say that the analyst must become the patient before the patient can become the patient. Now I know that can be carried much too far and is an indefensible thing to say, but I hope you understand how I mean it.

Further, in listening to Dr. Adler's presentation, I was struck by his references to borderline patients as "they." I am sure I write and speak that way also, but the major point I would make is that we all have significant degrees of borderline and narcissistic defense mechanisms, and I think that we will profit most over the years to the extent that we all come out of the closets in that regard.

Dr. Adler speaks of the bleeding heart type of narcissistic patient whom I am currently working with and have worked with, who is so closely attuned to everything the analyst says and does and is so easily hurt. I would make the point that such a patient feels totally responsible for the analyst and that there is a very gratifying aspect for the analyst in this, that is, the patient can be thought of as a holding environment for the analyst in one sense. The patient is as attuned to what he says and does as the mother is attuned to every least little thing her baby does. Now I well know not only the gratification of that, but also as time and work goes on how very constricting that is for the analyst, how very annoying, and the analyst must eventually cast off any gratifications the role provides him.

Early on I was getting the impression that Dr. Adler is more receptive to phone calls than some of us are. Now that is probably not the case, but this is an early impression I had and I was reminded of something Boyer said a year or two ago when I was in a conference with him. I think I asked him about the phone calls at home and he told me that he has not had a call at his home from a patient within 20 years and that, I am very happy to say, is the way my life also goes. I had a borderline patient maybe 35 years ago who had a searing impact upon me and one of the many things she did was to make phone calls at home. Dozens and dozens of them until it became evident that if I were to maintain any home life this must stop. It had to get that bad before I put a stop to it, and I have never been the same since then about phone calls to my home.

As to the projective material being taken back into the patient, it is one of the many questions raised here in this conference, to which we do not have answers, but which are enormously valuable and worthy of exploring and discussing. One of the techniques that I had found useful if the patient perceives me as being, let's say, afraid, is that I do not disavow that I may be feeling afraid, but I say, "Do you have any thoughts as to why I may be feeling afraid?" If the roots of my feeling afraid can be explored sufficiently, the patient can find something to identify with in those roots and can start taking back what is being projected. I have found that a very helpful kind of technique, which has to be felt, not simply a technique of words.

Dr. Adler spoke about times in the treatment when it feels stuck. Whenever I hear about stalemates in therapy, I think of two points I would make if called upon, and I am glad to have the chance. When in a stalemate over many months or even years, it is highly likely that the situation is unconsciously more gratifying to the analyst than he is consciously aware; something in him desperately wants things to not change. Dr. Adler makes this point beautifully clear when he speaks to the patient of his fantasy that they will spend the rest of their lives having sessions together. He said it obviously to convey that he could quite tolerably envision this, and my hat is off to him as it was many times when I heard him referring to his ability to be aware of his dependent and fond feelings toward the patient.

The second point I would make about stalemates is that we have reason to fear that things might change, but change a hell of a lot for the worse. For example, I am working with a patient currently, who has subtle paranoid processes, indeed subtle. He is an extremely obsessive man, tremendously obsessed and the work is terribly slow. There is just a bit more going on than a stalemate. But every once in a while, I glimpse his proclivities for a psychotic paranoid breakdown and I am glad that change is not occurring, if it has got to be change of that sort. So when we hear of therapists who are concerned about their patients being stalemated in therapy, I think the therapists are likely to be underestimating how afraid they are that things might change, but very much for the worse.

I desist from my comment. I could go on further because what I have heard has brought up many thoughts in my mind and I appreciate the chance to say some of what I have thought.

DR. ADLER: I would also like to respond to some of the questions and some of Dr. Searles' remarks. I want to pick up the holding theme. Do we literally hold patients? I, over the years, have seen a number of therapists in consultation that got into problems with holding patients and it usually is very problematic and not just in the way Dr. Searles spoke of it. I always wondered whether there are examples of it working well and the only one I know from the literature was that of Margaret Little who published a paper on her work with Winnicott in 1985. That was a holding in which he was not holding her in the way many patients are asked to be held. They want a skin-to-skin kind of contact; often in their histories there is a question about issues of past sexual abuse. Many of them were borderline patients. There is a significant literature that indicates statistics from the low 20 percent to 76 percent where there is a history of sexual abuse. Of course not all patients have those histories. I think some of these patients unconsciously wish to recreate some of the aspects of that in the treatment and they have all been placed in a dilemma in this regard. I had a patient like that who talked about a previous therapist who did, indeed, hold her. She saw this as a positive experience except that she was hospitalized and it led, I think, to her having to be transferred to another hospital. She wanted that from me and I felt that I could not do that for a number of reasons, both theoretical and because of the fact that she was a very attractive woman and I could see what problems would occur if I even considered something like that. The way I handled it was to say, "You know, when you work with me you are going to have to see some of my limitations. You have already seen many of them. Another one is that I cannot hold you." But there was a dilemma because she would do things where I would have to hold her. She would start banging her head against the wall. I have had many patients bang their heads against the wall, but she did it with such force that I had to step in and stop her, hold her hands. She was a woman who had had a sexual relationship with a parent, and I knew that as I touched her I was reenacting it. It is a real dilemma when you have to make an instantaneous decision. She had been psychotic in the past and became delusional in my office. When she went into the restroom, she began to pound her head against the mirror. She did not break it, but I had to go into the ladies room after her. I did not know what to do, so I said, I know that you do not want me to go near you, I know you are terrified of me, but I cannot let you keep banging your head against that mirror. You may break it and hurt yourself. You have to stop that right now or I will grab you even though I know that you do not want that. I want you to stop that right now. She stopped and we both walked out together. That is a kind of dilemma that such patients put you in. Outside of the Winnicott example, I do not know of any examples where holding works but it is a frequent longing and wishing. All my borderline patients talk about feeling dropped and longing to be held. The other point I want to make is that in talking about borderlines, I agree with Dr. Searles fully. If we are going to work well with our patients, we have to recognize "they" as "us." One of the nice things about the projective identification model is that when we use it well, it helps us acknowledge those projected feelings within ourselves. Elvin Semrad is often quoted as defining psychotherapy as a situation when one mess is there to treat a greater mess. I think that in part is acknowledging that "they" and "us" are the same.

DR. MEADOW: I love to participate in these conferences because I get a chance to examine my own countertransference and how I use it as a resistance. And now I would like to talk about the countertransference resistances of people on the panel if they would like to hear them.

I love the feelings that Dr. Adler gets with the patients. I like particularly the one of urinating on the patient. The fantasy is perfect and I think that we want to learn how to use these feelings and fantasies that we get. I noticed just one minor slip of resistance in one of his interventions. I think it is important to know that when we talk to patients we are going to reveal some of our countertransference, but if we can catch it ourselves and use it later, it will be for the benefit of the treatment. The mild one was "I will go first" with the patient who wanted to be with you always. I thought that was a holdout: "I will go first." If a patient needs me to be with him always, I am going to be with him in heaven, hell and always. So I think that intervention requires a little personal examination. Why are you planning to die and abandon this patient?

Now, with the case of the very battered abused woman whom Dr. Giovacchini presented, I feel and I believe that in the treatment of borderlines, the patient generally needs structure, not gratification. I think all the worry and guilt about gratifying them is probably a resistance to giving them the structure that they need. I felt the patient wanted to come and torture Dr. Giovacchini in the sessions, not ever have to leave and not ever be given an interpretation. That reminds me of one of Dr. Adler's patients, the woman who was very good at the language. She talked about empathy and she explained her character to him and it seemed to me that she probably did not need interpretations. I always think of interpretations as a breakdown in the treatment; when we finally have an excellent interpretation that is the point at which the patient's illness has beaten us.

DR. MADONNA: Dr. Giovacchini, would you like to respond?

DR. GIOVACCHINI: The patient certainly needs structure, I agree with that. The question is how to provide it. The only structure this patient had was her own artwork. She is a pretty good artist and she had a lot of drawings that she presented me with, which were helpful with the diagnosis of her character structure. But that was the only organized structure that she presented. I think we are dealing with such fundamental situations that it is very difficult to think in terms of sophisticated therapeutic techniques. This is a patient for whom the very act of living is painful and the only solution that such patients can present is suicide, to deaden their feelings, to soothe themselves and to escape from the terrible catastrophic torture that is going on. What can we do about this tremendous paradox?

I want to give an example of a patient who had these particular characteristics in a somewhat milder form, and was quite workable. This patient had a very traumatic childhood and was a fussy baby. Her parents hired a nurse to help her overcome her fussiness. The nurse handled it in a very interesting fashion. She gratified the baby's wishes immediately, but never the wish that was being expressed. If the baby were hungry, she would change the diaper; if the baby were wet, she would feed her. This was paradoxical gratification. The baby became very quiet indeed. When she grew up, she was an anorectic. She had a schizoid type of personality, very much withdrawn from the world. She got into treatment with a very skilled psychoanalyst who had somewhat similar problems to hers. One day this analyst said, "You know, psychoanalysis is dead. The only way to preserve it is to put it in a museum; so they will stuff me, put me in a glass case, and underneath will be written 'Psychoanalysis.'" The patient said, that will not really accomplish anything because you cannot be a psychoanalyst without a patient, so they will have to stuff me too, put me on a couch, and that way the two of us can go on together through eternity. That is the only way our existence could be preserved.

DR. GIOVACCHINI: You see the paradox, the terrible oxymoron: To be dead is to be alive; to be alive is to be dead. The only way that one can sustain life is through this feeling of deadness.

Unfortunately, from one point of view, the patient worked some of this through. She decided that she wanted to be alive on the basis of being alive. So, she got a boyfriend. The analyst killed himself. And now she is my patient. But you see what I am getting at. It is very hard to think in terms of sophisticated therapeutic techniques when you get involved in such thorny and fundamental issues as these.

Harold Searles—the many selves between analyst and patient: mutuality of the impulse for projective identification

Dr. Searles began his presentation by indicating that in his work with borderline patients, he had discovered that what was going on between him and the patient was often something that had actually transpired between two persons other than the patient himself, that is, two persons from the patient's childhood. He presented a clinical example of a woman who was quite identified with her father; a father who used to go four times a week to his mother's to have breakfast when the patient was a child. Similarly Searles' patient attended sessions with him four times a week. There seemed to be a parallel between how the patient used the sessions with Searles and how the patient's father had used his meetings with his mother. That is, the patient would come and speak to Searles about how things were going with her children. Similarly, the father's visits with his mother were concerned with how he was rearing his several children. The patient seemed to be indicating that her rearing and that of her siblings were really the grandmother's responsibility and that the father was merely a delegated agent. The patient's mother was very inadequate and could not be counted upon. Searles indicated that the feeling tone of the sessions left him with the impression that his patient's children were really his children and that he had merely delegated the care of them to his patient. He did not interpret this to the patient but gained comfort from arriving at that understanding of the patient.

Searles cited as a second example a schizophrenic woman who had played a passive role to her older sister who frequently quarreled with the dominant mother of this family. There were many stormy arguments. Searles said it was quite clarifying for him one day during a stormy session to come to the realization that the patient had been unconsciously identified with her sister in this regard. In the sessions, what were being lived out were the violent arguments between the sister and the mother. Searles has frequently seen that what goes on in this relationship with his patients is a replication of what has gone on between the patient's parents earlier in life.

Searles cited an example from his own early analysis. At the end of one of his sessions with the analyst, Searles got up and embraced his analyst warmly, saying to him, "Ernest, *when* are we going to get this analysis over with?" Searles recognized that he was treating the analysis as some sort of meaningless obligation imposed on him and his analyst, a sort of obstacle to be endured by both of them before they could consummate their relationship on another level. Searles stated that some 35 years later he did receive a clarification that he, Searles, was unconsciously identified with his father. His father, speaking to his wife, was saying, "Cora, *when* are we going to get this charade over with of me being the man in the family and you the woman?" Searles said that things were much more functionally turned about. His father was much more womanly in many regards and his mother was much more manly.

Searles went on to speak about the autistic defense of the analyst during sessions. He said that while the analyst may consciously be attempting to maintain a necessary therapeutic holding environment, there may be occasions when this is, in fact, only an illusion. That is, it may have genuinely begun as a therapeutic holding environment, but insidiously evolved into an environment that has become more geared to maintaining the defensive autism of the analyst. Searles gave two examples of this. One was from a record many years ago of Mike Nichols and Elaine May. It was a Christmas scenario with Elaine May playing the psychiatrist and Mike Nichols playing the male patient trying to explain why he would not be available for a session on Christmas Eve. The doctor in this scenario attempts to explore the situation, to understand the patient's motivation. On the surface, she is the epitome of kindness and gentleness and understanding. Beneath she is something else however, as is apparent when the patient remains determined to not attend the session on Christmas Eve. Her jealous and possessive witchiness emerges and she begins screaming at him. Searles also cited the classical psychoanalytic approach, saying that much is being swept under the rug in the interest of the analyst maintaining a neutral posture. In many instances this nonresponsiveness on the part of the analyst may be an autistic defense, a need in the analyst to remain self-preoccupied.

Searles next shared some of his thoughts about the projective identification process as it operates in work with borderline patients:

> Typically before I realize that the patient projects, what I experience is that my own true self, a self rarely glimpsed by anyone including myself, and never before revealed, so pitilessly revealed as now, has been uncovered. This is a very simple self, simply distasteful and unlikable to me, or simply detestable, abhorrent or frightening. Simply so, that it is not obviated or relieved by any attractive qualities that run this deep in my deeply true self. In these moments, I am not at all self-aware and self-accepting over any broad spectrum of personal identity feeling attributes. I do not at all feel basically comfortable, that my personal identity is like any human being's adult identity. It is comprised of a sample of everything: samples of

emptiness, sadism, futility, insufferably efficient and unfeeling know-it-allness, and so on. Nor do I feel that processes between self and patient have activated this. No, this one detestable self is subjectively my only true self. When then it later becomes evident that I am some aspect of the patient's unconscious self-projected into me, I am left feeling briefly, as if even this is not my own true self, then what is?

Searles seemed to be describing a totally enveloping process that begins from the roots up and leaves the analyst cut off from any sense of self-consistency. He rightly suggests that this process must be even more difficult for the patient who has fewer supports than the therapist.

Searles indicated that the analyst may react defensively to this projective identification process as it is experienced in the countertransference by prematurely interpreting aspects of the projective identification, in order to get rid of them or give them back to the patient. This, however, is not therapeutic, as the patient's ego is not strong enough to tolerate a conscious awareness of them. This premature conduct on the part of the analyst prevents the analyst from arriving at an understanding of the connections that exist between these phenomena and their more conscious correlates.

The projective identification process can, according to Searles, operate in reverse. He gives an example. During his first or second month at the Chestnut Lodge, Searles found himself in the presence of a threatening and quite frightening manic patient. There was only an effeminate attendant available who seemed quite insufficient to provide whatever assistance might have been needed. Searles was filled with a murderous rage toward the patient of which during the session he was unaware. Rather, he seemed to himself to be "the most passive of beings" in the face of the patient's rage and agitation. It was only when the session ended that Searles recognized his murderous fury and he was perplexed as to where those feelings had been while with the patient. He concluded that he had projected his rage into the patient and that the patient had been expressing his own fury as well as Searles'. Since that time, through his work and with trainees in supervision, Searles has continued to be reminded of the enormous patience and forbearance, which are required with angry borderline people. Anger is inevitably mobilized in the psyche of the analyst but may be kept from awareness by projecting into the patient who expresses it not only for himself, but for the analyst as well.

In a further elaboration on this process of projective identification as it evolves in either direction from patient to analyst and from analyst to patient, Searles sounds a warning. He said that if the analyst is "immobilized by omnipotence-based guilt, the analyst will not be able to sufficiently explore the phenomena being experienced, particularly projections into the patient." He stated, "Only as our feelings of guilt become modified can we examine this."

Searles indicated another facet of the projective identification process which warrants attention and which promises to be useful in analytic work. This emerged from his work with abused patients. He discovered that such patients not only identify with abusing parents and subsequently may brutalize their therapists during sessions, but to the extent that patients experience themselves as dissipating the aggressive sexual assault of their parents they experience themselves as preservers of the parents and even as healers.

It may well be that in the myriad of possible countertransference reactions the most difficult to bear is the unconscious need of the patient to help the analyst (the transference parent) to resolve the analyst's pathology. As Searles tells us, for example, "I am enormously difficult to help, especially when I am caught up in my own wish to help." Searles' unique contribution lies in his keen understanding that in order to truly become to the patient, the patient must be allowed clear and comprehensive entry into the psyche of the analyst, unobstructed by the analyst's own competing propensity for projective identification into the patient. For Searles, to become the patient seems to mean to allow the patient to activate and infuse all of those potentialities for pathology, which both patient and analyst possess. And the analyst, with eyes opened, must be willing to know it before the patient.

Phyllis W. Meadow—the salience of the mother-child, analyst-patient parallel—the power beyond words: synchronous and asynchronous states

Dr. Meadow began her presentation by stating that analysts have a great deal of feeling and may suffer in the treatment of narcissistic disorders. Such patients do not have object transferences and those working in the field have had to discover how induced feelings could be used to facilitate treatment. Such patients do not respond to words, but to rhythm or tone of the analyst's voice, to the emotional element of the analyst's communication. Borderline and narcissistic patients tend to respond to the gestures of the analyst and look for danger in the relationship. Any attempt to control the patient, persuade, convince or influence him will be met with the stonewall of narcissism. Such patients present to us as though they have no thoughts or feelings and we have no thoughts or feelings. They cannot rely on an introjective process. The patient appears to have no mechanisms. He is shut down, or internalizes his experiences, appears to be blotting our stimulation, appears to be fighting against letting the analyst in. An understanding of these primitive mental disorders can be found in drive theory. Meadow referred to Hyman Spotnitz's early work with child and adolescent schizophrenia at the Jewish Board of Guardians. One of the conclusions of that work was that deviant patterns of aggressive discharge were characteristic of the patients studied. Such patients evidenced a highly specific and ego-damaging pattern of self-protection against the discharge of destructive impulsivity within the analytic relationship. Schizophrenic behavior is to be considered a defense against the power of our destructive urges. The nuclear struggle for all such patients is "the will to live versus the will to destroy."

Patients who enter treatment would not be with us if they did not have a strong desire to live and "what we witness in the dynamics of the patient is all of the things that get in the way of that desire."

The analyst must remain in touch with the potential of a patient for destructiveness. Meadow indicated that she "experienced fear when with schizophrenic patients" as she gets in touch with the bottled-up aggression. "Patients appear detached, trying to block me off, out of touch with their own thoughts and feelings, they present as persons defended against impulses." It is the analyst's job to help patients gradually, over time, develop the ability to feel and then put into language, in the transference, those feelings they were unable to experience upon entry into treatment. Meadow says further that "whenever a mother or an analyst is able to stay in touch with feelings she may provide good-enough mothering." The needs of participants, mother and child, analyst and patient, will converge.

> The symbiotic reliving of intimacy, which is not possible in much of life, is possible in such a relationship, along with other rewards including the narcissistic pleasure in one's own creations – all serve to help the mother to respond emotionally to the infant.

Meadow warned that if the mother's:

> drives are blocked because of her own history, she may find such contact either disgusting or frightening. A strict superego may help provide the bottle at the right time but not related to the rhythm of the infant. The infant's restlessness or discomfort may further disorient the mother.

In the treatment relationship, especially at the beginning, the analyst needs to be at one with the patient who is at one with the universe. Meadow referred to Jane Goldberg who described the analytic environment as:

> like taking a bath at body temperature, feeling neither heat nor cold. The patient needs the analyst to be in tune as is the mother with an ability to gauge what is needed. Some patients will need distance, some words, some questions. Some need a good fight. Some need a silent and mild interest. Our feelings guide us in this area.

It is this intuitive power relying as it does upon the mother's ability to sense and share emotion which constitutes good-enough mothering and results in the necessary holding environment.

Meadow also referred to a twins study by Alexandra Piontelli, which gave early evidence of the life-and-death struggle, which is observed, in the consultation room. Piontelli studied twins before and after birth. Individual differences could be observed in utero back to eight weeks after conception. Each twin established a character pattern of behavior that continued after birth. Behaviors included choice of posture, repetition of certain actions, quantity and quality of body movement. Some twins showed no reaction to the strongest kicks or punches of their counterparts. This reminded Meadow of patients who seemed unaware that the analyst was in the room. Some twins reacted to perceived contact by withdrawing actively as do some patients in the analytic relationship. In some cases the contact from the other twin led to an instantaneous countercontact and immediate withdrawal, as if touched by an electric shock. This reminded Meadow of patients who become confused and disoriented if the analyst makes even the slightest move during the session. Some, when given gentle, affectionate contact, responded in kind. Others responded violently. Still another group sought out contact actively and these seemed to be the ones who were ready to know life and feel their feelings.

Piontelli concluded, therefore, that certain twins gave the impression of psychological birth while still in utero, while others seemed to refuse psychological birth even after there had been a psychical entry into the world. Character and temperament seem to predate any of the usual contacts with the mother. Some children welcome life and some dread it. The way in which analyst and patient experience and manage this issue during sessions will determine the quality of the treatment.

Meadow asked how we feel the feelings of the in utero fetus that already demonstrates either the wish to live or the wish to turn away from life. In one case, nothing seemed to help the patient to feel happy. Meadow therefore concentrated on how she and the patient could be together in a state of chronic dissatisfaction. To what extent could resolving her resistance to enjoying the patient, despite the chronic dissatisfaction, affect his enjoyment of life? The analyst gets induced with joylessness when the patient is joyless, feels detached, feels rage. These reactions need to be investigated lest the analyst be aroused to get rid of the patient or torture the patient with hurtful interpretations. According to Meadow, as the analyst struggles to understand her feeling states, she is struggling to understand what will arouse the life force which is being tenaciously resisted. Meadow asserts that the analyst needs first to achieve symbiotic resonance with the patient and then eventual asynchrony. The patient needs both.

According to Meadow, in countertransference states, the analyst moves between feelings of joy, oneness, states of deadness and impulsive and destructive urges. These primitive feeling states are contacts. They constitute symbiotic connectedness. By studying these states, the analyst can determine the amount of stimulation the patient is seeking. For example, some patients seem to be experiencing joy in the unity but are anxious about being squelched. Such behavior suggests that these patients felt welcomed at birth, that the desire for life was strong but their caretakers may have preferred that they be quiet. Such patients may induce in the analyst a desire for oneness, or the wish for the patient to be quiet. The analyst observes the countertransference reaction in order to understand the patient and does not take action until the patient makes verbal contact.

Meadow concluded that the therapeutic task is different when the analyst attempts to determine what introjects had led to pathology rather than perceiving the patient as being in a struggle, with a dominant destructive drive lowering the drive to live.

> What becoming the patient may mean is that sometimes I will experience the same feeling states as the parent or caretaker, but in earlier regressions I may experience the same feeling states as the patient when that patient was unaware that there was a 'me' and a 'not me.' In still earlier regressions I may simply experience getting in rhythm with the patient.

Meadow's unique contribution to our understanding of countertransference states lies in her ideas about primal synchronicity. According to Meadow, a synchronicity of rhythm and mood must predominate in the treatment and in this merged state of oneness; neither analyst nor patient is alone. Meadow believes this is a powerful building of force in this merger, which eventually leads to individual differentiation, psychological birth—the enhancement of the urge for life.

Panel discussion following the presentations by Harold Searles and Phyllis W. Meadow

DR. ADLER: There is one thing in Dr. Searles' work that helped me clarify something at the root of a lot of confusion with patients. I think when we get to know them well enough, we find that they are reliving some aspect of a very early or very painful childhood experience, often a relationship with a parent or a piece of a relationship with a parent or an observed relationship between two parents. Part of it can be viewed as an identification with the aggressor or an identification with the victim. And, in that, we are the one and they are the other and it goes back and forth. I think that a lot of the clinical material Dr. Searles presented very beautifully illustrated that. It is at the core of what we ultimately understand when we work with some of these patients. Dr. Meadow was also talking about some of these same issues. There is a paradox in our work with these patients in that they form transferences that are part-object relations. We are not dealing with separate people. This is the case pretty much from the beginning, with the patients we are describing. The paradox is that at the same time they may be beginning to relive pieces of whole relationships that are very painful, very charged, full of intense rage, primitive feelings of sexuality, rage in all kinds of combined ways. Both are present simultaneously and that is part of what makes especially the early work with them confusing, and part of what makes all the work with them confusing at times.

DR. GIOVACCHINI: I would like to raise some general issues stimulated by the presentations this afternoon. I want to look into the question of countertransference, the topic at this particular meeting, and ask why we get excited about it. Why has this become such an important subject? I notice that this year whenever I have been asked to speak it has always been about countertransference. This has become more popular than narcissism, creativity—other topics that in the past have gained top billing.

I think it is because we are beginning to recognize that there are feelings within us that can be extremely helpful or extremely damaging in the treatment relationship, feelings that we ignored before because Freud said that if we had such feelings we had to be reanalyzed—or something of that sort. We know feelings are a tremendous source of energy that we can harness somehow or other and I think all of the presenters today have been in one sense or another discussing that topic. Searles is intensely aware of his own reactions, but why was he even telling us about these reactions? Because somehow they affected the treatment of the patient.

More specifically, Searles has written and talked about the patient as the therapist to his therapist and vice versa. He has made the important and startling discovery that many patients want to cure their analysts— that all patients to some extent *want* to be psychotherapists. And it is true. Many patients do, in fact, become psychotherapists. They did not start out being psychotherapists, but there is a need on the patient's part to teach the therapist how to be a good therapist, in the same way that the infant has to teach the mother how to be a good mother.

Countertransference interferes in our relationship to our patients insofar as it gets in the way of our functioning as therapists and pulls us out of the therapeutic frame. The most difficult situation that we encounter in the therapeutic relationship is that of a psychotic transference. Psychotic transference, defined very simply, is the transference that occurs when the patient has destroyed the self-observing function. The transference is not dealt with as transference, but as reality, and we cannot work when that happens because we need the self-observing function. But sometimes we do that to ourselves. We destroy our own self-observing function because we are so involved in our own personal freedoms.

DR. MADONNA: Thank you Dr. Giovacchini. Dr. Searles, any final comments?

DR. SEARLES: One of the things that Dr. Adler mentioned this morning is that we cannot afford to treat too many borderline or narcissistic patients at any one time. It is too damaging to our self-esteem. I would phrase it that way, and it reminded me that at Chestnut Lodge for nearly 15 years, I was treating six chronically schizophrenic patients at any one time. A total of 24 hours a week. At the time I left there, I had no feeling of assurance that if I stayed there another 20 years any one of this bevy of six patients would ever be living outside the hospital. Since leaving, I have continued with two of those six, and both are outpatients. I am still working with them a million years later. One thing I see in retrospect is that during my years there, I lost the ability to see in perspective the role of their depre-catory mother-transference to me. I came to feel so deeply as reality my ineffectuality with them that I failed to keep in sight that they had brought into the treatment an assumption that I would prove ineffectual. Since I have gotten out of there and am working with weller patients I have regained the sense to see that transference in perspective.

I want to say one more thing about a case Dr. Giovacchini told about this morning of the man who had the wrecked sports car and who had had a socialite mother and a junkman father. Dr. Giovacchini told of his anxiety and of feeling treated as nonexistent by the patient. As I understood it he linked that up with an introject in the patient of the mother having equated the patient with his junkman father who deserved to be treated as nonexistent. The patient would project that subjectively nonexistent self, so to speak, into Dr. Giovacchini, which made for Dr. Giovacchini's anxiety. I do not think that Dr. Giovacchini would argue with this way of conceiving it, but I took it as one more very nice example of a transfer-ence in which what goes on is a repetition of something that went on between two persons in the patient's childhood other than the patient himself. That is, I felt that the patient was being identified with the socialite mother treating Dr. Giovacchini as the junkman father, which is simply another way of thinking about it. I find that way of thinking about it illuminating. But I want to remind you that the patient has within him both these inconsonant introjects, of the socialite mother and the junkman father, and we can get some sense of how nonintegrated the patient is within himself.

DR. MADONNA: Thank you, Dr. Searles. Dr. Meadow, we are going to give you the last word.

DR. MEADOW: Oh dear. Well first I would like to say that I agree with Dr. Giovacchini when he says that if we immerse ourselves in these feel-ing states we may lose our role as analysts. I think what we are trying to learn to do is to suspend the ego in the service of ego so that we can go down and come up, that is, temporarily suspending then having a functioning ego that will explain things to us, that we experience with the patient. I think that is probably very important for people to bear in mind.

I have two questions for Dr. Searles because I love his work and I want him to be a modern analyst, so these are both questions that concern how modern analysts work. Dr. Searles, on the patient you were seeing once a week sitting up, I wanted you to give up your belief in something that was interfering with you putting this patient on the couch. If he could only come once a week, why not do a couch analysis once a week?

DR. SEARLES: I never tried that. It certainly sounds virginal.

DR. MEADOW: Makes you very attractive …

DR. SEARLES: I think probably I am anxious about how attractive the patient is to me. I think that is a factor. I had occasion to tell this man, within the first few sessions, that I could imagine developing a crush on him. That is the first time I have ever told a male patient that; and he has to a degree taken me at my word and wondered what the future holds for us. I have had to scurry back and redefine my boundaries.

DR. MEADOW: If he were on the couch, you would have nothing to worry about.

DR. SEARLES: Well, he is an extremely interesting man, a very, very interesting man. I have seen him maybe a year now and he is an "as if" personality, right out of the books. He is somewhat troubled by whether the life he is living has any meaning, any inherent meaning, but what he induces in me is the question of whether I have any worth. This is where my immediate concern is session after session. I have experienced, after some months, a very troubled sense of doubt as to whether anything was going on between us, anything with any continuity to it. That is, one session will be of a certain sort, maybe quite intense, and the next session will be of a totally different sort and will seem to cancel out the first one. I have been interested to hear from him that the girlfriend he has taken up with was looking for a new car. She was with an auto salesman, and was a bit late coming back from looking at cars and driving them with the salesman. He said, "I wondered if something was going on between them." I was interested in the way he put that. It is a common enough way of putting it, but it is apparent that for him to have something really going on, between himself and another person, has a sexual meaning that he cannot accept as such.

DR. MEADOW: So the couch is a hot topic.

DR. SEARLES: Why don't I put him on the couch? I do not know. It may happen. It is possible. I have been slow to be convinced that once-a-week treatment in my hands is worthwhile. That has been one of my problems. I tend to offer interpretations much too frequently to this man in an attempt to make up for our comparative lack of time together. That is one of the mistakes I make. I give too many interpretations to him.

DR. MADONNA: I see that Dr. Giovacchini would like to respond to this question.

DR. GIOVACCHINI: I would like to respond to that question because actually, I am really promiscuous, not virginal, when it comes to once-a-week patients on the couch. I grant you I would rather see them more than once a week, in many instances as often as possible, but sometimes it is not possible. So I have tried once a week and I am utterly convinced about the timelessness of the unconscious. With many cases it does not seem to make any difference and I remember an extreme example of this. I had seen a patient for some time, for many years, once a week and then we terminated treatment because we felt that he was getting on well enough.

He came back six years later and he got right back on the couch and it was as if there had been no interruption whatsoever.

I will tell you a better story. One of my colleagues went on vacation and left my name as a backup person. Two of his patients, both once-a-week patients, called me for appointments. My colleague was gone about six weeks and I had his patients for that time. They came, they gave me no history, no introductory remarks, they just got down on my couch and continued free-associating as they had done with the colleague. Being who I am, separated and differentiated from the colleague, seemed to make very little difference. It was a ready-made transference. I do not strictly believe that. I do believe there are differences. But, from a clinical point of view, once-a-week patients on the couch work. I tried it and found it becomes more of an analytic situation because I feel so much more relaxed than when the patient sits up. It is a much easier situation.

I want to make one further comment about what Searles referred to when he talked about the bad mother. The patient was expecting that the analyst/therapist would also be a bad mother. At the beginning I used to resist the roles that patients projected into me until I realized that this was fundamentally transference. It is a difficult transference because you are reliving episodes in a patient's life where the patient has been failed, so to be a successful analyst you have to be a failed analyst and that is a paradox that is kind of hard at times to contain. But it can be done.

DR. MADONNA: Dr. Adler, any thoughts on this?

DR. ADLER: Just enjoying that last remark. That is the essence of a lot of the work with patients who had bad mothering experiences. They make us fail and I think we find ourselves making more mistakes with those kinds of patients than we ordinarily might make. Something gets unconsciously set up that makes us dumber than usual, that the patients are very aware of, and that causes guilt and shame and is part of the countertransference. I try not to rationalize it as only the reactivation of the negative maternal transference, although an important piece of it is.

DR. GIOVACCHINI: Winnicott once stated that the reason he would make an interpretation is to show the patient that he was capable of making a mistake, and that he was still alive.

DR. SEARLES: I want to mention that I have treated many patients twice a week who were on the couch ... so I am not that much of a Puritan.

DR. MEADOW: You are losing your appeal.

DR. SEARLES: I want to tell you that the patient whom I told I could imagine myself developing a crush on (which I never told any patient before) has an older brother who never married and is afraid that he is homosexual. I feel confident that I, to a significant degree, reacted to the older-brother transference that the patient formed toward me.

DR. MADONNA: Thank you Dr. Searles. Dr. Meadow, did you get to ask your second question?

DR. MEADOW: I have a second question. First, there are no drive theorists here, is that true? No drive theorists here? You do not mention drives very much.

My second question to Dr. Searles is a little difficult. When patients talk suicide and I get feelings that suicide is a controlling mechanism, a manipulation, and I get strong feelings of being manipulated, I frequently use such extremes (after investigating how they would kill themselves) as engaging in emotional communications instead of interpretations. The one I am wondering if you would be interested in trying is: "Could I help you to kill yourself?"

DR. SEARLES: Well, that is just dandy and very good stuff for the minor leagues. It is very good for patients who are more at the neurotic end of the scale. But not for the woman to whom I have been referring, whom I have been seeing going on eight years. When you are in the room with this person, you know that you are in the presence of major psychopathology. There is a feeling of electricity in the atmosphere, the knowledge that she attempted twice in her life to kill herself. She was in a coma for 24 hours once, for 48 hours another time. I once attempted to help her become aware of her disassociated murderous feelings toward her divorced husband, and within a minute and a half I became afraid she could kill him. I later learned that her previous therapist had feared that she would kill her husband. When you are dealing with psychopathology of that degree, you do not have the luxury of sharing your own fantasies with the patient. Similarly when Peter talks about various patients he has treated, I am very doubtful that he has ever treated a patient as seriously ill as those who are at Chestnut Lodge. They are a breed apart. Since I left there I have supervised dozens of their therapists, and every time I start working with a therapist who had a patient at Chestnut Lodge I find myself again awed at the depth of the psychopathology they are dealing with. So we cannot expect much of ourselves, for a long time, in the realm of sharing of fantasies with such a patient.

DR. MEADOW: These are the situations where the use of our countertransference is most important in knowing that the patient is truly manipulative and controlling, which is another kind of patient from the one described by Dr. Searles. I would like to give you the rationale for this type of intervention. If we believe that we are working with bottled-up aggression, then the purpose of such a communication is to get some of the aggression into the transference. Patients will either say, "You do not believe that. You would not help me," or they will be angry with you. They will have a little separation from the active outrage, and some of it gets put into language. But a very tricky intervention.

DR. MADONNA: I would just like to briefly ask if Dr. Adler and Dr. Giovacchini would respond to that issue and then we will conclude our conference today.

DR. ADLER: I agree with Dr. Searles and Dr. Meadow. Ultimately, it is tricky and very dangerous. For the kinds of patients who are scary in that kind of way one needs to be very cautious because there can be bottled-up aggression. There are people who so quickly misunderstand, who so quickly turn it against themselves. I would be concerned that that person would misunderstand that it is a potentially helpful thing and rather see it as a confirmation of their badness, which they are so wont to do anyhow.

DR. GIOVACCHINI: I would agree also. I am thinking of the patient that I discussed this morning, the patient with no skin, just a festering wound. To appreciate the kind of technique that Dr. Meadow is talking about requires a certain amount of ego structure. Even to be manipulated requires a certain amount of ego structure and we are talking about patients who do not have it. There is something witty and even humorous about making an offer of that sort. Wit and humor can be terribly beneficial but these patients have no sense of humor, have no sense of reality so I would think it is very, very tricky.

This chapter was originally published in 1991 in *Journal of Modern Psychoanalysis, 16*, 37–64.

Part II

Chapter 3

The third

Dan Gilhooley

I needed better defenses. During the last hour Ben smothered me with a blanket of rage. Today I felt that Ben was killing me. Psychoanalysts employ a clinical technique that is most elementally a set of defenses. Although analytic authority, anonymity, abstinence, neutrality, the use of the couch, and even interpretation were techniques created by Freud to assure the analyst's scientific objectivity and to protect the patient's independence, these techniques also insulate analysts from patients and the troubling feelings they arouse. The emotional distance provided by these techniques offers the "doctor a desirable protection for his own emotional life" (Freud, 1912, p. 115) and protects analysts from experiencing or acting upon their countertransference (Gabbard & Lester, 1995; Mitchell, 1997; Schachter & Kachele, 2007). Doing psycho-analysis is risky for both participants, and emotional insulation seems essential for patients and analysts alike. As Ogden (1989) says, "It is always dangerous to stir up the depths of the unconscious mind" (p. 172). As the analytic process stirs the depths of the analyst's and patient's unconscious minds powerful emotions emerge that can cause real harm. So we need strong defenses to manage these feelings during treatment. After spending an hour scorched by Ben's rage I needed to strengthen my defenses to withstand his powerfully negative transference. My problem was that I could not stop his murderousness.

My next hour was with Frank. "I miss him so much," he said of Anders, his 22-year-old son who died of cancer last year. Four years ago Frank first consulted me to get help for Anders who was depressed. Frank believed that if Anders could deal with his depression, then maybe he could fight off his cancer more effectively. I never met Anders, who did not want to speak to a therapist, but Frank stayed to talk about the fear, despair, and anger asso-ciated with Anders' illness. For the two previous years his son had been fighting cancer, first discovered as a lump beneath the surface of his cheek when he was 16. He had had ten major surgeries and a nearly continuous stream of chemotherapy. He lost his eye and the facial nerve on the right side of his head, and most of the last year of his life his face was disfigured by a large tumor. Anders suffered intensely, and so did Frank. During some periods Anders showed remarkable improvement, but nothing could ultimately stop the cancer that always returned, eventually spread to his brain and killed him.

Frank said that he was always an angry guy, but his son's illness threw him into rages of terrifying proportions. He would collide with a shopper in a supermarket and shove him into a rack of potato chips. He would be bumped by someone walking on the street who was talking on a cell phone and he would explode in anger. He would get into an argument over a cab and nearly end up in a fist fight. He was deeply bitter that he was losing his son. While his son's friends grew into adulthood, Frank watched Anders' broken body stagger from toilet to bed. When the cancer reached his brain, Anders began to have seizures causing him to sprawl convulsively on the floor until medicine could be administered that would calm him. These seizures were inescapable proof that his son's condition was wildly out of control, and they left Frank feeling deeply ineffectual. In the final months, on those days when he was home alone caring for Anders, he dreaded the possibility of a seizure.

During that last year of his son's life Frank talked often about killing himself. He wanted to buy a gun and blow his brains out. The realization that he was losing his son was unbearable, and after Anders' death, Frank's suicidal wishes only intensified. Having endured all this suffering, what did he have to live for? He figured he would join his son in death. Frank picked out a shotgun and studied it online. I told Frank he could not have a gun. He could look at them and talk about them, but he was forbidden to have one. He once went into a sporting goods store and placed his hand on a rifle stock and quickly left out of fear. Another time as he was driving home he began turning into the parking lot of a gun shop, only to veer just as impulsively back onto the highway. When he told me this he said, "I think Anders and you took control of the steering wheel and pushed me back out onto the highway, away from danger." Frank knew that his son wanted him to stay alive. On the last day of life Anders had made Frank promise that he would recover from his grief and grow strong again. Saying that his son and I both took control of the steering wheel made me realize that Frank identified me with the son who wanted to keep his father alive. Unknown to Frank, my father had shot himself in the head when I was 15. I knew the terrible pain of a boy losing his father, and Frank was experiencing the pain of a father losing his son. I certainly knew suicide inside out. As a boy I had once taken a rifle from my father, unloaded and hidden it when he threatened to kill us all. I wondered whether it was just coincidence that Frank ended up with me as a therapist.

"I do not think I would kill myself with a gun," he said. "What worries me is an accident, stepping off a curb into a bus, that sort of thing that my unconscious might do before I can see it coming." For example, the altercations he got himself into with strangers. Frank reported an interchange with a "junkie" in a small shop in Chinatown that he frequently visits. Though of European descent, Frank feels a strong affinity with Chinese culture, and suspects that he was Chinese in a previous life. Early one Saturday morning, just as the shop was being opened by a pair of young Chinese girls who spoke little English, Frank arrived to make a purchase. While he was there a young man came in and asked to use the restroom. In a state of incomprehension, the girls said, "No." The man persisted several times, and the shop girls resisted. Frank intervened,

"Listen, they have told you no several times. The answer is no. I think you should leave."

"What business is it of yours?" the young man responded belligerently.

"I am making it my business. I think you should get the fuck out of here," Frank said.

The junkie responded in kind. Frank stepped closer to the young man. Standing toe to toe, about a foot apart, Frank slowly raised his right arm.

Staring into the junkie's eyes he said dispassionately,

"This, my friend, is the right hand of death, and if you do not leave it is going to cut your fucking head off." The junkie stepped back incredulous.

"What are you talking about, what is going to cut my head off?"

"This hand, and the sword hanging at my side," Frank responded. The junkie looked at Frank's torso; obviously there was no sword.

"Sword? What sword? You are crazy, old man" the junkie said and walked out.

"That is right," Frank said smiling and following him out. "And if I ever see you in this store again, I am going to kill you."

Telling me this story, Frank was pleased that his craziness had taken hold in the young man and propelled him out of the store. I thought Frank was trying to provoke someone to kill him. I pointed this out to him, telling him that this was like stepping off the curb into a bus. This was another way his unconscious was pushing him toward death. Sometimes Frank wanted to be steered away from death, but at other times he wanted someone to put him out of his misery.

I wanted to protect Frank. I had failed to protect my father; I had not really seen it coming then. This time I saw it coming. I had a very real understanding of what Frank's suicide would do to his family and to me. I was surprised to find I had a strong desire to redeem myself. If I could drag Frank away from death's door, I would pay for the father I had lost through indifference. I found myself driven by 40-year-old feelings of guilt I had forgotten or never realized I possessed, and a deeply primitive talion principle of a life for a life. I began to realize that I depended on Frank for this opportunity for redemption.

Around this time it occurred to me that I was living inside a corpse. It is not that I felt dead. In fact, just the opposite. I felt energetic and alive. Yet

I began to feel that I was moving within this husk, a dead invisible hulk that seemed to envelop me, its material substance (the grainy texture of its walls) always just out of sight. It felt as though I was inside an organic version of the Nautilus, a small primitive submarine from 1800. I did not feel that it was weighing me down, but it subtly constrained me, and kept me submerged.

I felt as if I were the heart within that frozen corpse, half alive in the dead of winter. At first I thought that this corpse fantasy was a representation of my father, that I was living within his continual presence. Then I wondered if the emergence of this fantasy related to Frank, and whether this husk of death enveloped us both. Perhaps my beating heart was keeping us both alive.

I worried a lot about Frank. In the period following his son's death he would often be late or not show for his appointments, and this frightened me. When he missed an appointment, I would call each of his phone numbers and leave a message at one of them. If he had not called back in a few hours, I would call again, or I would wait until the next day and then I would call. I felt uncomfortable about making these second calls. On the one hand, Frank was in a desperate and dangerous state, teetering at the edge of life, and I felt I had to "go get him." But that was only one source of my discomfort. I believed that these second calls revealed a desperate, frightened feeling in me along with my redemptive need to save him. I did not want Frank to know about that. I was ashamed of this shadow peeking out from my past outlining the shape of my own loss and guilt. I tried to avert my eyes from it, and I certainly did not want Frank to see this painful reflection of me. One morning Frank did not show up for his appointment, and I called and left a message on his phone. Not hearing back from him, at three that afternoon when I had a break I called his cell phone. He answered.

"What happened this morning?" I asked.

"Oh, hi. Oh, ah, I forgot. I forgot what day it was."

"Where are you now?"

"Where am I? I do not know. I am in a bookstore looking at rows of books. I have just been wandering. I do not know where I am." He sounded out of breath, in a fog. "I had a presentation I had to make at work. I got out at one and never went back. I have just been wandering around since then. I do not know where I am." It sounded like he was looking around trying to get his bearings. He paused. "Look, I do not think I can do this, I cannot talk about this, it is just too painful."

"I know it is too painful, but I think that talking is the only thing that is going to get you through this," I said. As I spoke I wondered if he was right; maybe he really was better off not talking.

"I do not know. I do not know; I guess you are probably right. It is just so unbearable. It is unbearable to talk about." Frank took a deep breath and then was silent. "Ah, okay, I will see you next Friday," he said, and as an aside before signing off, "Thanks for calling."

Frank could not bear talking, so he was communicating through his actions. Frank made me feel as isolated, lost, disoriented, and frightened as he was; completely adrift with no shore in sight. I was angry with Frank. I was angry with him for filling me with these awful feelings of desperation, for his part in spilling out this shadow from my past and forcing me to see this humiliating shape of myself. I knew Frank must be angry at me for the same thing, for forcing him to experience feelings of loss and despair in my presence, and to be confronted by this pathetic image of himself. I was angry that Frank was not doing therapy the way I prescribed; not following what I knew in my heart would be a path toward life. He was doing it his way. But his way felt like there was no path, no way out. Frank filled me with feelings without showing up or saying a word. This method of communication was perfectly efficient. Perhaps these enactments really were a better way for him to do therapy, but I was having a difficult time with it. At some point during his next session when the topic of last week's absence came up I said,

"Look, this is impossible. I cannot stand this. You come in here and tell me that you are worried about your unconscious pushing you into an oncoming bus ..."

"And then I do not show up for my appointment," Frank completed my sentence with a smile.

"How do you expect me to react?" I said.

Frank responded, "No, you are right."

"And you are smiling about it," I said with frustration in my voice.

"I see what you mean. I think it is kind of funny. It is not funny of course, the position I put you in. It is not right," he said.

"That is right, it is not right," I agreed.

It was not right according to me, the pleasure he seemed to take in my discomfort was not right. But to Frank, it seemed just right.

The next week Frank reported a dream he had in which he opened the front door of his country home one Saturday morning and found me there having arrived as a weekend guest. Frank pointed out that it was the reverse of a well-known movie in which a patient followed his analyst on vacation; in this case the analyst was following the patient. We laughed about it together, but the image left me feeling uncomfortable.

"Do you make house calls?" Frank asked. "I could introduce you to my friends as my live-in analyst, always on call."

"I do seem to be chasing you down with those phone calls."

"No, that is good; you are keeping an eye on me. That is what I need you to do. I am so out of it sometimes."

Frank thought of me as someone looking out for him and ever-present. I was comforted by the image of Frank bringing me into his home. But I was embarrassed by that picture of me in the dream standing at Frank's doorstep. I would become the dependent therapist clinging to his patient who was trying to escape. I could not let him go; it was too dangerous to let him go. Frank's dream conveyed to me that he was unconsciously aware of my dependency on him, and I think he was aware of my discomfort and humiliation about it. It also occurred to me that Frank helped create these feelings between us because he felt uncomfortably dependent on me and humiliated to be seen in his desperately weakened state. Frank saw himself as a powerful patriarch leading his family. To be seen by me as incapacitated, not knowing which way to turn, was humiliating. Perhaps Frank found relief in knowing that I was uncomfortably dependent on him, and also felt humiliated and powerless. He seemed to need this symmetry. This fundamental sameness became the foundation of what Spotnitz (1969) called a narcissistic transference, or what Searles (1979) described as a therapeutic symbiosis. Frank and I were clinging to each other, uncomfortable in our mutual dependency, pulled together by the magnetism of loss.

A couple of weeks later I had a dream in which I woke up dead. In fact those words, "I woke up dead," echoed in my mind announcing the beginning of the dream. I hovered above my body that was lying motionless in bed. I circled it, checking for signs of life. Was I breathing? I reached out to lift my hand, to prod myself in order to rouse me. My body lay there motionless under a white sheet. I concluded that I really was dead. For being dead I felt fine, literally "carefree," and I seemed to move about effortlessly. It was easy being dead, and I was surprised that I was not a bit upset about my death. I guessed it must have happened in my sleep. I woke from the dream and sat up, swinging my legs over the side of the bed. I thought, "I really am dead in the mind of Ben." Weeks earlier, in a fit of rage, Ben had dramatically ended treatment. "Why do I have such difficulty accepting the reality of my death in his mind?" I wondered. "I am dead in this case. Get it, I am dead. It is the part I play," I told myself as I got up. But Ben's leaving was not a painless death like I experienced in my dream. In Ben's case I felt dismal, and I wondered if that was part of why it was so painful to let him go: A life sentence as a failure. "That is part of the transference," I thought as I trudged downstairs to make some coffee.

Later that week during his session Frank again described his awful despair at the loss of his son. "He is in my thoughts all the time," he said weeping. Near the end of the session Frank said, "I had a strange dream this week. I dreamt that I woke up dead."

I came to life. Frank went on to explain that he thought that this was a turning point, a signal from his dead son Anders who, having achieved angelic status, was now guiding Frank's mourning. "I think it means a kind of transition, a moving on. I think Anders is showing me the way." His dream was about life after death. Frank felt that his son had transcended the cycle of mortal pain and had moved on to heaven. Anders' role now, Frank said, was to help him recover from his son's death.

"When did you have this dream?" I asked.

"It was the beginning of the week, Monday or Tuesday," he said. "Why do you ask?"

"Tuesday morning I dreamt that I woke up dead," I told him.

Frank glanced over at me out of the corner of his eye. "Really?" he said.

"Really," I responded. "I have never had a dream like that before."

Frank looked at me with disbelief, perhaps some suspicion. I thought a part of him did not really believe me, or he did not know what to make of this. "I suppose that that is possible, that you are just connected up with all this," he said. "It makes sense."

It did not make any sense to me. How could I have had such a parallel dream? Where did it come from? Why now? By concluding, "It makes sense," Frank appeared to arrest further exploration. We did not say another word about it. The revelation about my dream seemed to upset him. It interrupted and confused him. So, I never described my dream to him, and he never described his dream to me. Instead, Frank focused on the meaning his dream had for him, how it was a message from his son.

Frank was right. This dream was a turning point. Frank began writing a story about life after death that begins with the protagonist announcing, "I woke up dead," the very phrase that heralded the beginning of my dream. The story is a dreamlike noir detective novel set in a timeless space between life and death, in which an unnamed man tries to find the path to eternal life. Every week Frank wrote more of the story and read a segment to me. I thought the story was a wonderful relief from the painful realities of mourning. Each week a portion of the session would be spent with the story. He would explain how he imagined the plot unfolding; he literally was making it up as we went along.

Each week brought curious surprises. For example, one of the main characters in the story was a German architect named Max who went progressively mad contemplating one of Zeno's paradoxes. Max's growing realization that no two lines could ever converge meant that the architectural structures he created (his entire life's work) were nothing but an illusion. Max came to realize that the manmade structures in the world were physical impossibilities held together by a mysterious collective unconscious, a kind of adhesive hallucinatory force that was now weakening. Max could see the fissures, the fault lines beginning to form in New York City's buildings. His awareness of this weakening adhesive force drove him to despair and insanity. Because of his persistent state of mental anguish, for some time Max had been seeing a Freudian psychoanalyst. They met twice weekly in the doctor's fifth floor, Bauhaus-decorated office. Max contended that they could not really be on the fifth floor because the building was merely an illusion.

The doctor formed a diagnosis of Max as obsessional and paranoid. The analyst disagreed with Max's convergence theorem and declared that the architect's belief in a deteriorating adhesive mental force holding the world together was "a delusion." This opinion threw the architect into a fit of despair. In retaliation Max hurled the doctor out the office window to prove to him once and for all the illusory nature of physical reality. Moments later, standing over the dead body lying on the pavement five stories below, Max said, "See what I mean. Get up!" Prodding the psychoanalyst's motionless body, he said, "Quit playing dead."

Listening to this I glanced over my shoulder at the office window, "It is lucky that I am on the first floor."

"Yeah," Frank laughed. "You are safe." I was struck by the image of a man standing above a dead psychoanalyst, trying to rouse him, disbelieving his death. It was just like my dream of waking up dead in which I circled my dead body prodding myself. As the story develops, Max and his psychoanalyst—who, being trapped in a space between life and death, never really dies—both share an apartment. They are destined to repetitively reenact the same scene of "living, dying, and living" again and again. Weeks later I remembered the phrase I told myself when I awoke from my dream: "I am dead in this case. Get it, this is the part I play," and I realized how perfectly that phrase fit the part of the doctor in Frank's story who dies again and again.

How could I explain Frank and I both dreaming of "waking up dead?" Who was the dreamer of this dream? Did our dreams cross?

At first, I thought that Frank was the dreamer and somehow I became aware of his dream. Or, perhaps in some mysterious telepathic way Frank became aware of my dream. As Freud (1933) says, "sleep seems particularly suited for receiving telepathic messages" (p. 37). But now I wonder if Frank and I dreamt the dream together, as one mind. Has some new identity been born through our therapeutic symbiosis, a convergence of shared aspects of our characters bound together by an adhesive hallucinatory force of our collective unconscious? By working together have we grown some form of shared mental structure, some portion of our minds which is "us" rather than "Frank" or "me?"

Ogden (2004) describes the analyst's and patient's co-creation of a "third" subjective representation in each of their minds, born out of an intersubjective process of projective identification, which is used for the purpose of psychological growth. Through this newly created "third" each participant is able to experience thoughts, feelings, and perceptions that had previously been outside their realm of experience.

> The individuals engaged in this form of relatedness unconsciously subjugate themselves to a mutually generated intersubjective third for the purpose of freeing themselves from the limits of whom they had been to that point ... The new intersubjective entity that is created, the subjugating analytic third, becomes a vehicle through which thoughts may be thought, feelings may be felt, sensations may be experienced, which to that point had

existed only as potential experiences for each of the individuals participating in this psychological-interpersonal process.

(p. 189)

In Frank's story Max the architect goes mad and then engages his psychoanalyst in a pattern of repetitive symbolic reenactments of death and rebirth. For Max, going mad appears to be the first step in the therapeutic process. Perhaps the symbiosis that developed between Frank and me is an evolving, encapsulated mutual madness created through telepathically communicated unconscious processes, creating a therapeutic healing space. Perhaps Frank and I unconsciously write this story together. At times our two minds appear to be working in unconscious synchrony.

How can I make sense of Frank's story of Max and his psychoanalyst? I suspect that the story represents an aspect of Frank's unconscious understanding of the therapeutic symbiosis developing between us. At first, the story of Max's obsession with Zeno's paradox appears to be nonsensical, a confusing mixture of two ideas drawn from ancient Greek philosophy. Max seems to confuse the geometer Euclid's postulate that parallel lines never converge with the numerous paradoxes of the philosopher Zeno. To my knowledge, none of Zeno's paradoxes involve parallel lines converging though many involve space, time, and infinity, and all conclude with the suggestion that reality is not what it appears. The fact that parallel lines never converge does nothing to undermine the integrity of architectural structures, so what is Max getting so upset about?

Yet Max is extraordinarily distressed by the logical impossibility of convergence. Max's delusion does make sense in a broader interpretation of Zeno's paradoxes where the concept of convergence is associated with our therapeutic symbiosis. Zeno's paradoxes are believed to have been authored as logical proofs in support of the notion that "plurality is an illusion" and that really "all is one" (Huggett, 2004). For Max, what threatens the integrity of man's structures is the logical impossibility of convergence; and for Frank, the integrity of his mental structure is threatened by this same logical impossibility. Without convergence of our two unconsciouses, without a therapeutic symbiosis that eliminates plurality and mixes us together as one, Frank unconsciously believes that the structure of his mind will fracture and disintegrate.

Just as Max believes the integrity of man's structures are held together by a hallucinatory adhesive force of our collective unconscious, the symbiosis that has developed between parts of my and Frank's unconscious minds—this intersubjective third that we have created—may be bound together by a similar hallucinatory form of adhesion. This caused me to think again about my fantasy of living within a corpse, an invisible husk that envelops both Frank and me, and I began to wonder whether this container is a three-dimensional representation of the third we have created between us.

What does this have to do with my defenses as an analyst? Everyone shares conflicting desires to be seen and known and to remain safely hidden (Aron, 1996). Being seen is risky. Very bad things can happen if you are seen. But being known and being understood brings with it a pleasure unlike anything else in life, so each one of us struggles against our most natural fears and takes risks to be seen. But do not underestimate these powerful, deeply rooted fears about being seen, and remember that we have evolved from people who for hundreds of thousands of years stayed alive by remaining hidden most of the time.

In psychoanalysis the patient is seen a little bit at a time and slowly becomes known, while the analyst tries to remain hidden. The analyst's technique is primarily a method of hiding; it provides the analyst with a set of defenses against the patient's intrusive vision. This is a good thing as far as it goes, but these defenses may only work on a conscious level. It is unclear what protection they provide against unconscious processes, and the therapeutic process, as we know, is a deeply unconscious one happening between the unconscious minds of the patient and analyst.

Freud (1912) advises the analyst to "turn his own unconscious like a receptive organ towards the transmitting unconscious of the patient," adjusting himself to the patient's transmissions, "so that the doctor's unconscious is able, from the derivatives of the unconscious which are communicated to him," to understand the patient (pp. 115–116). Employing Ogden's model of the third, patients need access to the analyst's unconscious to grow and to heal, and that can only happen if the conscious analyst can sit still (hour after hour) and allow that to happen. But this means that analysts have to endure a sustained level of continuously experienced anxiety over being seen. This is really too much for anyone to endure. So, I think the analyst's consciously employed technical defenses really serve as a form of "local anesthesia" allowing analysts to consciously believe that they are fully hidden, while their unconscious becomes accessible to the patient. Anonymity seems to be a necessary illusion fostering the analyst's participation.

What was the role of enactment in developing this therapeutic symbiosis between us? Frank needed to penetrate my defenses. He needed me to cast out this shadow of myself that was so similar to him. He did not need to know very much about me, but he needed to know this specific part, and it was important to him that I was consciously defended against giving it up. This was, of course, a mirror image of Frank's position. Frank was just as consciously defended against revealing his painful and shameful parts. Frank's enactments were natural experiments designed to circumvent my conscious defenses to obtain highly contextualized information about me. I think Frank believed that knowledge he acquired through actions he controlled, where my feelings of redemption, fear, and humiliation were revealed, was truer, more valid, and more reliable than anything I could have said to him. Importantly, if I had not been defended against providing this information, it would have had much less significance for Frank.

Modern analysts might say that Frank developed a narcissistic transference, but this only tells half the story. Meadow (1996) describes a narcissistic transference as the patient's regression to an infantile state of undifferentiation where there is an inability to distinguish self from other. Yet our apparently mutual dream of "waking up dead," and Frank's descriptions in his story so closely paralleling my dream, stretches the conception of narcissistic transference, suggesting that we developed a mutual narcissistic transference. Creating this symbiotic state appears to have been a process requiring the active participation of both of us. Though I was insulated by my consciously manipulated defenses, my unconscious was obviously permeable, perhaps easily accessible during Frank's skillfully crafted enactments. The symbiosis that has developed between Frank and me appears to have been formed from slivers of sameness drawn from a much larger world of differences that distinguish us as separate people. Frank seemed to have been searching for sameness in areas of intense vulnerability, and in these spaces Frank and I appear to have achieved a Zeno-like undifferentiated state where "all is one."

From the point of view of the analyst's defenses, it is important to acknowledge that this merger reflects a kind of insanity, a mutual psychotic transference. More than anything, analysts feel the need to protect themselves from their own and their patient's insanity. This seems to be a mistake. As Freud (McGuire, 1974) cautioned Jung about the dangers of countertransference, "it is best to remain reserved and purely receptive; we must never let our poor neurotics drive us crazy" (pp. 475–476). Yet this case suggests that the analyst's and patient's going partially crazy together is a necessary first step in a curative process.

Naturally it is frightening to experience and difficult to acknowledge these crazy states. For example, the esteemed psychoanalytic researcher Anders Stoller (Mayer, 2001) wrote a paper describing a number of telepathic dreams that were similar to my dream of waking up dead, though he never submitted the paper for publication out of fear that it would damage his career. It is easier to accept this process of mutual madness if you conceive of psychosis as a movement toward health—as the person's attempt to bring a troubling internal state into the world for its potential modification—that should be embraced, rather than seeing psychosis as the end-product of a psychological disease that needs to be disavowed, arrested, or eliminated.

Finally, why did I initially attribute my "waking up dead" dream to my painful difficulties with Ben? Perhaps there is a logical as well as an irrational explanation for this. As things developed, it became apparent that my dream had a lot more to do with Frank than Ben, and that my initial associations to Ben appear to have been a mistake. I think this reflects the dramatic split between my conscious and unconscious mental states and again highlights my defenses. As my conscious mind first looked at my dream, it related its content to my most pronounced emotion at that moment: the painful feeling of having been injured by Ben. Consciously I instantly tried to protect myself by making sense of the dream in a way that would help me cope with this injury.

For example, I comforted myself with the thought, "that is part of the trans-ference." Interpreting my dream in this way was like reflexively covering a bruised knee. Later, in a different defensive state, I realized a deeper and more complex meaning could be made of the dream with Frank.

That is the logical explanation; now here is an irrational alternative. Although my initial associations connecting my dream to Ben appear mis-taken, many aspects of my dream and Frank's subsequent story could also apply to Ben, and these lead to another possible explanation. For example, feeling perpetually trapped in a space between life and death, living in a world that is falling apart, the image of a figure standing over Ben's body wondering whether he is alive or dead, and the role of "playing dead," are all narratives that make sense in Ben's life. What meaning can be made of this? Are these themes so universal that they can apply to all of us? Perhaps, or on that Tuesday morning did Ben also have a dream of waking up dead? Of course, we will never know the answer to this question. But it raises the issue of what an analyst does with multiple symbiotic states occurring simultaneously with several patients. Furthermore, if Frank and I were drawn together by the magnetism of loss, who is to say that this magnetism would not have pulled Ben along in its wake.

In our session today Frank described a new kind of dream of Anders; this was the first one in which his son was healthy. Anders had regained his health. In the last year Frank has typically dreamed of Anders as still sick, sick but still alive, in the hospital. Today Frank said,

> This dream was different. For some reason he never looks at me in these dreams. I think it is just too much for him to see me in such pain. He said, 'Dad, will you shut the door?' He was on the other side of the doorway. I would not do it. I do not know why. The dream just ended.

Frank was momentarily overcome with feeling. Then he referred to a character in his story who serves as a guardian of a portal that allows the protagonist to traverse across time between worlds. Frank said, "That is what I am going to have the guardian figure say, his last line, it will be, 'Will you shut the door?'" Frank wiped tears from his eyes. Today as I often do, I announced the end of our session with the statement, "That is all the time we have for today." Frank laughed as he rose from the couch.

> You know, that is going to be the last line in this story. I do not know how I am going to work it in, but that is the last line. 'That is all the time we have for today.'

Frank rose from the couch and looking back over his shoulder said, "See you next week," before closing the door behind him.

This chapter was originally published in 2010 in *Modern Psychoanalysis, 35*, 68–84.

References

Aron, L. (1996). *A meeting of minds: Mutuality in psychoanalysis.* Hillsdale, NJ: The Analytic Press.

Freud, S. (1912). *Recommendations to physicians practicing psychoanalysis* (Standard Edition), 12, 111–120. London: Hogarth Press.

Freud, S. (1933). *Dreams and occultism* (Standard Edition), 22, 31–56. London: Hogarth Press.

Gabbard, G., & Lester, E. (1995). The early history of boundary violations in psychoanalysis. *Boundaries and boundary violations in psychoanalysis.* New York: Basic Books, 68–86.

Huggett, N. (2004). Zeno's paradoxes. *Stanford Encyclopedia of Philosophy.* http://plato.stanford.edu/entries/paradox-zeno/ (accessed April 24, 2010).

McGuire, W. (1974). *The Freud/Jung letters: The correspondence between Sigmund Freud and C. C. Jung.* Princeton: Princeton University Press.

Mayer, E. (2001). On "telepathic dreams?": an unpublished paper by Robert Stoller. *Journal of the American Psychoanalytic Association,* 49, 629–657.

Meadow, P. (1996). The preoedipal transference. *Modern Psychoanalysis,* 21, 191–200.

Mitchell, S. (1997). Introduction: From heresy to reformation. *Influence and autonomy in psychoanalysis.* Hillsdale, NJ: The Analytic Press, 1–32.

Ogden, T. (1989). The initial analytic meeting. *The primitive edge of experience.* Northvale, NJ: Jason Aronson Inc, 170–193.

Ogden, T. (2004). The analytic third: Implications for psychoanalytic theory and technique. *Psychoanalytic Quarterly,* 73, 167–195.

Schachter, J., & Kachele, H. (2007). The analyst's role in healing: Psychoanalysis-plus. *Psychoanalytic Psychology,* 24, 429–444.

Searles, H. (1979). *Countertransference and related Subjects: Selected papers.* New York: International Universities Press.

Spotnitz, H. (1969). *Modern psychoanalysis of the schizophrenic patient.* New York: Grune and Stratton.

Chapter 4

The look

John Madonna

Prior to entering treatment, J's life consisted of a long period of employment as an instructor at a junior college. Good looking, personable, and hard-working, he got along well with his colleagues and fit easily into the social life of the college, which, he said, "represented a family atmosphere." He engaged in many sexual liaisons with female staff. J was 30 years old when he sought treatment for a debilitating anxiety and depression following the break-up of a very intense love relationship with a woman. After less than a year he had found the woman to be emotionally unavailable, despite her sensuality. She had, however, left him. Around the same time, J also felt disappointed by a male colleague who had asked him to co-teach an interesting course, but then recanted. Both of these events had left him with the unbearable feeling that he was "alone in the world." Prior to commencing sessions with me, he had been hospitalized for his inability to manage his anxiety, which had eventuated into repetitive panic attacks for which there had been no relief. He dreaded that he would lose all control of his mind. He had been unable to work. Neither the outpatient psychiatric medication nor any attempt at social contact seemed to sufficiently allay his fears.

After an initial interview, he chose to continue with me because, he said, "I felt understood, like I had an ally." This was in response to my comment that he had been "going through hell." Fearful, agitated, and depressed, J cried deeply and often during that first session (and subsequently during the early months of treatment). He seemed shocked at the depth of anxiety and depression, which had overtaken him. His demeanor was one of desperation as he recounted the details of his "breakdown." He was frantic in his doubt about the prospects of getting better. Nevertheless, he accepted the couch without objection (and also agreed to participate in group therapy). I simply listened and encouraged him to talk. He did so, but I did not get the sense that he was talking to me, so much as at me. J's verbalization seemed like a nervous and sad soliloquy. It was as though he was almost totally engulfed in his fear and at a great distance from any real contact or capacity for connectedness.

When, during these early sessions, J spoke of his family, it was as if a silent movie was being shown and he, the projectionist, was a mere shadow in the dimly lit room. My occasional questions or comments seemed apparent intrusions, which did not much assuage his nervousness and grief.

As time passed, I came to discover a darker side to J's interests and conduct. In his calmer moments he revealed that he frequently flew alone to Philadelphia, where he had once worked, in order to visit the purveyors of live pornography in the sex shops, which flourished in the inner city. There, he would watch live sex shows involving straight or gay participants. On other occasions in lightless booths from which he could not be seen, he would masturbate as he instructed the female performing a few feet from him to engage in self masturbation. Often he would touch the woman on the buttocks and insert his finger into her anus. As he did so he would experience "a heightened sense of arousal." On a rare occasion, when he said he "felt more depressed," he would feel the anatomy of she-males who were performing. Invariably J would return home, filled with self-loathing.

Despite his subsequent torment over these escapades, J regularly sought prostitutes closer to home to expose their buttocks for him to touch and invade with his fingers. He said he found satisfaction engaging in casual conversation while asking these women to bend over and expose themselves so he could touch them in this way. "Talking with them about it was erotic." At other times he enacted fantasies in which he exposed his penis to the groveling and licentious admiration of real members of both sexes. At rest stops J occasionally, when intoxicated, engaged in homoerotic contact. These behaviors were risky not so much from the prospect of physical attack, as he said he had a knack for assessing the power differential between himself and the other, as from his being discovered and discredited. It appeared as though such behaviors were competing toward two ends. At one level his behavior reflected sadistic enactments aimed at shoring up what he felt was an ego under threat of dissolution; on another level it seemed pointed toward destroying his image, his "look" of respectability. The restorative aim of perverse behavior in ensuring ego integrity and self-preservation, despite the risk of ruin and destruction, which is also inherent, is comprehensively discussed by Robert Stoller (1976) and Joyce McDougal (1995). Though J always emerged from these episodes feeling badly about himself, viciously self-attacking and "empty," these behaviors persisted with some regularity through the initial years of treatment. As I got to know him his behavior did at times induce anxiety in me for his safety. This, I attempted to manage with diligent restraint, supervisory consultation, responsiveness to his extra-analytic contact (he began to call regularly between sessions when fearful or stressed), and careful questioning in response to his inherent and evolving desire to want to know the etiology of his destructive impulses in order to master them.

As J's commitment to treatment strengthened, his anxiety began to abate. He was able to meet and engage in more conventional ways with women, and formed excellent relationships with several of them. However, he was not able to bring to these a real commitment and they ended in disappointment.

Always his approach to women was marked by a significant search for the "right look," which was ever elusive.

J's insistence upon his women presenting a certain appearance was unrelenting. For example, he would want them to always wear makeup in a particular way and to wear their hair down and loose. If the woman did not comply he would become anxious, agitated, and angry. Similarly, J would spend, he said, "inordinate amounts of time" gazing in mirrors at his own reflection searching again and again for just the right view of himself—the one in which his features did not appear distorted and unacceptable. Frequently, he drove from store to store or from one restaurant to another until he found the perfect light in the perfect glass, which illuminated his image in just the right way. He would then for a while be soothed and feel "a sense of power and aliveness," and more viscerally to feel as though he existed. J had been, he said, engaging in this search for just the right view of himself for many, many years prior to entering treatment. It was, I believe, now a manifestation of how weakened his ego had become under the pressure of attempting to manage, what would be discovered to be, powerfully hostile urges which he was struggling to contain in the form of his perverse and dangerous enactments.

Eventually, when J seemed to become more aware of me, he would also comment on my appearance. At times he was concerned that I was "not properly attired," was "too thin," "looked old," was "too formal," "aloof" in my demeanor, and so on. These assumed deficits were reported with what felt like a mocking pleasure, yet there was some inherent distress in the tone of these utterances as well. It was as though if I as the analyst did not have the right look, J would be lacking in the authority and power with which he needed to identify, and so attain a soothing sense of security. He said as much. In the emerging transference, even at the early stages of treatment, the contest between this urge to identify with a potentially restorative object was counterbalanced by the need to minimize and denigrate. However, to the extent that the latter represented the beginning externalization of J's aggression, it may have represented a readiness to advance toward health. In fact, later J was able to say that his criticisms "became a way of making contact with you."

As I recall it now, I often felt as though I was being cast in the role of a spectator in a drama in which J displayed increasingly risky, and what seemed to me at the time, dangerous forms of perversity. It seemed as though I was being drawn tacitly into his fantasy life. I wondered whether he wanted me to experience his fear-wrought desire for help, or to involve me in voyeuristically witnessing his sado-masochistic efforts to destroy himself. In fact, there were times when I felt compelled to attempt to curb J's excesses. Consequently, on occasion I told him to stop the behavior, which was potentially treatment destructive. I told him that if he was to be arrested, contract an incapacitating disease, be assaulted or killed, treatment would come to an end or at the very least be interrupted. The assertive prohibition and the emotional concern conveyed by it diminished such behavior, and the anxiety and despair which was associated with it. J became more reflectively exploratory in responses.

Although I was ambivalent about issuing directives, this "active technique" first instituted by Ferenczi (Stanton, 1991) conveying unequivocal emotional presence, which Maroda (2004), Spotnitz (1985), and Meadow (2003) also utilized, seemed to help. In fact, J often called me between sessions to ask for help to control the impulse to act. These calls, he said, enabled him to "feel connected." My willingness to expand the usual treatment perimeters and to take those calls conveyed an important sense of my presence in a way that was sustaining for him, given how alone and intensely anxious he felt so much of the time. On those occasions when he succumbed to the impulse to act, it also began to seem related to perceived lapses in my ability to do so, that is, to be watchful and engaging in a way he needed. These were times when I could not be reached, failed to say the right thing the right way (i.e. "did not provide analytic insight"). There were instances, for example, when J would simply demand on the phone that I tell him what his behavior meant, why he was doing what he was doing. Though I did not usually comply, it was as though as long as I was there on the line and he did not feel ignored his anxiety was contained, as was his urge to act.

The very act of paying attention in the beginning and as the treatment progressed, regularly "seeing" J through the many details of his life beyond only the events mentioned, was important to him. That is, the analyst's interested gaze was upon him not only when he recounted the riskier transactions with the world, but also when he attempted contact with regular women. Despite the misses, I remained a constant enough witness to further the sense that I was both present and watchful in all domains. At this level it was not in interpretations given, as these were few. Rather it was in utilizing the patient's need to be seen, and fashioning that into an attitude and demeanor of attentional focus consistently conveyed. This was further augmented by including J in a group process in which many eyes were brought to bear. Later in the treatment when his desire to have even more contact with me developed, he would attend lectures which I conducted, conferences which I chaired, and classes I taught. One innovation was when J expressed a desire to attend as a student an advanced class in psychological dynamics in which I was a student. I did not object to this shared experience. Though at times I experienced some apprehension related to my own concerns about being negatively evaluated by him, and/or some worry about transferential contamination, I agreed to and even came to encourage this extra-analytic contact appreciating the importance of it in this case. It felt as though we were reconstructing a stage of early development in which the ever-watchful mother enables a necessary experience of separation and rapprochement (Mahler, 1968). That is, a regaining and repairing of an aspect of emotional presence, the co-construction of which had been initially poorly executed.

Experiencing me in this extra-analytic way was, according to J, "very important throughout the treatment." It was the security I think which he derived from this that enabled him to do the difficult work of reliving and renegotiating early sadistic strivings, as well as the primitive greed and frustration fueling them. He was able to regress, represent transferentially and navigate through these moments without being overcome by fears of abandonment. On one occasion, for example, J stridently said, "I want you to instruct me rather than doing analysis." He persisted in his demand despite my inquiries. Becoming enraged by my attempts to explore this, he said such things as, "I am paying for this. If I want you to bend over and drop your pants, then that is what I expect." The anal sadism formerly enacted with prostitutes had now become emotionally alive in the transference. It was to be heard and tolerated by me without retaliation, and without repeating the early abandonment he experienced by his mother. This process of repudiation of me by this man, my tolerance of it and the working through, time after time, examining and talking about what had just occurred, was to ultimately prove restorative.

As the treatment progressed, the attacks accelerated in frequency and intensity. He compared me unfavorably, for example, with other therapists he knew of, as well as professors with whom he had studied, accused me of being provincial, "a small town yokel." His observations of me in the academic settings mentioned provided him with ammunition for his attacks. The educational program with which I was associated was disparaged by him, as were my colleagues. He voiced a particular condescension toward the women faculty with whom I worked; he imagined them to be hostile and sadistic. He was unremitting in his condemnations of me for my association with them. All the while, he presented himself as superior. He, unlike me, had left a provincial city. He had, unlike me he believed, become a regular attendant at professional meetings and conferences sponsored by other and better academic departments. J, however, denied any malicious intent regarding such comments, saying he was "just having fun. I always had a deep, overall general liking for you." He added in a tone of gracious condescension that he in fact "wanted to have (me) join (him)" at those better institutions.

Later when J married and acquired property and status, he seemed to relish the impression that he had become worldlier than I. He was, he claimed, with some accuracy, in better physical shape, could "whip my ass" and was tempted to do so. He was also strident in his assertion that he read more than I did and dreamed that he would ultimately present papers in his discipline at teaching conferences, which I would attend as an intellectual inferior in search of his favor. There, as perhaps was the case with him when he was sent away as a child, I would be patronized and then summarily dismissed.

There were sessions during which he said he would fire me if I did not concede to his demands (i.e. to tell him how to conduct certain aspects of his life or give him advice on how to handle a coworker) and would devalue the quality of my interventions with him. Frequently, he referred to me mockingly by my first name. On at least one occasion he stormed out of a session, the fault he said being mine. On another occasion, he complained that I had been being cold and arbitrary in announcing an increase in my fee. Though he had stated early on that he never wanted to become friends with me, it bothered him that this relationship was apparently "all about money." Upset and bitter, he said he had serious doubts about whether the treatment was worth the cost, despite the fact that my fee was moderate and the first fee raise in many years. J's sadism eventually succeeded in arousing my own, which I was barely able to contain at times. However, I was aware that responding in kind would not be therapeutic for him. This condescending and attacking behavior went on for a long time and seemed to have the intent of debasing me, while simultaneously keeping me looking at him, although from the position of an unsatisfactory wounded supplicant, dependent, admiring and envious—a reflection of his own maternal rejection and its consequences.

During this phase of the treatment, it seemed that no matter what I said, no matter how reliable or understanding I was, nor how I extended myself, I was found deficient. The induced feeling was that I simply was not good enough. The point was for me to have the impression that I did not and could not measure up; others were much better than I. I was inconsequential and more poignantly, I was dispensable. It seemed as though this was an important transferential communication indeed, which he needed to make and which I needed to receive and tolerate. In fact, J's most vivid fantasy was of calling me up and saying, "Well, Johnny, you are fired." Psychologically savvy he, himself, was to refer to this type of communication as his urge to "act out sadistic transference needs." He was to later comment that I was actually "always good enough and had never let him down," a realization that, he said, was "very important to the overall success of our work together." Nevertheless, the induced feeling at the time was that I could and ultimately would be discarded, as he had been early in his life. He was, in fact, ultimately able to tolerate the conscious realization of this core dread and its origins.

That dread had its beginnings in his early family experience. J was the youngest son in a family, which also included a much older brother who left the family when a late teen, and five sisters. His father was "involved, but in a very passive way," his family being a matriarchy. His mother was dominant, and more interested in his sisters than in him. Illustrative of his sense of her lack of substantive concern for him was her expectation voiced during a family meeting when J was hospitalized for depression that he "snap out of it." "My mother became enraged during the meeting, that I would actually have needs." By so saying, she had demonstrated her reluctance to give him the right look, to affirm him, to be an emotionally resonant and supportive witness to his psychic well being at a critical juncture in his life.

J's pathos inherent in the tone of his particularly painful family recollections tempered my irritation, though at times barely, with his lack of gratitude for my many years with him. Years in which I missed very few appointments, provided phone sessions when I was away, as well as the allowance of other extra-analytic contact. Although he was expressing his thoughts and feelings in accordance with the mandates of the treatment process, I had endured sadistic denigration, time after time. I had been with him through his darkest days, through his menial jobs and faltering reentry into his field, through his many attempted and failed relationships, as well as the painful reliving of events in his family of origin. I had persevered with him through the uncertainty of intimacy with his wife. I had rescued him, I believed in my grandiose moments, from the underworld. I went through all of this with him, and he could discard me, or so it seemed. This annoyed and angered me and at times I entertained the fantasy of dumping him. I joined him on one occasion, perhaps with too much enthusiasm, encouraging him to engage another analyst when he threatened to do so. All was necessary and endured. We, neither one, left the other.

My interventions were guided by my growing awareness of J's dynamics portrayed time and again in the transference and the feelings which were induced in me, that he was someone who was not only not seen, but expendable. His basic fear of being alone, self-destructive, and ruined was apparent also in his report of his life and behavior in the often perverse encounters beyond the session. I felt moved and compelled to maintain contact. In addition to acceptance and toleration of transferential inductions, my interventions consisted of affirmations including the recognition of his emotional pain, conveyed in such remarks as the one I made during the very first session that he "had been through hell." My recognition of his desire, as well as his efforts to get well, seemed important to him. Many joining questions aimed at conveying presence in his struggle and aimed at understanding him (i.e. "Why do you suppose it is so difficult to find a woman who looks just the way you need her to?"). Such questions, which appealed to his intrinsic desire to know himself, enabled him to associate to important though long forgotten realities of his early life: "I could never get my mother to pay attention to me. She was more interested in my sisters." And at other times, he would ask poignantly, "Do you believe when one of my sisters was born, my mother sent me to live with a neighbor on the other side of the city for several weeks. I had no contact. I stopped talking and only began to speak again after a long time."

Other inquiries stirred references to his father: "My father is completely overlooked by my mother. He has been abandoned. It is all about females." He usually made such comments with a tone of frustration and a sense of pathos. My response was to express my understanding of how difficult it must have been for him, which seemed to reinforce the interpretive direction these interactions would take. For example, I would say "No wonder it is so hard to trust women. They often are not what they seem." To which he replied, "like my mother." On one occasion in response to his discussion about his anal interest in women, I said, "No wonder you do that; they are just assholes to you after all." This stirred a memory in him of how his mother seemed always to be turning her back to him, literally as well as emotionally.

When his acting out behavior posed what I thought to be an imminent and real risk to him, I commented that perhaps he was trying to get rid of himself by ruining his reputation, thus fulfilling what he complained of, that is his mother's emotional abandonment. Or perhaps, I said on another occasion, he was trying to get rid of me by ruining my reputation and so have a vicarious pyrrhic victory of sorts over the mother who had emotionally rid herself of him. On the occasions when I forbade him from engaging in nefarious rest stop encounters, he voiced relief and said he felt cared about.

I would also join him in his aggressive encounters. When he would threaten, for example, to whip my ass, I rose to the challenge with equal aggressiveness. "I am pretty quick for a man my age. You might be the one who gets whipped." This, I believe, allowed him not to have to worry about me; he could express the full measure of his sadistic rage, which he did do. Innumerable interactions of this sort seemed to enable J to define this primary dynamic, which governed him, and to eventually counter and diminish it in order to make better choices. Ultimately able to relinquish the need to control and torture the other, J eventually married a stable woman who truly had the right look and was capable of seeing him.

J continued his treatment for a number of years, and his relationship with me underwent a transformation of sorts. He became much more tolerant and forgiving of my shortcomings, both real and imagined. I became aware of an admiration for him as a result of his struggle for health, persistently waged. Though his competitiveness remained, it was much more humorously toned. J seemed to begin to feel that his life had become good as it was—and he knew that I saw that.

But there was more to the story. Some years after beginning treatment, J called in a state of panic. He said he thought he might be in serious trouble. The old behavior had emerged and he feared that his job and marriage might be at risk. He had descended into the "forbidden" dark again with behaviors like those with which he had struggled earlier. He confessed this resurgence had actually begun two and a half years previously and had continued sporadically, without his speaking about it in his analysis. When asked why he had not told me sooner, he said he was ashamed. He had done so well up to that point, he said, and he feared my judgment. It may well have been that my recognition of his successes made him unwilling to admit his "slide," as well as frightening him into thinking that our work was coming to an end and our relationship would be finished.

It should be mentioned that just previous to the resurgence of his problematic behavior, I had been struggling with an illness that was at the time debilitating. Although I continued to work, I required two years to make a full and complete recovery. During that time, however, my ability to be emotionally present to J was no doubt weakened. In fact, though he did not know about my illness, he cited my more frequent absences. I had also raised my fee just prior in a non-negotiated fashion, stressing him, and no doubt straining the contact. In addition, J spoke of his anxiety about how his wife's job promotions removed her from him. The suspicion that she might be preparing not to depend on him as much and was "building her own options" frightened him. Her emotional distance from him as she prepared for her new job, the loss of focused attention in this important relationship, pained him. Contact with his wife and with me had apparently both become compromised.

This was a concerning, disappointing, and humbling occurrence, for both J and myself. It prompted a close reexamination by us of the treatment, the heightened realization of the crucial importance of emotional presence and the tenuousness of the sense of security when contact is broken or diminished. This juncture in the analysis became, however, a moment for recommitment. There was a redoubling of analytic effort wherein it would be possible to proceed with fuller awareness of all of the facts affecting the psychic experience of us both in the context of the analytic relationship.

Subsequently, for a time, J seemed symptom free. In his sessions, convinced, he said, of the peril of not doing so, he would attempt to "say everything." He was, he asserted, determined not to allow himself to drift away from the truth, to be compromised by a repetitive compulsion to disgrace and humiliate himself, to destroy his hard earned "look" of respectability.

Although J appeared to be committed to making the most of this new phase of analysis, there was yet another interruption. This occurred when I mentioned one day that I was "thinking" about again raising my fee. J became furious, launched into a devaluation of the treatment, which seemed quite out of proportion to the tentativeness of my proposal. He complained that he was having financial problems, and that he had always had reservations about the fee and whether it was "worth it." Despite my attempts to analyze the situation with him, he appeared to fluctuate between a panicky objection, to outright anger and begrudging submissiveness. I refused to accept the new fee when he finally said that he would pay it. Despite my telling him that it was more important for us to understand his reaction, to talk about it, rather than for him to simply submit, he terminated.

Several months later I received a phone message from him thanking me for the work we did, saying he valued it greatly. About eight months after that I heard from him again. He complained that I had not returned his phone call. He said that it was quite "cold" of me after so many years together. I had not even wished him well. After several days, I called him and said that it was good to hear from him, although I did remember the termination differently (i.e. that I had at the time been very interested in trying to engage him in talking about his feelings and in having him remain in treatment to do so). I invited him to call if he wanted to talk more about this. I added that I certainly wished him well and have always done so.

Shortly thereafter, J called and left the message on my machine thanking me for my call to him. He said he thought that it would be a good idea to schedule an appointment. We did so for two weeks later. During that phase of the treatment, J admitted that the prospect of paying a higher fee had bothered him because he had again slipped into not telling me everything.

Consequently, he could not tolerate the idea of paying more when he had not been totally truthful, had not engaged in giving himself fully to the process. He had in fact been participating in online chat rooms and viewing pornography. When I asked if there had been more than this, he said "no." Then, when I asked why he would not tell me that, he again said he felt deeply "ashamed." He had achieved so much, but was not totally free of that inclination. It was as though, since he had not been able to maintain his vision of an ideal self, the proper look, he felt compelled to flee. I said to him that I certainly did not think, nor would I, any less of him for this, since I knew that this challenge was a difficult one. And I agreed with him that he had accomplished quite a lot in controlling his more overt and dangerous acting out.

This seemed to enable J to talk more about his longstanding fear that what he had attained would be taken from him, be it money or any of the achievements of his life. He suffered with the dread that he would be left alone, bereft, without resources, destitute, and homeless. I asked if he found that fear to be a surprising one, given the abandonment he felt by his mother. He said no. We then talked about the irrationalness of this fear in light of the reality of his life and his abilities, and how it, nevertheless, prompted decisions and actions which were counterproductive for him. These included his former anal sadistic and self-damaging exploits in the underworld, his tight and sometimes scheming attitude toward money which placed him at some risk, his envy of me, and the urge to restrict our work by withholding and then prematurely terminating, and thus truncating his chances for a full recovery.

J was asked if his fear was actually concealing a wish. He knew his behavior had the potential to bring about all that he dreaded. When pressed on whether there would be any advantages to "losing everything," he said he would then of course be free of the responsibility that was so much a part of the respectable life he had built. He could "hang out" at the public library for hours on end like the many "derelicts" he had observed doing so. He would be able to engage in the nefarious sexual encounters that he had engaged in previously. He would not have to worry about a reputation already ruined. He could, he said, be like some other men he knew who had not gainfully worked, but rather drifted through life. J seemed to be describing the tension free state that Freud (1920) spoke of in which impulse life was ascendant and free of the constraints of object relatedness. He acknowledged that this world had been an exciting one for him. But he said the pull of that frightened him as well; he did not wish to be ruined. The desire for the life he had built, which he now had, was stronger and he said better than the "thrills" of the past.

At our next session, J said that it felt "so liberating" to consider that this fear which had plagued him all of his life was irrational and that it need not triumph, that he could choose. He seemed to understand that the resources he had were substantial. These included his own will for health, the skill of his insight and psychological mindedness, a wife who had been consistent in her love for him, and an analyst who, though imperfect, had the capacity and a willingness to have been present for the struggles of the past as well as those that may lie ahead.

This case illustrates the lure and force of the repetition compulsion and the power of the drive toward self-destruction in this man's life and as it came to play in the transferential and countertransference experiences of the treatment. As Spotnitz (1969, 1976) noted, the ability to channel aggression away from the self played a vital part in freeing this man from his self-destructive enactments. Being able to work at attempting to denigrate and humiliate the analyst, who managed to remain emotionally present enough despite that, made it possible for J to stop so relentlessly denigrating and humiliating himself.

When the analyst gave his approval, J's wish to retain it led to a lessening of his attacks on the analyst, and silence about his escapades. When the analyst proposed raising his fee, a recapitulation of the maternal object's narcissistic self-centered disinterest, J at first felt stymied, humiliated, rejected, and for a while withdrew from treatment. When the analyst listened to J's criticisms and behaved in accordance with the patient's prescriptions (i.e. accepted being disparaged), J was able to return to the treatment and resume the work of attaining greater levels of awareness and further mastery of those dynamics, which had previously had the potential to place him at risk.

This man's recovery was aided by interventions of joining, reflecting, prohibiting, meeting aggression with aggression, interpreting, the allowing of extra-analytic contact, all of which fostered a feeling of a structure of being together, all of which enabled a sense of needed emotional connection between analyst and patient. This enlivened the transferential experience, as well as the work of reparation in the face of slips and imperfections. Always the sense of being seen and accepted, in an analytic relationship which came to have the "right look," wherein truth could be attained and ultimately empathy, admiration, and love could begin.

References

Freud, S. (1920). *Beyond the pleasure principle* (Standard Edition). XVIII, London: Hogarth Press.

McDougal, J. (1995). *The many faces of Eros.* New York: W.W. Norton & Company, Inc.

Mahler, M. (1968). *On human symbiosis and the vicissitudes of human individuation.* Vol. 1, New York: International Universities Press.

Maroda, K. (2004). *The power of countertransference: Innovations in analytic technique.* New York: Routledge, Taylor & Francis Group.

Meadow, P. (2003). *The new psychoanalysis.* Lanham, MD: Rowman & Littlefield Publishers, Inc.

Spotnitz, H. (1969). *Modern psychoanalysis of the schizophrenic patient: Theory of the technique.* New York: Grune & Stratton.

Spotnitz, H. (1976). *Psychotherapy of preoedipal conditions.* New York: Jason Aronson, Inc.

Spotnitz, H. (1985). *Modern psychoanalysis of the schizophrenic patient: Theory of the technique.* New York: Grune and Stratton.

Stanton, M. (1991). *Sandor Ferenczi: Reconsidering active intervention.* Northvale, NJ: Jason Aronson, Inc.

Stoller, R. (1976). *Perversion: The erotic form of hatred.* New York: Aronson.

Chapter 5

Symbolic imagery

An aspect of unverbalized communication

Theodore Laquercia

The evenly hovering attention recommended in the conduct of psychoanalysis by Sigmund Freud was a state of being which would, he posited, enable analysts to perceive better the unconscious communications of their patients. He used the word "Gleichschwebend" to describe this state of being for the analyst. This stance was achieved by a reduction in the sensory awareness of other stimuli and a heightened attention to the communications of the patient. "Poised attention" was the translation made by Theodor Reik (1948), which took into account the concept of "free floating attention" and other nuances inherent in the original German. Gerald Edelman (1992) describes attention as the human's ability to attend selectively to experience in a narrow band of perception, suggesting that this ability is likely to be a vestige of "evolutionary pressure" deemed necessary for survival. He goes on to point out that unconscious activity occurs simultaneously as the "global mapping" of consciously attended stimuli registers on perception. This interplay of conscious and unconscious activity is regulated by the demands of the situation for motor activity relative to the experience at hand. In the analytic session, the poised attention of the analyst and the attention potential of the patient, as defined by Edelman, create the setting for a unique dynamic and a particular kind of communication.

I have found times when the hovering, poised attention gives way or leads to a paradoxical condition, which, while appearing to create a disconnectedness, actually presents a way to become more deeply connected. In such moments, listening approaches a sleeping state, a kind of floating drowsiness. The poised condition, as recommended by Freud and Reik, is directed toward a listening that renders the analyst increasingly attentive to communications given by the patient. When one considers that the position taken by the patient when lying on the couch immobilizes him, the attention that Edelman describes allows for the interplay of conscious and unconscious activity without interference from novel or threatening stimuli. The patient is most free to communicate these elements. One might conclude that this condition makes the analyst a special kind of listener, keenly attuned to underlying messages emanating from the patient's psyche, and the patient an unknowing participant in communication from the realm of his unconscious.

In my practice, I have become interested in this state of connected-disconnection that is on the borderline of wakefulness and sleeping. While attending in this way, the mind of the analyst is moving into areas that are uniquely his and yet related to what is going on with the patient in a seemingly unconscious interplay. A French psychoanalyst, De M'Uzan (1976), describes the patient-analyst relationship as one where the defended patient affects in the analyst a "mild state of depersonalization" which allows the "analysand to 'take possession' of the analyst's mind." In this condition flashes of thought and fragments of images may come to the analyst's mind.

My interest lays in the connections such thoughts and images may have with the patient and with the process the analyst is engaged in—namely, the deciphering of communications that are coming to him.

I have speculated that a certain kind of communication emanates from a place in the psyche of the patient where the psychic structure does not follow clear, definitive, linear lines. There exist, nonetheless, although not verbalized, expressions of thought, feeling, and mood of which the attentive analyst should be aware. The task of resolving resistance, which would lead to progressive communication (that which has not been revealed) and thereby lead to a mature personality (Spotnitz, 1985), is ultimately a function of intervention that facilitates more and more communication, and in some way addresses repressed memories and feelings of the patient.

Central to the process of psychoanalysis is the concept of repression, and resistance analysis is concerned with the resolution of such repressions as they appear in the process of the sessions. Edelman defines repression as "the selective inability to recall" thoughts and memories buried from consciousness. According to him, these forgotten elements of the individual's consciousness are "value laden" experiences that are a "threat to the self-concept" of the person.

I will present several case vignettes to describe this phenomenon and to describe how communications are received in this state of suspension. Such messages, when recognized as unconscious language, can be utilized in resolving resistance to deep emotional expression or to memories previously unexpressed.

Vignette one

Paul had been in treatment with me for two years. Several weeks before Christmas, he was talking about going home for the holidays to California, where he had grown up. As he spoke in session, the free-floating, hovering condition I have described developed. I began to get drowsy and seemed suspended between wakefulness and sleep, hearing the patient, yet not fully. While in this state, the thought of a rifle emerged. Not actually a thought, but a figment; it appeared before my mind's eye as it would in a dream. At first, I was barely aware of it occurring, and I drifted off into a reverie, thinking of the rifle, allowing myself the idea of owning one and maybe even joining a shooting club. I had elaborate and fanciful ideas of shooting. Memories of my service experience in the Marines, of shooting—hearing the report of the gunshot, smelling gunpowder, feeling the kick of the weapon, and recalling how, as my hand cradled it into my neck, the rifle would spring back and almost bruise my face with its power.

When the conscious awareness of this reverie eventually struck, perhaps a few short minutes later, I asked myself, "Why are you thinking of a rifle?" The patient's process, apparently unrelated to the imagery, did not in any way suggest either the image or the power of the thoughts I was having. I pondered why my mind would take such a turn. Any connection between this man and guns or rifles seemed obscure. He was an artist, a pacifist, a creative, poetic soul. Yet the image was compelling; the fact that I had allowed myself to have such a rich fantasy kept me wondering whether there was an unknown connection related to the patient.

Fortifying myself with the idea, born from my training and supervision, that everything which goes on in the session is in some way related to communication with the patient or from the patient, on either a conscious or an unconscious level, I decided to risk a question. I asked, "Is there any reason why I should be thinking about a rifle?"

The patient's emotional response was immediate and intense. He stiffened on the couch and asked why I had asked him that. I merely repeated, in a mildly interested way, that I just wanted to know if there might be a reason why I was having a thought about a rifle. He said he did not know. But then he revealed that, while he was talking about going home to the west coast for the family holiday gathering, he had been experiencing a sense of dread and anxiety, which he was not telling me. Though he had said he did not like the idea of getting together with the family and would rather stay on the east coast, this had been presented with mild affect. He admitted he was just giving me the details and covering over the apprehension he was feeling about the meeting that was to take place on his older brother's ranch. He had not talked much to me about his family, and never about his brother. He described him as a typical red-neck rancher, with a pickup truck and a rifle in the window—a polar opposite of himself, with values and standards quite unlike his own. As he spoke of this brother, he revealed in more emotional tones the apprehension he had been masking, and he spoke of being terribly afraid whenever he was around him and all his guns. He verbalized his fear of this man's potential for violence, especially considering the easy access he had to all these instruments of killing.

As my patient told me these thoughts and feelings, I had the sense that my asking about the rifle had indeed resulted in this expanding description of himself and his relationship to his brother. And I was awake and connected to him in a keen way. Yet, a moment later he revealed information that really rocked me, since he had never to this point shared it. He said that when he was an infant, during a motor trip with the family, this same brother had thrown him out of the car window while they were traveling along a highway.

He had spent over a year in the hospital. Although he now had no conscious memory of this event, or of the long hospitalization, he spoke of both experiences in the session with intense emotional fervor.

This session prompted considerable speculation. The intervention, in the form of the question I had asked, born out of the image in the reverie, was not easily offered. There was much trepidation and concern that I might have been having a fantasy which had nothing to do with the patient and was merely something my mind was indulging. I had thought it might be my own thought exclusively, and unrelated to the patient. When I took the chance and posed the question, there was an immediate response and an emotional association to heretofore unpresented life events, which suggested that my thought was related to his apprehension about the current holiday trip he was about to make. I was faced with the disconcerting idea that I had somehow received a telepathic thought, disconcerting because of my own defensiveness, I suppose, for if this were really possible, then my own defended ideations might also be revealable; but likewise elating. The idea of defenses and how they are represented as resistances to thinking and feeling everything stimulated my curiosity about the events of this session.

Persisting with the exploration of these concerns, I began to think that such communications, hidden in symbolic imagery, might be possible. When Spotnitz and Meadow (1976) speak of emotional contagion, they refer to feelings which the patient and the analyst induce in each other, similar to the way the parent-child dyad contains a flow of feelings between them. Could the defense against the feeling likewise be represented as an image of an object, and could that representation be communicated, similarly to emotional contagion?

With these questions in mind, I began to observe the times when the poised attention attitude moved into the realm of this condition of semiwakefulness. I thought I would have more experience to confirm or refute the idea that I might be able to pick up images transmitted from the patient to me, in the way that emotional contagion, without words being expressed, has one person feeling the feelings that the other person has.

Vignette two

This kind of experience occurred with a man who had begun treatment with me after the sudden death of his analyst. Inasmuch as he had received years of analysis, there was a sense that I was supposed to know much of what he had already told his previous analyst. He would talk to me as though I understood about the people and circumstances he was describing. I essentially remained quiet if not confused during these times, not disturbing his perception that I should know. Yet, it was not easy to remain connected to his narratives. Prior to starting the analysis with me I had been his supervisor, and that probably contributed to his manner of presentation.

Early in the analysis, while the patient was lying on the couch and talking, I drifted into that "space" and pictured hands, with fingers pressed against a surface ... under great strain and pressure ... such that the fingers were bent, indicating that they were bearing great weight. Emboldened by my consideration of the "rifle" intervention, I investigated the image by questioning whether he had ever done pushups on his fingertips. I had embellished the image, and in my mind had come up with what I considered a plausible explanation of why fingers would be so strained.

As in the first example with the rifle, the image was so vivid that I felt the intervention to be compelling. He answered in a very positive way. With apparent pleasure, he raised his hands above his chest so that I could see them, and described how he did a particular kind of pushup. He talked about his military experience and the physical conditioning that was so rewarding. As he demonstrated with his fingers, he explained how fingertip pushups heightened the difficulty in the exercise, and then went on to say that he even did pushups with his feet on the seat of a chair and his hands on the floor, so that the angle of the pushup was extreme and greatly increased the degree of difficulty. His associations picked up, and he admitted to having been a "wild man," carousing, drinking, and brawling. He said he had been in great physical shape, and his pushups were part of the regimen for his conditioning. He then connected how his "nice guy" attitude was a cover for his negative energy that had been dissipated through physical activity and wilderness. Now he sits with tensions that seem to have no outlet, and he suffers with a duodenal ulcer and other somatic manifestations.

Vignette three

The way the "image" came to me in this instance was somewhat different. Rather than seeing or visualizing a specific object, this experience took the pattern of a visualized event—that of a childbirth. Layton was a man struggling to complete his Ph.D. dissertation. He obdurately refused to make progress in his thesis writing. He complained and fretted, but week after week, month after month, year into year, his work was not getting done. During the session in which I imagined the childbirth, filled with the details of a baby being born, I considered its implication in relation to the patient and decided to explore his experience. I asked him, "What was your birth like?" This question did not seem unusual; I was not as far out on a limb as in the previous illustrations. But still it was unrelated to the patient's conscious process. He responded by telling me the difficulty his mother had experienced in his delivery, and the concerns there had been for his and his mother's survival. He was late in term, and measures had to be taken to bring on delivery. He stated that he felt the impasse he had been experiencing with regard to his Ph.D. was related to a lifelong pattern of not wanting to move on. This was a breakthrough session for him. It allowed him to go deeper into the awareness of his recalcitrance, and to associate memories of his childhood and educational life that related to this condition of being stuck.

This same man later on in treatment and after having become "unstuck" moved on to other areas of interest. Since the time of the "childbirth" experience, he had gotten well into his thesis and had accomplished several other things he had been working on. Yet there were issues that impelled him on the deepening quest of his analysis.

In the session I am about to describe, he complained that he felt like he "just did not want to talk." He admitted that there was so much to say about events going on, but he felt a stubbornness which left him silent and irritated. This character trait had been a constant in the treatment, and I knew enough not to try to disturb it by suggesting he try anyway, or by cajoling verbal communication. Rather, I joined the position he articulated, and we both remained silent. I "hovered" through several images that varied in intensity. By now, I was able to discriminate between random images and more intensely communicated visions. Eventually I realized that one thought/image seemed more pervasive, and although the image was somewhat indistinct, the idea of a "ledge" kept intruding into my mind. Additionally, there was an image of "big heads," strange and unrelated to the idea of the ledge, and finally a brief flash of the number "2½." I immediately jotted down the thoughts and images, knowing that, as in a dream, the images and possible memory would be taken away by my unconscious sensor. I decided to wait to see if what I had experienced had something to do with the session, and its possible relatedness to the patient's silent communication. What I had written down exactly was: Ledge; on ledge; big heads (?); and 2½.[1]

Shortly afterward, the patient broke the silence by saying he felt he was floating like the astronauts who the day before had taken the first untethered space walk. The big head image of the space-suited astronauts immediately came to mind as I listened. He then associated to the movie *2001*, and the connection with 2½ was suggested. This floating sensation was not pleasant for him, and he complained that he should be talking about his successes. A report he had recently completed had been well received. A grant he had authored had been accepted by the federal government, which assured that an important project he was working on would continue. And he had learned that a previous grant he had written, although it had not been awarded, was reputed to be the best one received; the grant had been awarded to a competitor only to spread the work around. Additionally, he was writing well on the last chapters of his dissertation.

The primary image of the ledge had not been alluded to at all, even though it appeared to be the most vivid in my mind. It seemed not to be related to anything he was talking about during this part of the session. Now I was again left in the position of having an image that appeared to be absolutely obscure, and that could hardly be introduced into the process without my appearing absurd by raising a question about it.

The connection of the first two images, however, kept me pondering on how I could explore the third. Eventually I asked him about the ledge image, even though seemingly unrelated to the process. I asked, "Should I be thinking of a ledge?" He did not react with surprise, as I had thought he might, given the apparent unrelatedness. Instead he reminded me that at another time, when he was in a similar mood, he had written me an account of his feeling suicidal and had described climbing out of his office window. He did not use the word "ledge" in this account. He went on to connect the elements in the session, the feeling of isolation, floating, and symbolic imagery. He reported that when he had written about climbing out the window, he felt the same isolated feeling that he was experiencing now. It was not understandable in view of his present productivity and success. He elaborated on the positive things he was doing. Then he said, with some emotion, that he felt very isolated from the rest of the world, disconnected. I said, "The astronauts were untethered also." He replied with heightened emotion, "That would scare the hell out of me! I wish they would not do that." The sense of apprehension was very powerful at this point in the session, and the association between the astronauts floating away from the "mother ship" and his personal experience was becoming more evident. Now crying, he talked of space being like the womb, of how he must have felt then, and of how he wanted to be connected to the umbilical cord. He remembered the session when he had spoken of his difficult birth, and then associated to wanting always to hold on. He said that as a boy, when he was in a pool, he always held on to the ropes or else hung on to the ledge! The third image, and the most powerful, was now understandable. The relation to me in all of this was how he used the rest of the session. He admitted his fear of having to leave me when he finished his Ph.D. Why would he have to continue his analysis if he were so successful? Success was swimming in the open, without the ledge to hold onto. The astronauts' feat of the previous day so powerfully symbolized the relationship between success and being on your own that he had to attempt to neutralize himself from the consideration of leaving his analysis.

Vignette four

My final case is somewhat different from those already described. In this example, the image presented was the memory of a dream I had about the patient the year before, which came back to me during a session while he was talking. I started to think of the dream in the "poised attention" state as the patient was speaking of a present situation in his life. The dream I had the previous year, which had never been shared with the patient, was powerful and related to the underlying anger and rage that reside in this man.

My dream: I am in my office talking to a colleague. This patient is in the waiting room, waiting for his appointment. There is a violent crash, and

I realize that he has ripped the door off the hinges and is standing in the doorway. He is enraged that he has been kept waiting, and that the door was closed to him. I awakened at that point.

In the session a year later, I wondered why I remembered the dream at that time. I decided not to use this image, but rather to wait and see if the patient's process would give me a clue as to why I had the memory and the powerful image of his rage. Some time passed, and he continued to talk about the current relationship issues he was having. Then he began to associate to memories of his childhood and the relationship between his mother and father. Inasmuch as he had been talking about the difficulties of having relationships, he focused on problems and arguments that related to those times when he heard his parents fight. Then, with great emotion, he described one of his parents' scariest fights. He was quite young, standing in the kitchen with his mother. His parents had been arguing, and his mother locked his father outside. He described this fight in such detail and vividness of feeling that I could almost feel I was there. As the story came to a dramatic close, he said to me: "Do you know what happened?" I replied, "What?" He said, "My father was so furious that he actually ripped the door off the hinges." When he said that, I immediately connected to the dream. The use of the words that I had remembered—"ripped the door off the hinges"—was the compelling feature of his communication. I was left with the question, as in all the cases presented: how does this communication take place? In this instance, I had to consider that the image from the memory of my dream was in some way transmitted to him, unlike the other examples where the images seemed to have come from the patient to me.

Conclusion

In the cases cited, I have considered the utilization of nonverbal communication to understand the patient and to deal with resistances to mature communication. The task of "saying everything," as daunting as it is, may at times be facilitated by the analyst who might pay attention to nonverbal communication of the sort described. Freud (1915) had perceived the birth of the unconscious to be a function of the prehistory of the individual, the time before language had transformed experience, which is essentially diffuse and unformulated, into logical and coherent expression. It is during this time in psychological development that the individual records and expresses thoughts in fragmentary, unconnected ways. Only later, with the acquisition of language, can the necessary connections between idea and emotion be fused and communicated. Yet, one cannot deny that mentation of all sorts occurs before this time, and that memory exists in the prelanguage domain. It is likely, therefore, that communication at this level between a child and an attentive parent resides in an area that is not always explicable as logical language allows. Daniel Stern (1983) uses the term "unformulated experience" to describe this phase of primitive cognition. He recommends attentiveness by the clinician, that he be as aware of such communication as a parent might be with a tiny, nonverbal infant. Edelman shows us that the activity from the higher cortical levels is affected in a cascade of simultaneous brain activities coming from deeper levels in the structure of the brain. All this warrants an analytical stance which would allow the analyst to be receptive to nonverbal communications that are at first unexplainable.

This totalistic viewpoint is not new. We can cite many analysts who have recommended attentiveness to nonverbal gestures, such as body language and actions, to determine what the patient might be struggling with in regard to communication. But there are few who ask us to pay attention to visual images that spring to mind—to fantasies and to body sensations and arousals—as a function of something emanating from the patient. It is easy to see that such experiences are viewed initially as unrelated to the patient, because of the seeming nonconnection to what the patient might be expressing. Yet when examined, the analyst may find that there is a connection to the patient's unconscious process and to the defended state that the patient is in, that this defended condition is related to repressed material and, as Edelman suggests, contains "value laden" elements that would trigger brain activity. These elements may be communicated to the analyst and the emanations may be discerned by a listener poised to receive such communications. These repressed conditions may be resolved by the analyst's willingness to accept any manner of communication. With careful consideration of the patient's defenses and the formulation of an intervention centered on this awareness, the analyst could find such an approach leading to a fuller understanding of the repressions with which the patient is dealing.

This chapter was originally published in 1998 in *Modern Psychoanalysis, 23*, 23–33.

Note

1 The question mark related to the image as being strange. The heads I envisioned were big and round, with indiscernible facial features and no necks—yet heads in my mind, nonetheless.

References

De M'Uzan, M. (1976). Countertransference and the paradoxical system. In S. Lebovici & D. Widlocher (Eds.), *Psychoanalysis in France*. New York: International Universities Press.

Edelman, G. (1992). *Brilliant air, brilliant fire: On the matter of the mind*. New York: Basic Books.

Freud, S. (1915). *Beyond the pleasure principle* (Standard Edition). London: Hogarth Press, 18, 3–64.

Reik, T. (1948). *Listening with the third ear*. New York: Grove Press.

Spotnitz, H. (1985). *Modern psychoanalysis of the schizophrenic patient: Theory of the technique* (2nd ed.). New York: Human Sciences Press.

Spotnitz, H., & Meadow, P. W. (1976). *Treatment of the narcissistic neuroses.* New York: Manhattan Center for Advanced Psychoanalytic Studies.

Stern, D. B. (1983). Unformulated experience: From familiar chaos to creative disorder. *Contemporary Psychoanalysis*, 19, 71–79.

Chapter 6

The contact resisted, broken and restored in psychoanalytic work

Managing the pain and the pleasure

John Madonna

Spotnitz (1985) originated the notion of following the contact function of the patient in order to create the stimulus-free environment necessary for the emergence of the narcissistic transference. Others in the Modern School (Ernsberger, 1979; Margolis, 1994; Meadow, 1987, 1989, 2003; Spotnitz & Meadow, 1976) were able to discuss the central importance of this phenomenon as a prerequisite for understanding and intervening with measured questions, which joined, reflected and mirrored the patient's communications, unconscious intentions and tolerances. Yet following the contact also involves more than this. It requires the ability on the part of the analyst to regress, be induced, into the early psychic world of the patient, where libidinal impulses are strong and dangerous. In the course of this journey the analyst is inevitably brought to the re-experience of his own subjective transferential and countertransferential world, in whatever state of resolution or irresolution that may be in.

Establishing and maintaining this symbiotic connection is then fundamental to cure. However, the connection is resisted in various ways according to the pathology sustained by the patient. Sometimes also it is resisted or compromised by the analyst. In some cases the attempt to cast the analyst off is both salient and obvious. I am reminded of the older paranoid man referred by his physician because he had been difficult to treat due to his suspiciousness and the vociferousness of his accusations. When he arrived for his appointment with me on the wrong day and a half an hour early, he became quite irate when I informed him so. I was able to see him then as I had a cancellation and this placated him.

Presence in paranoia

Mr. Z's seven-year treatment with me was fraught with attempts at relationship oscillating with efforts to place me in a category of one who could not be trusted, in collusion with his physician who had tried to effect an inpatient mental health placement of him some time before. I was also seen in league with his brother who, he said, was trying to cheat him out of his money, his ex-wife and murderous stepdaughter who were out to do him harm. My early attempts to clarify his projections and place them in a realistic perspective were at best begrudgingly intriguing to him, though more often viewed with distrust, distain and dismissal. Bion's (1959) discussion of the paranoid attack on linking is aptly applied here. Frequently, Mr. Z lectured me in such a way as to convey a sense of superiority and so neutralize any impact I might have upon him. He seemed to cast me in the role of a neophyte to be instructed, less able, a good guy. And thus, less of a threat.

That Mr. Z and I were able to stay together for nearly seven years was probably due to several factors. First he was heavily besieged by actual as well as supposed threats, which waxed and waned larger than what he perceived emanating from me. At the outset of treatment, he had been recently divorced and engaged in settlement disputes with his wife. Having continued to live in one of his daughter-in-law's properties he feared he was under surveillance, which may well have been the case. In addition, Mr. Z had a significant history of heart disease, having suffered several heart attacks. He also had gastric problems, which eventuated into stomach cancer necessitating an invasive surgery. All of this was successfully treated despite his emotional agitation and the suspicion he harbored toward his healthcare providers. Given the existence of these external enemies, and the desperateness which he experienced as a result, he sought and allowed himself to receive the interest and support which I offered enabling some semblance of a connection, albeit not very complete. This receptivity may to some extent be in keeping with Goldberg's (1981) notion that physical injury or illness can result in an abatement of psychological symptomology even in severe cases, thus allowing a better level of object relatedness.

For my part, though they sometimes made me nervous, I was able to withstand well enough the paranoid projections toward me because despite, or I should say in between his accusations, I found him to be likeable. The roguishness that was a part of his presentation did at times convey a sense of humor.

Of relevance also was the convergence of two salient phenomena. The first was how much Mr. Z in his facial expressions looked like my dead father, loved and lost, but now before me again each week. And though the similarity ended there, I must confess, I looked forward to the sessions in part for that reason. Of more significance, however, Mr. Z's particular paranoid personality was personally familiar to me. It reminded me of my experience with my mother. She was a woman who was intelligent, generous, good-hearted and humorous when not distraught. However, she was easily hurt, quickly provoked to suspicion, combative, emotionally volatile and dramatic in her capacity for condemnation and disavowal. In the early years, she had moments in which she could also be violent, self-attacking and quite self-destructive in her behavior. It was my job as a child, which I came to execute with convincing skill, to soothe the beast which troubled this mother I loved, a beast which I feared could take her from me. Even many years later the bittersweet remembrance, the worry, sorrow, anger and love begotten of that travail remained.

As with my mother, accepting and joining Mr. Z's mistrust of others for a long time enabled this man to navigate through the fear which beset him and he was able to attain a wary tolerance of me. He seemed accepting of my assertion of "incompatible realities" (Kernberg, 1992) in the face of his paranoid beliefs about me. He also seemed to accept my incredulous utterances of "what would I have to gain by that?" in response to his assertions that I had spoken to and conspired with his brother to defraud him of his funds. When I urged that he ought to consider leaving his inheritance, which was considerable, to a charity of his choice rather than family members, he seemed reassured. There were times when I simply met his charges with blatant outrage and denial: "absolutely never!" and challenged him for "lumping me in with everyone else." The emotional tone of my comments gave him pause and he would relinquish his imputations, seem to relax and readjust his efforts with me, speaking in a more relational way.

I, nevertheless, remained concerned about his potential to act on his perception of threat, as for example when he would provocatively confront men half his age while alone at bars. Or when he once went to an ex-girlfriend's apartment armed with a small crowbar, anticipating that he would be assaulted by her new boyfriend. His recounting of such episodes at the time seemed to me like overblown attempts to assuage his own fear, to prove to himself, and me, that he was not weak, nor ineffectual, not someone to be trifled with. That is, as Cooper (1993, p. 440) indicated, these seemed like attempts at "explaining … (i.e., demonstrating) to a ferocious superego" that he was neither weak nor a failure. Mr. Z took great pride in himself, as he related his prowess to me, on not backing down to those he believed had violent designs toward him, in fooling them in being able to read their intentions and preempt them. Though he never attacked anyone, or precipitated an attack, he did succeed in getting himself classified as a persona non grata and was not welcomed in some places, and sadly in some relationships which were important to him.

When our relationship reached phases in which it was minimally encumbered by his distrust of me, Mr. Z was able to voice how lonely he was, and how sad. He was able to consider and comment that he might have "a problem with paranoia," and "might at times have reacted in a paranoid way." He was able to accept my reflection of what he himself had offered on how the brutalization he had received in childhood (i.e. his father kicking him so hard in the back that his spine was damaged, his older brother's sadistic demeaning of him, and most hurtful, his mother's predatory reliance on him, including cheating him out of thousands of dollars later in life) had made him susceptible to distrusting others, especially those in positions of authority. He was able to recall many of those traumas and talk about them; he saw the relevance of their connection to his inclination to be "paranoid."

He asked me to let him know if I saw that happening with this or that person or event—including with me. In these moments the contact between us felt like a close, familiar working alliance. I was encouraged. On three occasions, he gave me small gifts, which in keeping with the need to reinforce his sense of facility, and after much discussion, I accepted. I insisted on paying for one gift, which he allowed. On one occasion, knowing his love for music and dancing to World War II era bands, I gave him a ticket to a "Forties" music concert which had been given to me. While this may be seen as a countertransference enactment on my part, it was done with some deliberation and at the time it seemed right. It was a reflection of Mr. Z's contact with me; it appeared to reduce his agitation and promoted self-reflection and the progressive communication apparent at that period in the treatment.

The specter of paranoia, nevertheless, loomed like a shadow in the background often in the form of a discerning stare or sideways glance. Ultimately Mr. Z was to break the connection. He discarded me, ending the treatment convinced that by the tone of my voice, I had judged him unfairly, supposing him to have pedophilic interests in relation to a story he told about a young relative. I deeply regretted that ending, though for a while I oscillated between relief and resentment. I took some consolation in the belief that the treatment served, through the seven years that it lasted, to enable his cooperation with his medical providers. It also forestalled his acting on his hostile impulses which could at times be intense, and, I believe, provided him with a consistent period of relationship with someone which he would otherwise not have had. As with my mother, I had been a constant companion in the darkness and the light.

As I look back on it, I do not recall exactly what I also may have done in this case to contribute to the dissolution of the contact that Mr. Z and I had attained. His discarding of me seemed to come unexpectedly and subsequent to a lengthy period of mutual affinity, more open revelation and discussion. But it may have been for that very reason; our relationship may have become "too good" and thus the threat of harm therefore more insidious and dangerous. Perhaps, in what he may have experienced as a growing closeness to me, an intolerable sense of passivity accompanied by a perverse sexual impulse may have been aroused. He left, after all, because he believed I thought him a pedophile. However, in his paranoid process, I may have been unconsciously experienced as that perpetrator. I may have simply not been thinking so clearly in these terms at the time, choosing rather to live in the apparent success and comfort of the moment, as I had done so many times in the distant past with the mother of my childhood. Overconfident, I may not have conducted sufficient inquiry. Though this I cannot say for sure.

Presence through the self-returned

The emotional connection comes under great strain in other ways when working with obsessive-compulsive individuals. In such cases the intellectualizing, compartmentalizing of affect, repetitive communication, the doing and undoing of thought and feeling obviates and precludes a resonant emotional contact. Often intelligent, hardworking and perceptive such patients can be appealing. They give the appearance of engagement. But caught in their repetitious, ritualistic thinking they make it difficult for others to feel in good contact with them. In addition, in their effort to also attain certainty, absolute control, excellence and superiority, as well as invulnerability, they wall themselves off from attempts at relationship. As one such man, Mr. Y, a dentist in his middle forties, whom I had seen many years ago when I was starting out, said during a session, "Dr. Madonna, I like my own thinking more than that of anyone else. I just want to be alone with my thoughts."

This man's difficulty maintaining connection with me was notably reflected in a constant refrain of his: "Are are you there?" When I asked about this in the beginning of the treatment, he said it was because I had fallen asleep on him. In fact, I had in an early session been suffering from a sinus infection and, medicated, did close my eyes and did for several seconds zone out. He had turned on the couch and noticed. He had wondered whether he had bored me to sleep. Though I had not thought so at the time his communications had been repetitive and egocentric and may well have contributed to my sleepiness. Subsequently, he was to question my interest in him, as well as my competence.

Many months after this occurrence, his queries continued: "Are you there?" "Did I lose you?" "Are you with me?" This annoyed me. It caused me to question myself. Was my singular episode of sleepiness so large an error, so strong an injury? Certainly my patient's self-esteem had not seemed to have been at all diminished; he did not seem to be suffering in any discernible way. In fact, he carried on the story of his life with an intensity of purpose. At times he did so with elation and pride. Often this was in relation to his recounting the many sexual triumphs he enjoyed with a succession of girl-friends. When he felt pathos about an event or person this was often delivered as though to himself, indeed as though I was "not there."

When he did address me it was to ask a question, the answer to which he seemed already in possession of. Mr. Y would sometimes complain that the treatment was not going deep enough. His tone was at times condescending. I felt irritated with him for this, and frustrated. Perhaps I was not a substantial enough analyst to enable him to go deeper. Did my falling asleep represent not just the vagaries of seasonal flu, but age and the fatigue consequent to not being able to intellectually keep up with this younger man? Certainly my pride in performance in the face of my awareness of advancing age had been a sensitive issue for me. Mr. Y was an extremely sophisticated, intelligent and successful dentist. He was also quite competitive in his life and work, owning and managing two dental offices. While I was aware of his competitiveness, the subtle intensity of it did remain somewhat obscure to me. Perhaps this was because my attention was drawn to the fact that his productions were mixed with a genuine desire to know himself and a facile capacity to look within. He could also be quite quick witted at times, which I liked, and this did help in those moments to affect a sense of connection.

Mr. Y's quest for dominance and superiority was exemplified in two inter-actional sequences which occurred one day. He had entered my office and taking the couch, asked what we should talk about. I asked him what he wanted to talk about. "I do not know," he said, but then referred to the recently re-contracted fee. He had started his treatment at a low rate during his residency period, but had long completed that commitment and had quickly done well. The re-contracted fee that we had agreed upon was 90 dollars, up from 65, still quite moderate, and due to begin in two months. "Eighty-five sounds good to me," he challenged. "One hundred and twenty-five sounds good to me. You are a successful professional," I volleyed back. "I do not think so," he said with a self-assured tone. I asked what motivated this attitude. He smugly asserted again that he liked 85 rather than 90. He then went on to say that he had actually managed to acquire ten new patients requiring various rather expensive dental procedures, at one office site, since we had met two weeks earlier. His income, he said in a somewhat self-satisfied way, would increase considerably. I tell him that I am impressed with his achievement and say that it sounds as though he will be well able to pay my usual fee of 125 dollars per session. He curtly retorts that after taxes and office expenses he will "not actually be taking home that much."

Mr. Y abruptly changed the subject to speak about his patients, the power differential between adult medical professionals and the patient in pain, how he experienced the difference of position as highly influential. His insight and candor seemed impressive. He went on to speak about his relationships with women, his desire for conquest and his proven success in achieving it. As always, he was robust in the presentation of his capacities. He talked then about the humble origins of his parents and his own birth "not" being a grand or "princely" one. As he compared himself to his parents, he said in a somewhat superior way how he felt "able to reconstruct their psychic life with some accuracy." He expressed confidence in his ability to do so, but on reflection, felt discomfort in saying it.

It was at this point that Mr. Y asks if I am there. I say "yes" and ask why he asks. He says he wishes I were more active. I say "how curious that is, given how active I have been during the session" (having asked many ques-tions as well as having engaged him vigorously on the issue of the fee). He does not say more about this, but goes on to talk about how he came in eighth in a recent five-mile one-man scull race in which there were 500 con-testants. I compliment him. He says he had hoped I would have been there "not as a contestant of course, on the sidelines." I understood the demeaning intent of that remark and said, in a teasing, joking way, though perhaps feeling my own competitive potential stirred, "you know I am in pretty good shape for a man my age." Incredulously he responds, "are you, a rower?"

Shortly after that he asks again if I am there. I say to Mr. Y that I have been "very much here" and will be when it comes time for him to pay his 90 dollars per session. I add in a playfully challenging tone, "however, I think that you should bite the bullet, be a professional and pay 125 per session." He reminds me of our agreement that he would pay 90. I say that I think it was a mistake on my part to agree to that. He asks why I did. I respond that he seemed to be in such a state of despair about money at the time, but now I believe that may have simply been his competitive maneuvering.

Soon after, he once again asks if I am there. I ask if he keeps asking if I am there because he is being so aggressive with me, referring to his interaction with me regarding the fee, and to the demeaning remark about the race and how these comments seem to represent his overall desire to assert his dominance. Has he been wondering, I say, if he hurt me, or angered me enough that I have become injured, provoked to perhaps retreat from and abandon him? He seemed to muse on this and did not respond as he had done so many times in the past, by indicating that it was all about my having fallen asleep on him several years before. I wondered out loud if Mr. Y's question of, "are you there?" was the result of his oedipal strivings with me in the transference, an analyst he admired and liked but would like to surpass. That question, I said to him, seemed a screen communication for, "are you there or have I injured and/or killed you?"

The question subsided, although it did not disappear entirely. When he asked it again sometime later, it was as though he were also inferring a pre-oedipal fear: "Dr. Madonna, I think I ask you that because I get so involved in my own thinking that I feel I lose you. I get afraid. I get afraid that I will be alone." Articulating this deeper underpinning of experience, and the sense of true vulnerability inherent in it, a new period of analysis began. One in which he was able to voice more clearly and directly the realization of his envy and resentment of me, as well as his love, without the fear of loss obstructing him. He was able to talk about his desire to surpass me, his father and others, and how that desire represented a strong wish to feel special, as he had felt earlier in his life, as an only child, in relation to his mother.

Related to this, it occurred to him that his repetitive talk about his sexual conquests, as well as his inevitable dissatisfaction with those women, also reflected his oedipal dilemma. With these realizations, connected as they were with the deeper awareness of how his mode of thinking isolated him from and jeopardized his connection to others, the contact with me became more emotionally immediate and productive. Less fettered by obsessionally self-centered, repetitive, intellectualized thinking, or the drive for domination, Mr. Y was himself able to be "there" in his interactions with me, and consequently more secure, as we went forward, in the feeling of my presence.

Presence in dream states

Schizoid psychopathology presents particular challenges to the establishment and maintenance of therapeutic contact. Mr. X, a man in his fifties, applied for treatment complaining of chronic depression which made him "unable to get started." He had been unemployed for the preceding 11 years, living on disability benefits. He read fitfully from a large collection of books he never finished, watched late night TV talk shows until the early hours of the morning and then fell asleep. He would not awaken till two or three o'clock in the afternoon. Each afternoon would be spent lying on his day bed fantasizing for hours repetitively masturbating, sometimes reaching orgasm, sometimes not. Mr. X had no friends and maintained little phone contact with his family.

At the outset of treatment, Mr. X frequently engaged in controlled and repetitious diatribes toward his elderly father whom he resented, he said, for rejecting, denigrating and humiliating him. In one session he said he wanted "to punch the son of a bitch in the face. He is a fraud. I hate the son of a bitch." Mr. X was also enraged with his father for alienating his older brother from him. The father did this during the adolescence of the boys, by cajoling the older brother to be more like Mr. X who was smart, studious and passively compliant. During one session when he spoke of this, Mr. X slammed his fist into the couch and half sitting up cried out, "I would like to kill him."

During another session Mr. X sarcastically voiced his contempt for what he perceived to be the unfair treatment he received from past employers and other authority figures. In a therapy group of which he was a member, Mr. X stated that he felt "belittled and manipulated" by a succession of "withholding, intrusive," "condescending" and "dictatorial" group leaders. Though the emotion he expressed seemed palpable there was a forced quality to it and his verbal contact with me was virtually non-existent. It would be more accurate to say that his verbalizations were more like soliloquies chronicling what sounded like oedipally driven hatred alternating with self-attack. His negations of himself included such frequent remarks about himself as that he was an "ineffectual pushover," "disgusting," "bald," "old," "worthless," "weird," "weak," "ordinary," "bizarre," "a milk toast creep," "timid," "melodramatic problem child," "not grown up," "incoherent," "ineffectual as a man" and "a coward who would never get better." In addition, at various times he said that his "muscles were shrinking," his "gums were receding," his "brain cells were dead" and his "penis was small." It was as though he was trying to discourage me from regarding him as a viable person. And I must admit that under the barrage of such images, I did feel some disgust, as well as the onset of extreme frustration at his lack of direct contact.

The preoedipal origins of Mr. X's difficulty eventually became apparent in his relentless lack of engagement with me which went on for so long that an environment was created which was affectively motionless. This I believe was fostered by strong undercurrents of Mr. X's controlled rage and an, at the time, unrecognized, fear of that on my part. The chronic and utter lack of contact had a disabling effect on me. I felt as though the potential for understanding, therapeutic intervention and effective relationship was impossible. An incipient feeling of uselessness eventuated into a shroud of paralysis. Over time, anesthetized in a near death stupor I was even unable to move my fingers without great effort. The life support system which did seem to operate were Mr. X's fantasies which were floridly sensual and interesting. He himself appeared to live in these fantasies, the story lines of which depicted him as an alpha male vampire who thrived on sex with incestuously related females. Though I was sustained in some strange way by these, they nevertheless seemed like emanations from a great distance, discernible flickers of light through a dark haze.

The fibrous threads of the preoedipal defense rose like shadowy yet over-powering flora. My incapacitation was reminiscent of the process of projective identification described by Ogden (1991) and Geltner (2005). That is, I was having the feeling which was "originally the patient's" and though I felt different from the patient, I felt nevertheless painfully bonded through the induction in a situation which he controlled. I was suspended and encapsulated in what felt like a tightly woven chrysalis which continually stifled emotion, replicating his own insulated psychic world and insuring that though held close to him, I would not intrude upon him. Arnold Modell (1976) spoke of this many years ago in describing the preoedipal sensitivity of the narcissistic person to the world of others as a cocoon defense. In this case I was being wrapped in a cocoon, paralleled to his own.

This impasse was only broken by the desperate necessity to arouse myself after many months from this ever-tightening bind. After a series of particu-larly numbing sessions, I was able to mirror and join with forceful conviction Mr. X's life, as he described it. As he commented on how useless his existence was, I interjected that, after all, he had been quite successful at constructing a safe and secure life for himself and he should not change it. I added that both he and I had been, and were, failures regarding any effort we had, or could make, to effect change and we should accept that reality. He did not like hearing this and was able, somewhat surprisingly, to focus his rage upon me. After angrily telling me that he did not like my attitude, he stormed out of the session and did not return for several months. In much the same way as Spotnitz (1985) had described how treatment impasses get breached via emotional communications which release a patient's bottled up rage, our joint chrysalis seemed to have been broken. To his credit Mr. X did finally respond to my calls and returned. When I asked him why he had done so, he replied it was because I had called and, as if to keep the authenticity of his annoyance with me alive, and I think to keep any sense of facility I may be experiencing in check, said somewhat sarcastically that I was "the only show in town." We were, nevertheless, able to talk about what had happened as a result of the feelings that had been stirred. It seemed a turning point.

Mr. X has remained in analysis for a number of years without interruption. Though his relationships outside of sessions continued to be somewhat impoverished, his emersion in fantasy as a primary defense during sessions has become greatly diminished. His contact with me became more affectively alive, and at times even congenial. Our interactions during sessions are better.

The humorous exchanges which I have become able to initiate, and to which he has responded, are now common. To some extent this reflects, I believe, the emergence of an anaclitic countertransference (Liegner, 1995), which facilitated a level of object relatedness. I have come to laugh together with Mr. X, feelings of playfulness and joy which this somber and aloof man had previously not attained.

Conclusion

These three cases illustrate how therapeutic contact, though needed and even consciously desired, is, nevertheless, resisted and at times broken. The establishment, maintenance and restoration were achieved via emotional communication, although in one instance quite desperately begotten. In the case of Mr. Z, it was the directness of my assertion of our incompatible realities, the bluntness of my denials of collusion with the enemy that seemed key. I was able to tactfully demonstrate, I think, what was a reassuring force to match his own. As his inclination for violence was strong, this was important. It was also my flexibility in the face of his erroneous certainty, as when he showed up on the wrong day and time. I saw him nevertheless. And I was, of course, genuinely interested in him, in part based on my own psychic history, and able to relate in friendly ways when he sought to do so, and could tolerate that. It was a difficult case, nevertheless, and ended sadly.

Though it had taken some time to do so, Mr. Y's continual provocations inspired me finally to recognize the aggressiveness of his question, "are you there?" This recognition subsequently led to a more direct consideration on his part of the aggressiveness of his drive for oedipal triumph/superiority and also put him in touch with a more basic underlying fear. This enabled him to engage in progressive communication. I was simply unable to appreciate the full measure of his aggression because for a while I was blocked in the recognition of my own. His issues were too familiar for me to separate myself enough to quickly acquire the emotionally felt experience of his aggression. This countertransference resistance delayed effective intervention. I certainly felt attracted to and stimulated by this bright man's thinking about matters analytic. His commitment to the inner exploration, diligence and candor were admirable. His occasional humor and capacity for banter were appealing and disarming, particularly as it stood in contrast to the virtuosity of his self-reflections.

With this patient, I came to remember again how aggressively competitive I had been, and was in my own life and relationships, although now subtly so. It seemed as though I was seeing the reflection of myself and caught in that, wishing once more to live again in that way, and in that time. It can feel good, although it may not be clearly recognized in the moment, to be with ourselves again—to be again in the company of our own youthful, competitive, energized and sexual presence. However, the pleasure of that can be distracting. Related to this, the elation of knowing the patient, having the feeling of being ahead of the game, of course lends itself to the possibility of precipitous or poorly focused interventions.

Maybe too, my realization of Mr. Y's aggressiveness was provoked by the subtle yet poignant sense of superiority toward his parents, especially his father. It might well have been that I did not allow myself to know the dark side of Mr. Y because, as Bernstein (1993) indicated in her discussion on counter-transference resistance, I did not want to see again my own. It was noteworthy that he had said he was uncomfortable comparing himself with his father, because he was afraid of what that would mean about him, what he would see of himself. Interestingly, as I sat there with him, I was flooded with memories of my own past and current strivings to attain eminence and superiority, my own discomfort with having surpassed my father, issues known and long forgotten.

With Mr. Y, it was my mirror image that mesmerized and in so doing resulted in countertransference resistance which worked for a while against the analytic contact and mission. In finally recognizing all of this in myself, in us, the level of contact could eventually be deepened. The recognition of his aggressiveness, and my own, was the door through which we passed.

The complexities of the contact with Mr. X seemed much more pernicious and potentially lethal in nature. I felt as if I were being bound in a chrysalis, unable to move, to think, rendered affectively numb, at a great distance from the world, near death, surviving only on the far away pictures of Mr. X's fantasies and a few of my own. Moreover, it was as though this chrysalis was being spun not only around me but from within me, from the fibers of my own psychic propensities, but not by me. That is, not under my control, but his. With the stillness, there came a terror. It was the desperate intolerableness of this fear which ultimately propelled me to engage Mr. X as I did to break free, and to begin the long march toward something more akin to object relatedness.

I think that it is not always because the resulting countertransference states in certain cases feel so difficult, so toxic, but because they can feel so good, that we find ourselves in a state of resistance. For all the desperateness of being bound the way I was, in a chrysalis dried of affect and emotion, I am more clearly aware now of the hypnotic appeal of being in that state. In it there was, after all, freedom from the labor of working in the analysis, of the strenuously difficult task of attempting to understand and relate. During sessions the responsibilities associated with life itself were diminished dramatically. The object world vanished to be replaced by a stupor of deep dimension which was spiced with the porno-erotica of Mr. X's fantasies. When with him I felt the listlessness of the opium den, the sustaining stimulation of pipe dreams. There were times I did not mind it, indeed I looked forward to it. Though my fear became intolerable, the addictive lure was fundamental in contributing to my inability for a long time to think and act analytically.

I believe that in a case of this sort it must be this appeal that makes the experience so much more obstructive in its potential. Though the induction is to some extent being done to the analyst by the patient, giving it the feel of projective identification, the desire to linger in that state, indeed even to seek it, was, I believe, an unmetabolized propensity for that within me—deep and existential. This propensity thickened the resin, further gluing and tightening the experience. In fact, something quite pervasively fundamental seemed satisfied. Because of this, the experience of the chrysalis state encompasses and moves a bit beyond projective identification. Though it seemed that what I was experiencing was a primitive form of psychic sharing, merely what the patient was capable of at a particular life juncture, as well as an understandable attempt to neutralize intrusion, it was an excursion which seemed to take me perilously and inextricably close to nirvana, cessation, death. Such cases can be intoxicatingly dangerous, insofar as individual psychic vulnerability and somatic susceptibility may be stirred in ways we cannot imagine or anticipate.

The visceral experience of the contact resisted, broken by both patient and analyst, inevitable in treatment, can nevertheless enable a more thorough knowledge of the patient than otherwise could be achieved. In order to attain this, however, we must be willing, and have the stamina, to suffer familiar and unfamiliar pains and terrors, as well as the inherent allure, fascinations and pleasures of the countertransference experience, in effect, to become the patient (Madonna, 1991). Navigating between the Sylla and Charybdis of that polarity can be difficult and at times potentially injurious. Attaining the kind of contact that promotes full analysis takes time, in some cases much time, and this can tax the analyst's patience, skill and humility. It requires the ability, and a willingness, to move beyond our pain—and our pleasure.

This chapter was originally published in 2009 in *Modern Psychoanalysis, 38*, 275–291.

References

Bernstein, J. (1993). Using the countertransference resistance. *Modern Psychoanalysis*, 18, 71–80.

Bion, W. R. (1959). Attacks on linking. *International Journal of Psychoanalysis*, 40, 308–315.

Cooper, A. (1993). Paranoia: A part of most analysis. *Journal of the American Psychoanalytic Association*, 41, 423–442.

Ernsberger, C. (1979). The concept of countertransference as therapeutic instrument: Its early history. *Modern Psychoanalysis*, 4, 141–164.

Geltner, P. (2005). Countertransference in projective identification and sadomasochistic states. *Modern Psychoanalysis*, 30, 73–91.

Goldberg, J. (1981). *The psychotherapeutic treatment of cancer patients*. New York: The Free Press.

Kernberg, O. (1992). Psychopathic, paranoid and depressive transferences. *International Journal of Psychoanalysis*, 73, 13–28.

Liegner, E. (1995). The anaclitic countertransference in resistance resolution. *Modern Psychoanalysis*, 20, 153–164.

Madonna, J. (1991). Countertransference issues in the treatment of borderline and narcissistic personality disorders: A retrospective on the contributions of Gerald Adler, Peter L. Giovacchini, Harold Searles, and Phyllis Meadow. *Modern Psychoanalysis*, 16, 35–64.

Margolis, B. D. (1994). The object-oriented question: A contribution to treatment technique. *Modern Psychoanalysis*, 19, 187–198.

Meadow, P. W. (1987). The myth of the impersonal analyst. *Modern Psychoanalysis*, 12, 131–150.

Meadow, P. W. (1989). How we are to be with patients. *Modern Psychoanalysis*, 14, 145–162.

Meadow, P. W. (2003). *The new psychoanalysis*. New York: Rowman & Littlefield.

Modell, A. H. (1976). The holding environment and the therapeutic action of psychoanalysis. *Journal of the American Psychoanalytic Association*, 24, 285–307.

Ogden, T. (1991). *Projective identification and psychotherapeutic technique*. New Jersey: Jason Aronson, Inc.

Spotnitz, H. (1985). *Modern psychoanalysis of the schizophrenic patient*. New York: Human Sciences Press.

Spotnitz, H., & Meadow, P. W. (1976). *Treatment of the narcissistic neurosis*. New York: Manhattan Center for Advanced Psychoanalytic Studies.

Chapter 7

Til death do us part

Hatred, love and emotional communication in a case of obsessional neurosis

John Madonna

There was never a patient who induced the level of love, as well as the concerning quotient of murderous hate, in me as Mrs. A. She arrived at my office nearly 20 years ago. Cautiously, she opened the door of my consulting room with a new white handkerchief. Her heavy coat remained sternly buttoned throughout the initial interview. Mrs. A tearfully told me that she had a "problem with germs." She said that she had become preoccupied with the fear that she would become contaminated and had found herself instituting more and more precautions.

Although innately social, Mrs. A had been avoiding public places. When she shopped she spent enormous amounts of time inspecting the condition of the food items she purchased. Mrs. A was also meticulous in her concerns for cleanliness of her home, washing and rewashing counters and floors—much to the consternation of her husband. More seriously, and in true obsessional style (Salzman, 1973), she had become preoccupied with her own personal hygiene, to the point of repetitively bleaching her hands. There were occasions when she literally bathed in bleach and her skin became defoliated, cracked and bled.

Mrs. A was concerned that her life was diminished and restricted. In fact, this well-spoken woman had become educated despite the impediments imposed on her by her religion. She had secured a position in a marketing firm where she was competent, successful and well thought of. Nevertheless, she worried continually about not being good enough and anticipated discipline for imagined infractions. Prior to her marriage several years before her entry into treatment, she had traveled throughout Europe. "While traveling," she said, she "found freedom from repression ... could be the person I secretly wanted to be. There was no one there to severely and harshly judge me. I was becoming a citizen of the world, a Renaissance woman."

Despite these accomplishments, Mrs. A looked so limited and defeated that I was unable to imagine her actual complexity. I was to discover that she possessed many strengths, not least of which was a capacity to analyze herself, and me. Nor did I guess at the intensity of her affect, the murderousness of her rage.

Mrs. A was the youngest of seven children, having one sister and five elder brothers. She was born into a Middle Eastern American family and lived much of her early life in a tenement in an ethic enclave of a large city. Her father eschewed material gain on religious grounds and the family was of modest means. Her mother lived the domestic life of the women of her time. Her father had become a practicing member, and elder, of a fundamentalist religious sect. He and his wife argued because of this, she having remained true to her conventional religiously orthodox upbringing. Mrs. A remembered being caught in between the pull of one or the other parent. She was led to believe she would not be saved if she did not attend the religious services of her father's faith. Yet she felt terrified that her mother was "doomed to hell" for her failure to comply. Both parents played upon the child's loyalty and both parents were unrelenting in their punishing attitude and remarks when they believed their daughter had sided with the other parent. In those instances her father referred to her as Satan's child; her mother referred to her as "a mistake" who she wished she had given up for adoption ... Mrs. A commented: "I could not be a part of the world due to my father's religion. Thus I spent a great deal of time alone. No dating, no long term male relationships."

Mrs. A relied on food to soothe herself. This reliance was fostered by her mother who, remorseful after her tirades, would stuff the child with food. Mrs. A found some measure of her mother's acceptance through eating. She was overweight when she applied for treatment and has struggled with weight control all of her life.

A structure of therapy, which provided ample clinical contact, was initiated. This included two individual, one group and eventual marital sessions each week. Contact was also made beyond sessions. Mrs. A's phone calls were received and encouraged. In addition, she would sit for long periods of time on a stone wall across the street from my office. This provided her a sense of constancy and, she said, a feeling of security. In addition, insofar as she lived in the neighborhood of the office, she frequently walked nearby, sometimes encountering me on my walks. On occasion, when she requested it, I walked together with her for short periods. Of this she was to say that she "felt she belonged here." She "felt welcomed." She felt someone "truly cared about her for the first time" in her existence. She was sitting near "someone who loved" her, who "did not use her." She perceived my acceptance of her as "unconditional." Often Mrs. A experienced these extra analytic contacts as positive connections, which seemed to facilitate analytic communication. Later in the treatment, however, they seemed to become brutal attacks against me, as a person who was despised both for failing to gratify her desires, as well as for having stimulated them.

In the beginning, the story of rejection and abuse from her parents, siblings and husband, which Mrs. A recounted, evoked in me both compassion and rage. It was easy to feel sorry for her. Her hurt was so poignant, her pain seemed so genuine. She cried openly and often. In the very beginning of treatment, her anger at the abuse of her family was, however, oddly absent, bound by her obsessional thinking and restrictive obsessional behaviors. In retrospect, it was apparent that my contempt for her tormentors was exceedingly quick and suspiciously thorough. I wished her free of them and they vanquished. Scenarios of a fitting revenge filled my thoughts.

Mrs. A frequently complained of an impatient, volatile and violent husband. Unable to tolerate his wife's obsession with cleanliness, he reacted by screaming and threatening. On a number of occasions he pushed, restrained and struck her. In one incident he attempted to "cure" her of her fear of germs by dragging her into the bathroom and splashing toilet water in her face. She trembled and wept in individual and group sessions as she talked about such scenes. Group members were incensed and stirred to vengeance. In fact, so powerful was the wish for revenge that it remained in force even as Mrs. A's part in the creation of this behavior became apparent. It was as though, in her presence, the emotional inclination toward violence was inevitable. This was exemplified, for example, when one group member, a rather large, burly man, offered to accompany Mrs. A outside after one session in order to pummel her waiting husband.

An intense rivalry also apparently existed between her and her sister, a woman who Mrs. A believed owed her a debt of gratitude for the gifts and attention she had given her children. Her brothers were depicted as selfish and self-indulgent. They had all, she said, abandoned Mrs. A to care alone for ill, demanding and unappreciative parents. She spoke, for example, of her frustration with her widowed father whom she had visited, bringing him a supper she had prepared before leaving for the weekend. He had insisted that she change a dental appointment to which she would have to bring him, without any regard for the fact that due to her work schedule she would have difficulty doing so. "He does not appear to appreciate the fact that I orchestrate his life. He does not even see the sacrifice."

Though the callousness of her family seemed credible, her self-pity became relentless. It seemed to serve as a justification for a vindictive attitude, which she came to increasingly verbalize in treatment. She indirectly expressed this in her unremitting requests for family members to "pitch in" and help her in the care of her parents and invariably found fault with their efforts. As she became more overt in her discontent with them, she was met with rejection.

The sense of deprivation experienced by this patient during her formative years resulted in what Spotnitz (1969) called "frustration aggression." That is, the increase in the level of aggression, and her inability to discharge it resulted in a vicious cycle in which she repeated her early longings for nurturance with consequent escalating frustrated aggression (pp. 46–51). It came to seem as though she was demanding that her husband, relatives and analyst give her the love and acceptance that a fortunate newborn gets from its parents. At the same time, her inability to appreciate anything in her life, and her lack of consideration for the limitations or desires of the people in her life, increased the intensity of this cycle. Her repetition was truly beyond the "pleasure principle," a flagrant example of the need to repeat the past, no matter how unpleasurable (Freud, 1920).

Illustrative of her need to see herself as a victimized "have not," Mrs. A began one session by announcing that she was "massively irritated." She stated that she did not want to be at her vacation home or even back home. She had a "to do" with her husband. And she was feeling "massively put upon" by her boss who had assigned a number of difficult projects to her. Although she had a reputation for being able to manage such assignments, she thought it unfair that she be given so many, when another employee was given so few. She was struck by the unfairness. I commiserated with her stating that she "had a lot to put up with."

She then spoke about how she had asked her husband to do a few things the night before so that they could leave earlier to go to their vacation home. Her husband had refused saying he had other things to do. They argued. She said, "We told each other to 'go fuck yourself.' Handing me his paycheck is all he feels he has to do." She recalled another time at their vacation home, when after having worked very hard with him in the yard, she asked him to accompany her to a favorite scenic area, which offered a particularly beautiful view of the mountains. He refused, as he had so often in the past, wanting to work on their property instead. She sobbed saying,

> We have no sharing of anything. I do not think I am feeling sorry for myself. I just do not know how long I can stay living this way. I am tired of being me. It would be nice to have a companion. I ate three quarters of a pound of spaghetti to soothe myself. It was the only thing that helped me to feel good in that moment.

Along with the amplifying stories of family abuse, Mrs. A was making increased demands for contact with me. Of this, she was to say,

> due to my religious upbringing, I never had any physical, sexual feelings. My first sexual longings were for you. I had fallen in love with you. You were my first love. After my lifetime of deprivation it was so difficult to do what you asked, to express my feelings and then go home.

Excited and ashamed by her transference, she was reassured that it was all right to express all of her thoughts and feelings. She resented this permission when it became clear to her that her longings would not actually be gratified. Feeling denied she, like the women who are "children of nature" in Freud's (1912) discussion of transference love, seemed at this phase of the treatment only "accessible to the logic of soup, with dumplings for arguments." (p. 167).

Her oscillations between adoration and rage became pronounced. She would offer herself sexually, then accuse me of abusing her the way her family had, tormenting her with my refusals. She wished death to my wife, a gregarious woman whom she had met in another circumstance and with whom she had courteously spoken, although she recalled the encounter with a seething fury. In subsequent sessions, tormented by her own envy, she would say vicious things about "the bitch." To be emotionally present during these tirades was difficult and I only managed it due to the realization that her anger was necessary and its expression, even in this way, was a vitally important movement for a woman who was accustomed to binding, in a strangulating obsessional defense, any traces of that affect. Her desire to have "a life" was, after all, at the core of her frustration. Her feelings were driven by that desire. She came to be able to say, "I wanted to have the life I perceived I would have with you. I wanted to be with someone who could show love to me as you do."

She continued to complain during sessions about my commitment to, and imagined preoccupation with, my family. I reminded her that "those people" were only in the consulting room when she brought them in. Though not always convinced, at times this intervention and the unequivocal tone with which it was delivered helped her to be more settled. She could then talk about her own sense of deprivation and her sadness at not having a primary family of her own. Mrs. A was also able to understand how this sense of deprivation and sadness compelled her to strive to make others feel comfortable, entertained and nurtured by her, in the hope that she would be accepted, valued and included by them. She was often indiscriminate in these efforts, and frequently disappointed in the results, experienced resentment, self-pity and rage.

On some occasions Mrs. A so vehemently berated and excoriated me, while simultaneously issuing demands which made me feel as though I were being devoured, that I felt the urge to deny even her most reasonable requests. She threatened me with a suit for faulty treatment and presented such a convincing scenario as to how she would proceed legally that I found myself concerned. On numerous occasions she filled my answering machine with scalding messages. Not only did I feel that she was attempting to "burn" me with these communications, but it was as though she was literally crowding out anyone else from having access to me. In fact, she complained vociferously in our individual sessions about the attention that I gave other group members. Despite this, and though in group she took much time, she was also extremely dynamic in facilitating the communication of others. To her credit, she was helpful to many.

Nor was her disdain confined to the verbal. She sometimes had a look about her when she entered my office, which made her loathing tangible. And lest I misperceive, she was not averse to giving me the finger with both hands. She was truly operatic in her delivery. I could tolerate her because she was reminiscent of the delinquents I worked with earlier in my career and to some extent of my own children during the worst moments of their adolescence. It became apparent to me that my efforts to symbolically gratify this woman's maturational need for love by letting her accompany me on walks only increased her frustration. Though it led to a temporary idealization and disarming of her aggression it eventually just added fuel to the fire, since she could not in reality satisfy her demands for the perfect ideal object.

There were moments when I wanted to kill her. This reaction seemed similar to that of Harold Searles' (1972) fear (i.e. desire) to kill one of his patients and Spotnitz's (2004) offer to do so as a counter to the self-attack of a hateful patient of his. I had satisfying fantasies of suffocation, or smashing her head, throwing her out the window or simply dismissing her from treatment as she launched into one of her vitriolic tirades. I conveyed these to her with relish. Some of these emotional communications that "felt far more powerful than explanations" (Bernstein, 2009, p. 107) would have been clearly guided by my experiences with Mrs. A and her formative transferential inductions up to that point. Her delight that like her, I was "vile," foul mouthed and murderous seemed a confirmation of Spotnitz's (2004) assertion that "in the presence of a person who is like themselves, patients feel liked, understood and thus free to proclaim their hostility and rage" (p. 45). Indeed, in those moments, she had transformed me into a sadistic, vengeful person who exulted in the prospect of administering a painful and brutal murder. I had become the patient, a process that was so aptly discussed by Adler, Giovacchini, Meadow and Searles in 1990 at Clark University (Madonna, 1991).

Through my feelings, I came to understand her murderousness and her need for restrictive obsessional defenses. And I understood her kinship with Lady Macbeth, the need to wash, actually bleach, away the guilt from her hands to substitute, as Freud (1895) indicated, a driven concern for physical purity for the moral purity/righteousness, which has been lost. Eventually, Mrs. A was able to trust me enough, that is, believed me greedy enough, "a money mongering fuck," vile enough, "a selfish, self centered, and uncaring son-of-a-bitch." That is, enough like her to be felt by her to be truly with her. Through the enactments, we were consequently able to talk about and begin to resolve the obsessional constraints.

The reliving of her infantile needs for exclusivity in the transference and the verbalization of her rage at not getting what she wanted allowed for the gradual discharge of her bottled up frustration, aggression and the modulation of her demandingness. Her discovery that she could be vicious to the analyst and that he could be vicious in return allowed her to create the object that she needed, one just like herself, what Spotnitz (1969) has called the "narcissistic transference." Meeting hatred with hatred, I had perhaps demonstrated not only kinship of sorts, but strength stronger than her own.

Just as quickly as they began, the emotional attacks on me and on her shifted, and Mrs. A became the hurt child and then the reflective adult whose analytic associations and interpretations of her motives and behavior were impressive. And I would be the recipient of admiration, fondness and affection. It was exhausting. One session could pluck every emotional cord, simultaneously. Her conflicts were reworked on the anvil of the transference, and I was worked over on that anvil too. Not always emotionally flexible when I began this treatment many years prior, working with her, I became more so. I hated her and loved her for that. And it was this gift that enabled me to remain engaged.

Mrs. A's commitment was profound. Her own assessment of that commitment was accurate:

> I have never missed a session in all these years. I sacrificed to come to my sessions. I gave you the deepest love, commitment, caring. I never gave up, no matter what I needed to do. I never held back. Told you everything, let you be a complete part of my mind, life.

Her realizations and revelations brought her not only a sense of sorrow, but frequently, tranquility. She came to view her attacks on me, and her attempts to destroy the treatment in order to maintain her repetition, as actually attacks on herself. It was her ability to analyze, her diligence and ultimately her consistent devotion to the process that held us both through difficult times.

Having come into awareness of her need for revenge, Mrs. A posed a question that poignantly conveyed her dilemma when her desire for control was thwarted. "What does a woman do who wants to kill everyone, including herself?" This was also part of her growing realization of the magnitude of her need for others to behave as she wished. Her wish to please others led to abuse, self-pity and anger:

> I have been so predictable. Everyone in my life always knew what I would do. I am too damn predictable. Do whatever you want to her. She is coming back. She is holding on, not letting go. She will bounce back. She is resilient. And I think I practiced on you, because you said I was unpredictable.

Poignantly illustrating Spotnitz's (1969) frustration-aggression theory, she tells how the frustration of her natural impulses led to an increase of aggression and the need to employ ever more severe restraints upon her.

> I was never allowed to hate, did not hate, could not hate. I could not hate God. I would take whatever God said I had to take. You are not part of this world. You will not do this. You will not do that. You will not! Okay. Okay. You are God, so that is it ... Sure! That is me. And my father used to say you must deaden your body members. So that is what you do. You are just dead with your feelings, dead with them. They are gone.

Previously compelled to contain powerful hatred in specifically obsessional ways, Mrs. A's epiphany came in her ability, finally, to perceive and acknowledge with unrestricted feeling what Liegner (1980) referred to as the hatred that cures. The recognition of her attempted use and victimization of me and the holding environment of the analytic situation, which we shared, are illustrative:

> All that hatred came out. I hate! I hate. I hated the silent treatment. I hated the box they put me in ... the box. You are in a box now. You are going to live in this box. And there is an avenging, destructive God that is going to whack you the second that you are human. You are not going to be human! If you are human, you are the devil. I hated my father and I hated my mother. I hated myself. And I took all of that hatred out on me. All that hatred. As you know, I put shit away. It is sad to say, but you were the person I could show that hatred to. I just did not know how much I had, have in me. It is all right with me that I know the hate; I know the hate that I felt. I know the anger. I knew the rotten things I could do. I knew how I would get you with my messages. The things I knew which would infuriate you. I could murder someone with these hands. You know how strong these are?

As she became more open and expressive there were occasions in which banter and humor were apparent in the exchanges between us. A sense of emotional connectedness occurred through the irreverence, which emerged as an important part of Mrs. A's attitude and with which I was able to resonate. Moreover, the ability to laugh together, even in the throes of her rage and mine, seemed normalizing, and added an impetus in the momentum for healing.

She announced, for example, that she had seen my name on the list of providers in her insurance book and would have liked to have "put a gun to your temple and pulled the trigger and blown your brains out. It said you were an expert in treating eating disorders." She demanded, "Why have you not helped me lose weight!"

DR. M: We have been talking about weight for a long time. How come I have not helped you lose weight?

MRS. A: I want to put a picture of myself in that pamphlet and say this is what you can expect from the expert on eating disorders.

DR. M: You will let them know how incompetent I am.

MRS. A: That is right. How come? (She said this with considerable sarcasm.)

DR. M: Even Leonardo DaVinci needed something to work with. But tell me. How come I have not helped you?

MRS. A: I sometimes think that you are part of the reason I cannot ... because I cannot have you.

DR. M: What do you mean? You have me regularly. We are married in a way in what we do.

MRS. A: Oh sure. Would you like to go with me to the lighthouse?

DR. M: Can you take me with you? I would love to go there with you.

MRS. A: Right. I will put a dummy in my car, a manikin. I will talk to it all weekend. You know what I envision with you. You would take me to the theater. You would say, "I have some tickets to the theater or a concert. Would you like to do this or that?"

DR. M: Should I help you find someone to do that with and you could still have me too?

MRS. A: But I do not think I want anyone else. I trust you.

DR. M: Obviously not enough to forego the weight defense. And to be thin like me.

MRS. A: I do not know.

DR. M: I think I should help you to find someone and still have me as your companion in what we do.

MRS. A: I did not want to talk to you as I was driving over. Now I do not want the session to end.

In this sequence, Mrs. A began by expressing discontents and focusing on her relationship with me. First, she spoke of her frustration and anger with family members, and then the sadness she felt as a result of how they had disappointed her. It was only after she expressed her frustration and anger with me and her impulse to kill me, followed by her ridiculing, her joking desires to malign me in public, that she could express her true desire. It was in accepting her anger/ridicule and echoing her sarcasm with my own, appreciating her heartache and the fervor of her wish to be cared for and loved, that she felt some measure of relief. And so, she concluded with her desire not to have the session end, not to leave. Many of our encounters went this way.

It was within an emotionally resonant and safe analytic context that this woman came to realize that her obsessional behaviors were an effort to control the intensity of her murderous impulses and her emotional bondage toward her parents, her siblings and her husband. She was able to voice the profound disappointment with and consequent hatred of her siblings and her husband for not meeting her ideal of the close and happy family for which she longed. Her expectations were ultimately cast in more realistic terms, though with a considerable sense of sadness. She came to consider that her preoccupation with germs was in large part a painful self-attack, an effort to cleanse herself of destructive urges and the guilt inherent in them. And she also came to realize the insatiableness of her emotional hunger and how that aroused the sadism of others. These realizations seemed to some extent to have a relieving effect. But it was the opportunity to experience desire and hatred in the transference, without retribution, which facilitated her being able to reach higher and more defined levels of awareness, and to ultimately achieve healing.

Mrs. A possessed the desire and the drive to get better. Consequently, when the resistance to the expression of hatred was resolved, the forces that lead to maturation became active. The washing and bleaching greatly diminished and then for long periods of time stopped altogether. Mrs. A's analysis released a measure of creative energy and there appeared to be a fulfillment of Spotnitz's (2004) theory of recovery. He said that with sufficient recovery "there is a notable increase in the patient's capacity for self fulfillment and happiness, and s/he can sustain the impact of traumatic events with considerable resiliency" (p. 206). Mrs. A obtained a master's degree in marketing. She acquired a home at a vacation resort, which to some extent mitigated her view of herself as the unwanted, inferior child, the unworthy "mistake," always on the outside looking in at other people who have, she having been the perpetual "have not." She was able to construct a satisfying, somewhat tranquil, less conflicted marital and professional life after much time spent in feeling inferior, maligned and at risk. Both she and I enjoyed her satisfaction with these accomplishments.

Prompted to think more deeply about the course of her life and treatment, Mrs. A did not consider her story finished. She expressed determination to strive to become even more independent of the regressive "pull downs," as she called her self-attacks. By having been enabled to express her aggressiveness in the transference, Mrs. A was able to moderate the viciousness toward her and others and to gain some control of it. Having done this, she was able to become passionate in her resolve to achieve her potential for greater joy. She would continue to use her analysis, she said, toward this end, to be aware, present and expressive. And she would expect the same from me—"til death do us part."

This chapter was originally published in 2011 in *Modern Psychoanalysis, 36*, 95–108.

References

Bernstein, J. (2009). Consciousness and interpretation in modern psychoanalysis. *Modern Psychoanalysis*, 34, 106–116.

Freud, S. (1895). *Obsessions and phobias: Their psychical mechanisms and their aetiology* (Standard Edition), 3, 69–89. London: Hogarth Press.

Freud, S. (1912). *Observations on transference love* (Standard Edition), 12, 157–171. London: Hogarth Press.

Freud, S. (1920). *Beyond the pleasure principle* (Standard Edition), 18, 1–64. London: Hogarth Press.

Liegner, E. (1980). The hate that cures: The psychological reversibility of schizophrenia. *Modern Analysis*, 5, 5–95.

Madonna, J. (1991). Countertransference issues in the treatment of borderline and narcissistic personality disorders: A retrospective on the contributions of Gerald Adler, Peter L. Giovacchini, Harold Searles, and Phyllis Meadow. *Modern Psychoanalysis*, 16, 35–64.

Salzman, L. (1973). *The obsessional personality: Origins, dynamics and therapy.* New York: Jason Aronson.

Searles, H. (1972). The function of the patient's realistic perceptions of the analyst in delusional transference. *Countertransference and related subjects,* 197–223. New York: International Universities Press.

Spotnitz, H. (1969). *Modern psychoanalysis of the schizophrenic patient,* 46–51. New York: Grune and Stratton.

Spotnitz, H. (2004). *Modern psychoanalysis of the schizophrenic patient.* New York: Human Sciences Press.

Chapter 8

Intuiting the unknown

Listening with the unconscious mind

Adrian Jarreau

Freud's "evenly suspended attention," in my opinion, provides the foundation for effective psychodynamic treatment. According to Freud (1912):

> Evenly suspended attention consists simply in not directing one's notice to anything in particular ... In this way ... we avoid a danger which is inseparable from the exercise of deliberate attention. For as soon as anyone deliberatively concentrates his attention ... he begins to select from the material before him; one point will be fixed in his mind ... and some other will be disregarded, and in making this selection he will be following his expectations or inclinations. This, however, is precisely what must not be done. In making the selection ... he is in danger of never finding anything but what he already knows ... It must not be forgotten that the things one hears are for the most part things whose meaning is only recognized later on ... He should withhold all conscious influences from his capacity to attend and give himself over completely to his "unconscious memory" ... He should simply listen and not bother about whether he is keeping anything in mind ... Those elements of the material which already form a connected context will be at the doctor's conscious disposal; the rest as yet unconnected and in chaotic disorder, seem at first to be submerged but rises readily into recollection as soon as the patient brings up something new to which it can be related and by which it can be continued.
>
> (pp. 111–112)

Another way of stating what Freud is recommending is that, as listeners, we must wait until we have a bigger picture of what is going on to be able to sort things out. As we are listening and waiting, he recommends we let go of our theories of what is happening and be receptive listeners. We do not want to jump to premature conclusions about what is transpiring and risk leading the patient. Access to the "unconscious memory" is achieved by letting go of the ideas that come into our mind as we listen.

Freud says that when the chaotic disorder of the patient is stored in the unconscious mind of the analyst and is not consciously tampered with, it becomes available for links to other pieces of the patient's material. In this way we gradually come to understand the unconscious of the patient. At the same time, however, this closer connection may trigger emotional turbulence that feels disturbing, even dangerous, on an unconscious level to both parties.

Others who came after Freud, such as Bion and Meltzer, developed his ideas further and wrote about the centrality of the emotional experience. When we are subject to our patient's projections of unwanted experiences and then potentially become an adversary in the patient's mind, we are impacted emotionally. It may be a painful and difficult experience and often forces us to deal with our own anger and hate. Bion (1965) said this emotional impact may feel catastrophic but may also be the source of intuition through transformation.

If the manifest content of the patient's material is usually designed to hide primitive states of need and to hide the fear that those needs will not be met, then how can we know what is going on? How can we come to an intuitive sense of the patient's unconscious state? Freud, followed by Bion and Meltzer and others, says that the conscious mind must be kept out of the way until intuition emerges, and then it can be used in the service of communicating what has become known. What does it mean to keep the conscious mind out of the way and how does one do that? Bollas (2002) writes: "The analyst is not meant to reflect on the material; not supposed to consciously construct ideas about the material; not encouraged to remember anything" (p. 12). So what do we do? Bion (1970), referring to Freud, states that we must be blind to capture the darkness. To discover something new we must let go of what we remember of the patient, what we want to happen, and what we have learned about how to do our work: we must surrender memory and desire.

Why is this necessary? According to Bion (1970), it is essential that we listen in this meditative state to be able to transform the O (psychic reality) of the session into K (knowledge). If we think too much we will be too protected from the unconscious primitive parts of the personality. Bion believes we must subject ourselves to the primitive turbulence of the patient's unconscious, his hallucinations. This is a vulnerable state for the therapist because we are subject to our own primitive and chaotic unconscious as well.

How then do we function as clinicians? What are we left with? According to Bion (1970), nothing but faith. He writes about the necessity of developing faith in O, the unknown and mostly unknowable psychic reality of the encounter between patient and analyst. He explains that this is a faith in the receptivity to the hallucinosis, the darkness, and the formlessness. This is a faith that some order can be found in the chaos that uncertainty and confusion can lead to understanding. This faith makes it possible to subject ourselves time and time again to the catastrophic nature of the emotional impact of the session.

In another paper, Bion (1963) points out that the mind learns and develops through the oscillation between emotional upset and containment. It is an integral part of the self to repeatedly fall apart and come together. Bion believes the disturbance to equilibrium is as valuable as its achievement. This is where Bion's idea of faith comes in, but faith in what?

Eigen (1993) writes of Bion's idea: "Faith is the medium of access to psychoanalytic data. It undercuts and transcends our controlling needs and enables us to experience the impact of emotional reality in a way that allows the latter genuinely to evolve" (p. 219). He seems to be saying that access to our theories in our unconscious mind comes through faith that the turbulent encounter with the patient can yield understanding.

Britton (2005) says that relinquishing a state of equilibrium is more important than gaining it. To have some sense of security, the analyst must have "a belief in the probability" that "some sort of resolution not yet known or even conceivable will emerge." Britton's belief in probability seems quite similar to Bion's notion of faith.

Also writing about Bion's thinking, Meltzer (1983) states: "It is in the emotion that the possibility of a meaning being extracted from this experience resides" (p. 68). I believe he is saying that receiving the split off and projected parts of the patient's personality triggers an emotional experience for the therapist. This experience, an amalgamation of the two subjectivities, is the countertransference. With our open reception to this relational experience we have the creative potential to transform it into "a configuration or form that he [the patient] can think about" (p. 67).

This transformation is not a conscious inner activity. We cannot try to make it happen. However, we can perhaps prepare for this creative transformation by making contact with the primitive unconscious through our particular way of listening. As Meltzer (1983) writes: "Mental health and the development of the mind derives from intimate relationships in which the primordial events are emotional experiences. Bion's work places emotion at the very heart of meaning" (p. 44).

Preparing to receive meaning

How do we get to the meaning? How can we be receptive to this transformation of emotion into understanding? According to Bion (1970), our psychoanalytic attitude is important. It means holding in esteem the emotional experience of the patient and what that evokes in the analyst. We must be willing to come under the influence of the patient and be affected by his way of relating. There are pressures from the patient to be treated in certain ways: to be comforted, to be treated specially, to be agreed with, to take sides, to be advised, and never to be left. When we do not give in to the pressures, then we may be perceived as cruel deprivers and felt by the patient to be a withholding adversary. If the analyst can tolerate being this way with the patient, the experience may yield understanding.

My work as an analyst is to be receptive and to be a container of the patient's projections. I do not have to think or search for meaning. I do not have to generate understanding by trying to remember theory. I do not have to work hard except at being open to the painful and possibly disturbing experience of being with the patient. This is hard work. It takes discipline and vigilance to go against the old habits of avoiding disturbance. Being the object of primitive catastrophic fears, and the anger and hatred they trigger, can be quite disturbing.

When the analyst tries to comfort or take control in order to defend against these feelings, the analysis is impeded. The patient gets the message that his primitive mental states are not acceptable and should not be part of his humanity. Another consequence of soothing is the obstruction of a creative process. If an understanding can arise from experiencing the emotion, but that emotion is comforted away as if it were merely a childhood scrape, then the understanding is lost with it.

We cannot completely suspend memory and desire, but we can train ourselves to let them go when they intrude. This is similar to what occurs in meditation, a practice I have found helpful. When thoughts are released, our feeling state becomes more apparent. Thinking, at a preliminary stage, can be defensive and can insulate us from the bare emotion.

We gather the raw materials for our work by listening with our unconscious mind. It is similar to dreaming, which we do when our conscious mind is not interfering. It is in these states that we receive creative productions that can be very useful. It has been my experience that when I can release my thoughts, then I invite a "dream." It might be an intuition or something I did not know I knew that came to mind because there was space for it. It is like going to sleep in reverie. The conscious mind is kept out of the way so that the dream/intuition can emerge from the emotional turbulence.

What I have noticed in my practice of "no memory or desire" is two similar but different experiences. In the first, after listening for a while and not paying much attention to the thoughts that come up, I become aware of something that seems like an important new discovery like finding the missing piece of a puzzle. I feel grateful, but I may also feel anxious because my patient may feel deeply understood and then have an envious reaction that could lead to its negation.

The second and much more common experience is that after listening for a while, relinquishing thoughts and feeling the turbulent effects of the encounter that often include a pressure to say something, I may speak for any one of several reasons. There may be some derivative in the material that seems important because it provides information about something happening in the present. I may want to affirm what my patient has said to strengthen it or I may want to point out that some harsh, self-destructive attitude has been expressed. Or I may simply succumb to the pressure to say something.

However, something has already happened in my period of listening that has affected my patient and me. Gradually I become aware that the experience has deepened for both of us. I seem to have a clearer and keener sense of what is going on. My intuition is active, meaning that creative, insightful thoughts occur to me while engaged in a dialogue. I can make links among things. Thoughts come into my mind about how my patient is relating to me, and I can develop and expand on them as I speak. In listening I have learned something that enables me to be more interactive while retaining my psychoanalytic function.

This development has often surprised me, perhaps because I have been waiting for something like the former experience of suddenly having a clear, well-formed understanding. When that understanding has not occurred and a lot of time has elapsed, I have given in to internal and external pressures and said something. It has felt like a compromise, and perhaps it is, perhaps I have not wanted to be subject to the pressures any longer. At that point, it has seemed like my investment in the waiting has not paid off; I wanted something and did not get it. I got caught up in desire.

But all has not been lost. I have seen, as the session progresses, that I did make a good investment in my period of listening with my unconscious. In having done so I provided space for my patient to think, and I opened myself up to the unknown of the experience we shared. It has seeped into my unconscious mind and become more available to me.

My primary work in the session, therefore, is to be willing to be affected by what my patient does not want to experience. Then I may be identified as a bad object, defined by the hatred and projected experiences. This triggers a primitive emotional response in me. However, if I am thinking constantly about what is going on and trying to figure it out with the use of theory, I can be easily overwhelmed by the difficulty. I do not think we need to work this hard. If we do, it could become frustrating because the understanding we are striving for may remain just out of reach.

Striving in a way is a defense against the emotional impact of the encounter with the patient; it is an enactment of desire as opposed to an experience. Practicing no memory or desire is a way of getting the defenses out of the way long enough for meaning to develop. I do not think Bion meant that we should not have desire. I think he meant that we should let go of trying to procure what we want. Desire may still exist as a felt experience, but it is not distracting or being acted upon.

Clinical examples

It is difficult to illustrate with clinical vignettes how listening with the unconscious mind can lead to intuiting the unknown. One needs to be there, so to speak. Nonetheless, I will describe two such experiences. You may find these even more meaningful if you imagine yourself in a similar situation.

These clinical examples are intended to show that as clinicians we can come to know something about our patient we did not know before if we are willing to let unconscious material accrue and coalesce without "the exercise of deliberate attention" (Freud, 1912, p. 111).

To begin I will describe a session with a 40-year-old man with whom I have been working for about three years. He is the oldest of three children, all 18 months apart, and as an adult has always lived alone. He reports many instances of being overlooked or ignored by his family. He has told me the same stories many times probably assuming I will not remember. He has described several periods of extreme depression in his past. With me, he is very agreeable and compliant.

I have occasionally gotten sleepy during our sessions. One time when I had not been sleeping well because of an illness, I fell asleep for a moment several times during the session and lost track of the interaction. It was disturbing to me, but the patient did not comment on it. In the session I will describe, I again became sleepy, but since I had been sleeping well, I could consider it my unconscious response to him. Although that was helpful, I still did not know why I had that unconscious response. I tried to figure it out in order to help myself fight off the sleepiness but then gave up. Then I discovered I was able to pay attention to the experience of being sleepy and not fall asleep. I thought that attentiveness to the sleepy experience might be the only way to learn why I was reacting to him this way. At that point I had nothing else to go on.

I said nothing for at least ten minutes as I struggled with the experience. As I listened, it seemed as if he was working hard, perhaps feeling that he had to since I was silent and sleepy. I suspect he was afraid he was losing me and was trying hard to get me more involved. His associations, however, were very helpful to me. We had been talking about times when he dissociates from painful relational experiences, and he was telling me about a recent visit with a woman he had become interested in who he feels is attracted to him. A relationship of a rather flat nature has developed. He has been mostly unable to express his attraction. She mentioned in passing that she was dating someone new. He, of course, was disappointed but unable to acknowledge the hurt or inquire into it.

He was also telling me about a therapist friend who had asked him if he had ever been angry with me. What began to filter into my consciousness through the fog was the recognition that the sleepiness stemmed from a lack of emotion in the session, which created a deadness. I also felt overlooked emotionally. It seemed as if I had no emotional effect on him, as if I did not exist. As he talked to me about himself, his words felt vacant, like a disembodied expression as though he were talking about someone else.

He has never expressed dissatisfaction or frustration with me, nor has he failed to be a good and friendly patient. He always has something to talk about, trying to make me feel like his time with me is important to him. He almost always agrees with me, wanting me to feel as if what we do is working for him. This has given him some security in the endurance of the relationship, without which he may fear I would ignore or dismiss him.

The relationship with the woman is not happening. He has been with her as he has been with me: more like an outside observer, not emotionally engaged, but hoping to be acknowledged. The content of his material was revealing but since it lacked affect, I became sleepy. Allowing myself to make space internally for the fear of falling asleep led me to the awareness that he was expressing himself to me without emotion. This seemed like an intuitive understanding. It had the quality of quiet surprise as if I had discovered something about him that I had not consciously known. I said to him that he may fear being dismissed if he had an emotional response to me. He agreed as always, but also seemed to be genuinely affected by what I said. We talked about his fear of being frustrated with me when I was inattentive or inaccurate.

Bollas (2002) describes not knowing for long periods of time what patients mean by what they say, but being "genuinely lost in the movement of the patient's communication" (p. 35). I was lost. I had come under a spell. I had to overcome intense internal conflict in order to face my fear of relaxing with the sleepiness. I dreaded falling asleep. The session was important for me in terms of building trust. I was afraid it would become like the previous one. I had to let go of my memory, which put me more in touch with the fear and the sleepiness. At the end of the session, the patient reflected on times he had been frustrated and angry with me. He expressed gratefulness as he left. I also felt grateful.

I reflected on his history of being the oldest sibling by only 18 months and how painful it must have been to be overlooked at such a young age. I thought about how that has shaped his personality. He seems to expect to be overlooked, and I think he is when he cannot have emotional responses to people. Initially my sleepy response was the way in which I overlooked him.

He started the next session by saying, "I think you know something you are withholding from me, or you do not know but should." He was able to express his frustration. Perhaps he could now project into me and be angry because I had become a withholding object to him. He said he thought I withheld from him because I could then have manipulative power to keep him coming and be my ATM (automatic teller machine). He was depositing something with me in the form of his projections, but he felt I was withholding something from him. I felt better being a bad object than an overlooked one. I was awake and alert.

A law regarding the conservation of energy states: "energy can neither be created nor destroyed"; it can only be converted from one form into another. For example, when we plug in a heater, electricity is pushed through resistance wires and converted into heat. Perhaps this is what happens in humans with the energy of our emotions. There is the potential for transformation into another form that is useful. If, however, we are not receptive to our emotions and project them internally, they can transform into symptoms. I think this happened in the session when I became sleepy. However, I could not ignore the sleepiness. I wanted it to go away, but it was something I had to pay attention to.

I did not think about my sleepiness; I simply paid attention to it rather than denying or trying to get rid of it. Fortunately, that made me less sleepy.

However, I had been quite afraid of falling asleep again and losing track of the session. As I listened, many thoughts occurred to me, any one of which could have defensively gotten me out of my predicament.

In my experience, when the emotion of a session is not attended to but instinctively rejected, then not only is transformation and creativity obstructed, but fiction can be created. I call this "selected fiction" in contrast to Bion's (1962) "selected fact" (p. 72). It happens when I unknowingly do not want to be emotionally affected by the encounter with my patient. In this defensive mode I am likely to say something before I have a clearer sense of what is going on. I am trying to protect myself from the intimate relational impact of being together. Uncertainty becomes the enemy and in my striving to understand I am likely to grasp at anything in my patient's material that triggers a memory of theory. The interpretation from this defensive state becomes the selected fiction. I change the reality of the session and both of us are off on a wild goose chase. It becomes very difficult to differentiate between what my patient genuinely feels and how I have made her feel. Projection into the patient, producing distortion, makes it very difficult to know what is going on.

To further illustrate what I am discussing, I will describe another clinical experience. This patient is a 50-year-old single woman with few friends. Her mother died suddenly when she was six. The oldest sister took over many of the maternal functions for the patient who was the youngest of five. A few years later that sister died suddenly in a plane crash. When the patient was in her early teens another sister, to whom she was very close, died in a horse-riding accident. After this death my patient withdrew from life for several months, hardly speaking to anyone. All this time her father, with whom she had been close, had been withdrawing through alcoholism. He died when my patient was in her late teens. It is apparent that my patient has been trying to protect herself from loss for most of her life.

I have been working with her for five years. Our time together has become very important to her. It is one of very few relationships, including those with her remaining family. We increased from one to three sessions a week quickly, and I have been seeing her four times weekly for more than three years. Periodically, she has reacted rather violently to not having a special relationship with me and having to end our sessions. During these times she gets angry, sullen, withdrawn, and unreachable. The good work we have been doing becomes useless and ineffectual, and she becomes adamant about finding something that will work for her. She has said that I do not care about her and that for her to feel better she must find someone who cares. Knowing that I care and that this must be some distortion, I have interpreted that she may be afraid of my care and cannot receive it if she is certain she will lose it. I have also said that she may want me to be the family she lost, and that she is afraid it will all end suddenly and badly, which may be all she knows.

Over time these angry collapses increased in frequency and intensity. Gradually, I came to realize we were at an impasse. I was having trouble containing her frequent threats to quit. She could not let herself work with me. Progress was abhorrent as it meant relying on me, and I was so undependable. We were stuck. Her threats to quit became a daily occurrence. Every session was full of intense upset and angry withdrawal. Unconsciously I was unwilling to let myself experience this pain. I interpreted too much. My interventions were, for the most part, accurate, but they were unconsciously intended to deflect the angry threats. With the help of supervision I was finally able to confront the reality of the situation. I faced the fact that I was not only feeling impotent but had become so. I realized that something had to change or she would end the analysis.

I had to be the one to change since, as the clinician, I am responsible for the impasse. I do not mean that I am solely responsible, but the impasse was a difficulty I could not get through (i.e. I too was at impasse). I became painfully aware that I had not let myself be impacted by the powerful destructiveness that was unfolding before my eyes. It was as if I had blinders on and my vision had become narrowly restricted. When her threats become imminent, I realized I could no longer keep the blinders on. It became clear to me that the only way to save the work was to surrender to the painful impact. I became diligent in my practice of no memory or desire. I had to give up these defenses if I was to save the analysis.

In the session that broke the impasse, I decided that I would wait for something to seep into my unconscious and gather significance before speaking. She was angry and sullen, saying she was hopeless about getting what she wanted and without that nothing would work so there was no reason to continue. After an initial mistake, when I fell into the same defensive trap, I was silent and patiently waited for my openness to the experience to produce some intuitive sense of what was going on. Nothing occurred to me so I remained silent. I was afraid my patient was going to have a lot of trouble with my silence as she had in the past. I was aware that enduring the fear might indicate to her that I could tolerate her annihilating rage and threats to quit. It also occurred to me that she might experience my silence as a sign of my impotence, my inability to respond. I had to take that chance. I had nothing to say, and if I spoke it would likely be defensive. I thought to myself I would be okay if she did not continue even though she was my last training case. Did I really know what was best for me or for her at that point?

We remained in silence for 40 minutes. I was struck by her quietness. I expected her to be quite upset and angry, reiterating her intention to quit. I thought she would pressure me to speak. However, she calmed down. Just before the end of the session she said in a surprisingly light way that it was time to go. We parted in a much more relaxed and relational atmosphere than I had anticipated. Perhaps she felt relieved that I had been able to tolerate her anger and the underlying fear of losing me, along with my fear of losing her.

When she returned the next day she reported having had a better day and attributed it to "some different way I had been with her." I was quite surprised that my efforts had made a difference so soon given the stubbornness of the impasse. I felt grateful that my willingness to face what initially seemed catastrophic had paid off, strengthening my faith in the creative process. I was also somewhat disoriented since I had not expected this change so soon. I was prepared and actually looking forward to enduring the onslaught because I felt like I was really working and accomplishing something, a feeling I had not had for some time. This was an important lesson for me. It taught me that it is just as creative to be silent when there is nothing to say as it is to have an intuitive understanding.

Thinking about the experience, I wondered where my expectation of her having trouble with my silence had come from. It did not seem to happen so it must have been my fantasy. I expected the past to repeat itself because I had been having trouble locating myself in the present with her. This indicates the importance of clearing away the impediments and returning to the emotional present.

Returning is the key word here. It is impossible to fully relinquish memory or desire and remain emotionally present. I got caught in my defense of remembering what had happened in the past, fearing it would happen again. As I defended myself from what we were going through in the present, the emotional turbulence intensified. My patient became increasingly frustrated and angry, making it more difficult for me to continue to defend myself. I found myself in a conflictual dilemma. My defenses were not working, or they were working too well. Nothing was happening in the therapy.

My increasing resistance to the fear of losing her was indicative of a corresponding resistance in my patient. The emotional impact on me had to intensify to the point of overcoming my instinctual resistance before I could understand my patient's conflictual state. I had to go to the place of fear with her, the fear of loss.

Letting things go in order to pull them together

When I was trying desperately to hold on defensively as my patient was angrily threatening to quit, I felt as if I would be inviting catastrophe were I to give up my defenses. It seemed as if the destruction of the analysis, which I was trying to prevent, would finally happen. But having become aware of the impasse, I was faced with the realization that my approach was not working. Something had to change. I had to let things fall apart, let go of the analysis. But paradoxically, when I shifted, the catastrophe I feared did not occur. Letting the work fall apart psychically had the effect of pulling it together. I had to experience the terror my patient was feeling in the separations. Her survival felt threatened, and she did not feel safe even when she was with me. When I let myself go there, let myself experience the fear that I would lose her and not survive, she felt understood and no longer felt compelled to leave analysis. The fear was coming from my defenses, and it diminished when I could relinquish them.

Freud's and Bion's technique of listening with the unconscious sets us up to be emotionally affected, which initially can feel catastrophic. Faith is all we have when we let go of memory and desire. Without faith we cannot let our equilibrium be upset and therefore cannot get a sense of what our patient is going through.

Bion does not seem to have much to say about where this faith comes from and I do not know why this is the case, because he has a lot to say about learning from experience. Perhaps it was obvious to him. In my opinion, the faith develops early in life when one learns, with the help of others, to trust oneself, and it develops further during treatment. As a patient, one oscillates frequently between difficulty and containment and is helped through these transitions. With this help, faith is developed in the ability to return to a state of equilibrium simply because it happens so frequently in the treatment. Developing faith in being able to return to a state of containment is necessary for working at the frontier of primitive relational experience where equanimity can be upset.

I have attempted to describe and illustrate the necessity of experiencing emotional turbulence in order to do the work of analysis. As Bion (1967) writes: "His interpretations should gain in force and conviction – both for himself and his patient – because they derive from the emotional experience with a unique individual and not from generalized theories imperfectly remembered" (p. 272).

I would like to close with an excerpt from a speech given by Meg Harris Williams (2004) at Donald Meltzer's funeral:

> In his view theory was always subordinate to practice, and the practice of psychoanalysis he saw not as doing things to other people but as a "state of rest" in which if you listened sufficiently quietly, the miracle of your internal mother and father and all the knowledge they contain, would simply present itself to you.

This chapter was originally published in 2012 in *Modern Psychoanalysis, 37*, 66–81.

References

Bion, W. R. (1962). *Learning from experience*. London: Karnac.
Bion, W. R. (1963). *Elements of psychoanalysis*. London: Karnac.
Bion, W. R. (1965). *Transformations*. London: Karnac.
Bion, W. R. (1967). Notes on memory and desire. In J. A. Lindon & A. Coodley (Eds.), *Psychoanalytic forum*. New York: International Universities Press, 271–280.
Bion, W. R. (1970). *Attention and interpretation*. London: Karnac.
Bollas, C. (2002). *Free association*. Cambridge, UK: Ikon Books.
Britton, R. (2005). *The pleasure principle, the reality principle, and the uncertainty principle*. Unpublished manuscript.

Eigen, M. (1993). *The electrified tightrope*. Northvale, NJ: Jason Aronson.

Freud, S. (1912). *Recommendations to physicians practicing psychoanalysis* (Standard Edition). London: Hogarth Press, 12, 111–120.

Meltzer, D. (1983). *Dream life: A reexamination of the psychoanalytic theory and technique*. Perthshire, UK: Clunie Press.

Williams, M. H. (August2004). *Speeches at Donald Meltzer's funeral*. www.harris-meltzer-trust.org.uk/pdfs/FuneralSpeeches.pdf (accessed 2012).

Part III

Chapter 9

An approach to the management of treatment impasses

June Bernstein

The aim of modern psychoanalysis is not to provide a corrective emotional experience, to offer insight, to reconstruct the past, to afford catharsis, or to repair the ego, although all these things may occur. The purpose of treatment is for the analyst to resolve the patient's resistance to feeling, thinking, and remembering everything—and putting it all into words.

What Spotnitz and his colleagues call "modern psychoanalysis" is an expansion of classical technique that evolved in response to the impasses that tended to develop in the treatment of preoedipal conditions. Finding that interpretation was not usually effective with such patients, modern psycho-analysts extended the range of their interventions. They regard a most significant contribution to technique as being the emphasis on the role of emotional communication, especially in the analyst's interventions.

Freud's writings have provided the source for two lines of development of psychoanalytic technique. In one, described by Sterba in 1934, the analyst helps the patient to dissociate the reasonable part of the ego from the drives and defenses that arise in the transference. The analyst and patient together examine the events of the transference in a state of affective detachment. This procedure is reminiscent of Wordsworth's definition of poetry as emotion recollected in tranquility. Sterba's approach derives from Freud's structural theory and is the preferred one in psychoanalytic ego psychology. It requires, however, that the patient have a reasonable ego accessible to intellectual conviction.

Strachey (1934), writing in the same year, put an emphasis on the emotional interaction between analyst and patient rather than on intellectual insight or the therapeutic alliance. In describing the conditions necessary for a mutative interpretation he said: "A mutative interpretation can only be applied to an id-impulse which is actually in a state of cathexis … a charge of energy originating in the patient himself" (p. 149). Since the id-impulse must be directed at the analyst within the transference, the analyst is "exposing himself to some great danger … deliberately evoking a quantity of the patient's id-energy while it is alive and actual and unambiguous and aimed directly at himself" (p. 159). Thus, a mutative interpretation is neither given nor received in a state of affective tranquility.

In such a situation, the patient's reasonable ego is not likely to be available. Freud (1958) noted how, under the influence of transference resistance, the patient is "flung out of his relation to the doctor," and "he regards with indifference logical arguments." He said, "Just as in dreams, the patient regards the products of the awakening of his unconscious impulses as contemporaneous and real; he seeks to put his passions into action without taking any account of the real situation" (pp. 107–108).

Under such circumstances, the effectiveness of interpretations tends to be particularly impaired and the use of emotional communication is most crucial.

Emotional communication is a communication given from within the transference-countertransference interaction, rather than an interpretation from outside it. According to Margolis (1978), it is "a form of exchange between people which conveys information, transmitted and received emotionally rather than intellectually, concerning their conscious and unconscious feeling states" (pp. 146–147). Thus, a patient who has been expressing self-hatred may be told, "You are despicable!" rather than being informed that he suffers from low self-esteem. The emotional communication is used to promote further verbalization and to resolve or mobilize resistance rather than to offer insight. If the patient believes that he is unlovable, the conviction will be activated in the transference. The patient will believe the analyst does not find him worthwhile, that he is boring and unwanted in the here and now. By agreeing with him, the analyst accepts his perception and offers him the opportunity to examine it at some distance from his own ego. Meadow (1974) says:

> To tell him he is not in touch with reality, as we do when we interpret his projection as belonging to relationships of the past, denies his emotion. Telling him he deserves our hatred accepts his projection. Asking him why the analyst is so mean also accepts his projection. Feeling accepted, the patient could learn to say: "I do not deserve your hatred and if you were a decent person you would treat me better."
>
> (p. 93)

Modern analysts believe that every transference provokes a reciprocal countertransference. The analyst's willingness to experience and tolerate the feelings that the patient induces, without acting upon them, is an index of his ability to work with the emotional force of the countertransference. Treatment impasses may occur when the analyst resists having, or letting the patient have, some unpleasant feeling.

Freud considered negative transference an obstacle to treatment. He dismissed as untreatable those patients who were incapable of forming a positive transference. Freud (1958) observed that patients enter treatment with certain conditions for loving. These conditions are bound to infantile imagos in which the patient's libido is regressively invested. The analyst meets the patient's requirements for loving when the infantile prototypes are reactivated in the transference. But for Freud, if the withdrawn libido cannot be reanimated and redirected toward the transference figure, the patient is not a suitable candidate for psychoanalysis. Freud says, "Where the capacity to transfer feeling has come to be of an essentially negative order, as with paranoids, the possibility of influence or cure ceases" (p. 107).

Later psychoanalysts found that these patients, in whom the conditions for loving cannot be met, either run away from treatment themselves, or induce the analyst to get rid of them. They cannot find the right object, and they prefer no relationship at all to the kind of relationship they characteristically have. Their resistance to forming and maintaining a relationship may first be expressed in the difficulties they make about the simplest arrangements for coming. They attempt to give up treatment before it begins. The modern analyst tries to make the patient comfortable enough to state all his objectives to coming: "It is too far. There is no parking. The time is not right. The fee is too high."

The analyst deals with these objectives in two ways. He accepts them at face value, that is, he does not interpret their unconscious defensive significance, and he explores them in order to get the patient to expand on them more fully. How does the patient get here? Can he take public transportation? Is there a parking lot nearby? What fee would he like to pay?

A patient who asks about the analyst's credentials may really want to know whether the analyst is a person with whom he can have a relationship. The analyst who answers the question without further investigation may be foreclosing an opportunity to discover what kind of object the patient needs. If the patient inquires, the modern analyst explores the request to clarify how the patient views the relationship.

One new arrival wanted to know whether the analyst was familiar with Gestalt therapy. When the analyst asked what he should know about it, the patient explained that his mind was in fragments and he needed someone who was interested in making things whole. He thus gave his presenting problem and told what he wanted from treatment. The patient is still defining the object he needs. At present he wants someone who will help him to feel an emotion and is explaining what the analyst would have to do to enable him to feel one. His usual form of discourse is highly idiosyncratic and incomprehensible, but the need to instruct the analyst involves him increasingly in secondary process thinking.

A successful and apparently forthright businessman asked if the analyst had been trained in any specialty. What he wanted to know was how he should begin. Would the analyst structure the interview or just let him flounder around? He wished to know about the analyst's training so he could cooperate with it. Asking him to tell the story of his life was sufficient to get him started.

It is important to explore the patient's questions to discover what kind of object will meet his conditions for investing his psychic energy in the task of psychoanalysis.

Since narcissistic patients have serious difficulties in forming intimate relationships, treatment begins at a frequency the patient can tolerate. Patients have been known to start treatment on a once-a-month basis. Others may ask to be seen several times a week, but indicate by lateness or missed sessions that they are seeing too much of the analyst. Spotnitz (1969) recommends that the patient be kept in a mild state of object hunger so that he will work most productively in sessions.

Some narcissistic patients arrive in treatment in an essentially objectiveless state. They demonstrate by self-absorption and withdrawal that they have not yet cathected objects as a means for reducing tension. Their main requirement seems to be a need for insulation. For the person who defends against emotions by sensations of deadness, numbness, or emptiness, the analyst provides ego insulation to protect the patient from overstimulation and the consequent necessity to employ even more radical defenses.

Overstimulation is dangerous to such patients because the tension it generates is not discharged in interaction with the outside world. Instead, it is turned back onto the patient's own psyche or soma. Originally, Freud (1957a) saw narcissism as the withdrawal of libidinal cathexis from the outside world and its reinvestment in the self. In 1917 he described how in melancholia the self is attacked in lieu of the abandoned object. In 1920, with the introduction of the dual drive theory, the self is seen as the original object of both libidinal and aggressive impulses. Since that time there has been increasing recognition that it is the disposition of the aggressive, rather than the libidinal drive that is the nuclear problem in narcissistic disorders. Modern analysts believe that what is needed to help a patient move from narcissism to object relations is an object that can be perceived as being like the self. Spotnitz and his colleagues facilitate conditions, which promote narcissistic transference by limiting their responses to the patient's direct attempts at contact. Spotnitz (1969) describes how he begins treatment by providing a neutral, non-stimulating atmosphere in which the patient will feel comfortable enough to form a relationship with the analyst. Spotnitz times his interventions to the patient's attempt to contact him. His responses are not only cued by the patient, they also mirror the patient's style of contact. Meadow (1974) says:

> Contact functioning replaces the subjectively determined timing of classical interpretation with what might be called "demand feeding," in which the timing and type of communication are what the subject asks for. When the analyst responds to a question with a question, a devaluation with a devaluation, the subject is in control of the quantity and type of stimulation that he receives.

(p. 92)

According to Spotnitz (1976):

> When the therapist limits his own communications to responding to the patient's direct attempts at contact, and responding in kind, the narcissistic defense is reactivated rather quickly and promotes the development of transference on a narcissistic basis. In other words, the patient is permitted to mold the transference object in his own image. He builds up a picture of his therapist as someone like himself – the kind of person whom he will eventually feel free to love and hate.
>
> (p. 109)

An object who can be hated or loved like the self can be used as a substitute for the self, and may be the first step in acquiring object relations.

Although in 1912 Freud spoke only of the patient's buried love emotions, toward the end of his life he became increasingly aware of aggressive impulses. Eventually, he said that all of psychoanalysis would have to be reformulated in terms of understanding the aggressive drive as separate from the libidinal drive. According to Spotnitz and Meadow (1976), modern psychoanalysts have used this as their starting point.

Many modern psychoanalysts use Freud's early energy concepts, but emphasize in preoedipal cases the bottled-up aggression rather than dammed-up libido. Spotnitz and Meadow (1976) offer examples from published case histories to support the thesis that patients protect their object and defend themselves against recognizing their destructive wishes. They report on a patient (Reik's) who said: "Instead of knowing that you want to kill someone else, you wipe yourself out" (p. 6).

The inability to find acceptable and adequate methods for the discharge of the aggressive drive is often considered responsible for narcissistic disorders. Because libidinal energy is tied up in object protection it is not available for other purposes. According to Spotnitz (1969), libidinal energy "is overwhelmed as the organizing force of the mental apparatus" (p. 30).

The infant first discharges tension in random, unfocused movement or in somatic conversions. Gradually he learns more adaptive ways of discharging energy, culminating, if all goes well, in the establishment of object relations and a structured psychic apparatus. The narcissistic patient, however, still presents the problem of energy discharge. Because his psychic structure is incomplete, it is useless to appeal to his ego with intellectual insight. In modern psychoanalysis the aim is not insight, but discharge of thoughts, feelings, and memories into words—a process of psychic ego development and integration.

Narcissism may be viewed as a form of self-attack. Such narcissistic defenses as autism, ego fragmentation, depression, and somatization are methods of turning aggressive impulses against the self in order to protect a valued object. The objectless state is, paradoxically, employed to protect the object from the feelings the patient would have were he to acknowledge the object's reality and importance. Spotnitz (1976) suggests that such patients experience too much stimulation and too little discharge, and that the analyst must support the defenses until the patient has developed the ability to engage in the rapid, verbal discharge of all feelings, particularly negative ones. Until that time the analyst insulates the patient from experiencing more feeling than can be dealt with in the session. Encouraging the emergence of hostile feelings at too rapid a pace may lead to psychosis.

Freud (1966) suggested, in his "Project for a Scientific Psychology," that discharge of energy is the first requirement of human life. Objects are acquired in association with drive reduction. Every infant who survives the crib has acquired some rudimentary object. It was Freud's (1957b) hypothesis that the first object was indistinguishable from the self. Furthermore, he speculated that hate might precede love and be the older form of relating. He wrote, "at the very beginning, it seems, the external world, objects, and what is hatred are identical" (p. 136). When, in 1912, Freud emphasized the patient's conditions for loving, he had not yet formulated his theories about aggression and the death instinct. At present it appears that conditions for hating may be even more crucial in the treatment of narcissistic patients. Modern analysts find that the narcissistic defense (self-attack) can be mitigated by resolving the patient's resistance to expressing hatred in undisguised verbal form. Such a resolution of resistance releases libidinal energy that is otherwise tied up in protecting the object (Spotnitz & Meadow, 1976). To facilitate the expression of both love and hate, the modern analyst does nothing to interfere with the spontaneous development of transference.

Although the oedipal-level patient reactivates infantile images of real objects, the narcissistic patient creates an object in his own image, blending self and interjects from the undifferentiated state. He externalizes early self and object impressions from the period before ego boundaries are formed. Such a narcissistic transference fulfills the patient's conditions for having a relationship.

Narcissistic patients are treated on the couch. The immobility this imposes, like that of dreaming, allows the patient to freely verbalize aggression without fear of actually harming the analyst. Face-to-face treatment inhibits the development of transference and substitutes nonverbal communication for speech.

The couch permits a more desirable control of regression by what is said rather than nonverbal cues or reliance on familiar reality. Verbalization is ego building, whereas discharging feelings in gestures and facial expressions circumvents the ego. Restricting both patient and analyst to speech permits greater range and flexibility of verbal expression. Most patients become freer to express all their feelings if they do not have to "face" the analyst while doing so. Face-to-face treatment keeps the patient oriented to the social realities, but social reality had already failed to resolve the patient's resistances.

Early in treatment, emotional communication is used to make the patient feel understood and to facilitate narcissistic transference. Instead of confronting the patient with reality or correcting his distortions, the analyst joins the patient behind the stonewall of narcissism. In essence, modern analysts follow the procedure recommended by Anna Freud (1965) for the treatment of children:

> Did he come to his appointment in a cheerful disposition, I was cheerful too ... I followed his lead in every subject of talk ... I did nothing but follow his moods and humours along all their paths and bypaths ... if he were serious or depressed I was the same.
>
> (p. 9)

The patient is justified in experiencing any emotion in the presence of the analyst without being contradicted. If the patient feels uncomfortable or frightened and the analyst tells him he has nothing to fear, it inhibits the expression of the feeling without dispelling it. Therefore, it may be preferable not to contradict the patient who says, "You hate me," or "You think I am terrific," but to explore further. A patient, who commented that the analyst was yawning the week before, was asked, "Why did I yawn?" and not, "Why did you think I yawned?"

In describing the treatment methods developed by Spotnitz and his colleagues, Meadow (1969) says:

> They reflect the feeling of the patient as a way of joining him in his type of verbal contact – answering his questions with a question of the same type, agreeing with him in his hopelessness and feelings of inadequacy, and by devaluating the person of the analyst that he has over-evaluated, thus bringing the analyst down to the patient's own ego level where he is not too powerful to criticize.
>
> (p. 19)

She also says:

> In classical psychoanalytic interpretation, the psychoanalyst brings the unconscious reason for the maladaptive response to the attention of the patient's rational ego; in psychological reflection, the psychoanalyst agrees with the subject's maladaptive distortion so that it may be examined as in a mirror.
>
> (p. 20)

Thus, a patient who repetitively attacks himself may be "joined" by being told he is even worse than he realizes, that he is hopeless. Or the analyst may "mirror" the patient by saying that the patient is doing fine, the problem is that the analyst may not be adequate. In the first case, the analyst joins the patient's feelings by agreeing with him. In the second, the analyst mirrors the patient by describing himself as inadequate like the patient.

Whether mirroring or joining, the analyst limits these responses to requests from the patient for some feedback. Modern analysts call this "contact functioning" because it relies on the patient's contacting rather than on the analyst's desire to say something. It puts the patient in control of the amount and type of stimulation he receives.

Patients may have been over- or understimulated in the past, and they may require a similar or different experience with the analyst. They will indicate what they need by the amount of contact they seek from the analyst.

Thus, the patient who wants to fight can get a fight. Patients are relieved to discover that the patient can be as rude, silly, coarse, or argumentative as they are. One patient threatened to bash in Spotnitz's head. Spotnitz, who by this point had plenty of negative feelings to employ for emotional communication, retorted, "No you will not, because I will bash yours in before you get off the couch!" (Spotnitz & Nagelberg, 1960, p. 193). Another patient declared solemnly: "If you can take what I have dished out here and give it back to me, you are my friend for life" (Spotnitz, 1976, p. 112). This patient found just the person he needed for a long-term object relationship, someone who could hate and be just as vicious as he was. When the patient creates an object in his own image, it does not necessarily mean that the analyst is perceived as a nice fellow. Most narcissistic patients have a low opinion of themselves.

The ability to offer emotional communication depends on the analyst's willingness to have countertransference feelings. Unacknowledged, unfelt countertransference is much more likely to be impulsively acted out by the analyst. If the analyst blocks a feeling, the patient may block it too. A treatment impasse is often solved by the analyst resolving his own resistance to having some feeling, or to letting the patient have it. Each transference resistance is likely to provoke a corresponding countertransference resistance. The first resistance is resistance to transference. Neither the patient nor the analyst wants to have an emotional relationship at all.

After the patient's conditions for having a relationship have been worked through, and a relationship has been established, the patient may find the whole situation too valuable and potentially precarious to allow his inevitable negative feelings to emerge. Usually, establishment of a narcissistic transference is followed by a period of having any negative feelings for the newly found, self-confirming object. Idealizing transference has been described by Kohut (1971), and he emphasized its curative aspects. Modern psychoanalysts would agree that the "syntonic feeling of oneness is a curative one, while the feeling of aloneness, the withdrawn state, is merely protective" (Spotnitz & Meadow, 1976, p. 67). However, this benevolent transference and its corresponding countertransference does eventually become an impasse to experiencing the full range of feelings.

The modern analyst does not interpret the latent negative transference, but he does work on resolving the patient's resistance to expressing it himself. The patient who is trying to maintain the status quo may nonetheless indicate in disguised ways that he is dissatisfied. Why does the patient not simply say, "I suspect the treatment is no good and will not help me at all?" Usually the patient attacks himself in some devious and disguised way that also implicates the object. This is due, partly, to the lack of discrimination between self and object. Among narcissistic patients, it must be remembered that any attack upon the object is also an attack upon the self. It is also true that self-attacks, stories of failure, and assertions of hopelessness are attacks on the unhelping object. The depressive characteristically attacks the object by attacking himself; the paranoid believes the object outside is attacking him. In both cases, treatment impasses occur when the patient inhibits his own expressions of rage against the analyst in order to save a valued relationship.

In a case study provided by Meadow (Spotnitz & Meadow, 1976), a series of impasses are described along with their eventual resolution. The patient, a withdrawn schizophrenic girl, was first helped over her initial resistance, which was to avoid treatment altogether and to evade contact with the analyst.

Meadow helped the patient remain in treatment by providing a neutral, non-stimulating environment and by respecting her need for distance. Her resistance to transference was supported by the analyst, who reflected back her style of contact. During the first period, the patient was self-absorbed and seemed unaware that the analyst was in the room with her. Under such circumstances, modern psychoanalysts ask one to three object-oriented questions. These are questions designed to take pressure off the ego by directing attention to something, or someone, external. Questions about neutral subjects discussed by the patient counter introspective tendencies and provide ego insulation for those patients who are unable to talk about themselves without increased anxiety, defensiveness, and withdrawal. Modern analysts are willing to discuss any topic with the patient, no matter how apparently trivial or removed from the reasons for which the patient sought treatment.

Meadow occasionally called attention to herself (as object) by asking what she might be doing to make the patient want to stay away from her or come late to sessions. According to Meadow (1978), caution was used in introducing herself as a transference object before the patient had spontaneously turned her attention to the analyst as an object of interest. She believes that the introduction of transference, or any other subject not initiated by the narcissistic patient, is experienced as an intrusion. It was done in this case rarely, and with dramatic emphasis. The patient's usual response was to blame herself for lack of progress in treatment. This narcissistic defense both saves the object and eliminates it as a real presence.

Meadow finally joined her patient by agreeing that the patient was not getting much out of treatment. She then mirrored the patient's self-criticism by asking her to help her understand why she, Meadow, was not doing a better job. These interventions supported the patient's perceptions of failure but were experienced as intrusive. As a result, the patient externalized the attack. She vigorously blamed the analyst, not for the failure of the analysis, but for her intervention, which made a demand on the patient. The rare and dramatic use of this technique resolved a major impasse—repetitive self-attacking and ignoring of the object. It precipitated the first undisguised expression of the patient's covert negative feelings toward the competent analyst who was not helping her. Resolving the resistance to expression of the negative narcissistic transference permits the otherwise withdrawn patient to attack an object, thus externalizing the self-attack.

As this patient moved from self-attack to observations on the object, she improved. As a further resistance, she resisted being influenced by the analyst. Meadow noted the secondary gain in keeping the analyst helpless to help her. The patient expressed the rejection of all outside influence by a session of complete silence. Neither patient nor analyst said anything. Following this, the patient reported a sense of relief. She had been afraid that she would be forced to do what the analyst wanted. Such a transference may reach an impasse when it serves as a resistance to expressing awareness and desire for the analyst's benevolence.

As the patient increasingly directed her attention outward, she also began to cathect the analyst with libido, and to want things from her. When the analyst became valuable to her as an omnipotent mother, she reverted, when frustrated, to the defense of self-attack. This time Meadow emotionally joined the self-attack in an ego dystonic way. Since the patient's ego was no longer so fragile, and a firm transference had been established, Meadow was able to use some of the negative feelings the patient had induced in her. She demanded to know how the patient could expect anyone to care for such a cold and unfeeling person. The patient was amazed and relieved to discover she had inspired such strong feeling in the analyst. It made her feel real, cared for, and understood. She began to thaw. Confronting her with emotion had given her a new model with which to identify.

The emotional communication that Meadow used is an example of what Spotnitz (1963–1964) calls "the toxoid response," in which the feelings that the patient characteristically induces in others are fed back to him. As the patient progresses in treatment, the analyst puts him under increasing strain and exposes him to a greater range of emotions.

The patient not only needs to be able to hate the object, he needs, at various points in treatment, to be able to tolerate being hated, without recourse to self-destructive maneuvers. He needs to be hated by a real person, not by a conspiracy or by a delusional object. Because the paranoid was hated by a parent during his formative years, he is apt to create an omnipotent object who hates him in the transference. Some paranoids defend against this by believing they are particularly valued. Kohut, the Chicago group, and modern psychoanalysts agree that narcissistic patients need to have the infantile omnipotence confirmed by an idealized object. But since they need to be able to experience a full range of feelings in order to mature, they must also eventually have the experience of being frustrated, disliked, and even hated, without being devastated. Modern analysts are willing to be bad objects as well as good ones.

In the epilogue of her case, Meadow's patient says that the most important thing the analyst did was to overcome her desire to leave. Meadow attributes the patient's impulse to leave to her having been an unwanted child.

Fairbairn (1952) describes how the schizoid defense is employed by patients who believe that their libidinal attachment is unacceptable to the object. These are patients who would literally rather die than ask for help.

Rosenfeld (1971) reports on a narcissistic patient who dreamt of a small boy who was in a comatose condition, dying from some kind of poisoning. He was lying on a bed in the courtyard and was endangered by the hot midday sun, which was beginning to shine on him. The patient was standing near to the boy but did nothing to move or protect him. He only felt critical and superior to the doctor treating the child, since it was he who should have seen that the child was moved into the shade (p. 174).

Rosenfeld confronted the patient with the meaning of the dream:

> I showed him that even when he came close to realizing the seriousness of his mental state, experienced as a dying condition, he did not lift a finger to help himself or to help the analyst make a move toward saving him, because he was using the killing of his infantile dependent self to triumph over the analyst and to show him up as a failure.
>
> (p. 174)

Rosenfeld notes in his commentary that the patient's response to interpretation, even when momentarily effective, is ultimately to become detached and sleepy, to drift away from the consulting room and to avoid closer contact with the analyst. Thus, although the analyst understands the dream and offers a brilliant interpretation, the patient is unable to profit from it. Even when the reasonable part of his ego awakens momentarily, it is not stable enough to form a reliable alliance. The patient reacts to the narcissistic injury of a correct interpretation by resorting to the comatose condition he describes in the dream. Kohut (1972) describes how narcissistic rage arises in response to injuries to self-esteem. This patient appears to defend against expressing rage toward the analyst by further withdrawal.

Spotnitz and Meadow (1976) believe that the manifest content of a dream may be a disguised expression of preverbal wishes. To understand the hidden meaning of the dream, they recommend concentrating on the manifest content as well as on the associations. The manifest content expresses, symbolically, primary process thoughts and feeling states that cannot be put into words.

The associations consist of material that is preconscious and thus capable of being expressed through secondary processes of thought and language. Associations usually reveal the preconscious defenses against the wish expressed by the dream. The patient dreams what he cannot state openly or reveal in his associations. The modern analyst's aim is to get the patient to say what he wants in adult language instead of merely dreaming it. The dream may be used to understand what the patient wants from the analyst and why he cannot get it. Rosenfeld's patient reveals his wish to be taken care of without having to lift a finger. His defense against such a regressive and infantile desire is to feel critical and superior, and to die rather than ask for help. The superficial feeling of triumph is really a pyrrhic victory since the patient expects to die. He will attack his own body if he is neglected by an uncaring object.

One might assume that he wants the doctor in the dream to take responsibility for him, but does not wish to ask or to be exposed to too much warmth or probing. He may want an object who is cool and remote, like himself. Any such hypothesis would have to be confirmed by finding out from the patient why he does not advise the analyst.

In the process of externalization, paranoid patients divest themselves of the feeling and self-concepts their egos are too weak to tolerate, thus indicating that confrontation is likely to have a negative therapeutic result. They reactivate an infantile image that is valuable to them. An object that persecutes or neglects is better than no object at all. In treating the analyst as a personification of the early, uncaring mother, they preserve the original relationship. It may have been a deficient relationship, but it is the only one they had and they cannot relinquish it.

To help this patient discharge feelings into words instead of discharging them against his body or mind, the modern analyst might draw attention to the object by asking why the doctor in the dream does not take better care of the patient. The dream expresses negative narcissistic transference in disguised form. The patient is resisting telling the analyst how much he hates him for not taking better care of him. When the patient has been trained to verbalize his feelings freely, the analyst may respond to such dreams by asking ego-oriented questions. Why does he want the boy to die? If the patient protests that he does not want that, it is simply what happens in the dream, he is asked why he dreamed it. It is, after all, his dream. Why does he choose to dream this rather than something else? Finally, the patient may be asked, "Do you hate me so much that you would rather die than see me win?" The last intervention conveys the analyst's interpretation in the form of an emotional communication. It invites the patient to describe the transference to the analyst instead of subjecting him to the narcissistic mortification of having the analyst tell it to him.

How one responds to the dreams depends on where the patient is in treatment, how close to the surface the dream appears to be, and what contact the patient makes. If the patient tells the dream without further comment, and without asking anything about it, the analyst may remain silent, if the patient does make some request relating to the dream, his form of contact—hostile, polite, distancing, placating—may provide a clue for the analyst's response.

Interventions are aimed at helping the patient to talk rather than to understand. According to Spotnitz (1967): "Any type of intervention that helps the patient say what he really feels, thinks, and remembers without narcissistic mortification is designated as a maturational communication" (p. 107).

The modern analyst evaluates his interventions on the basis of the patient's reaction to them. If the patient responds to a brilliant and correct interpretation by threatening to leave treatment, feeling suicidal, or decompensating, the interpretation is not judged effective. Only if the patient responds with progressive communication, putting more feelings, thoughts, impulses, and ideas into words, is the intervention considered successful. One patient, with a paranoid character disorder, had been complaining for years about how difficult it was to have a relationship with a woman. Homosexual material had been presented in disguised form throughout treatment. Asked why he did not have a relationship with a man, the patient discussed the merits of the question in a reasonable way, but the following week could not remember anything about the session. He also wondered how much longer he should continue treatment. This was a clue that he was not ready to consider the issue of homosexuality. The intervention had led to increased defensiveness.

The paranoid is only an apparent exception to the rule that the narcissistic defense protects the object. It is true that he reactivates a bad infantile object. However, although he projects the aggression, it is still being directed at himself. The bad object persecutes him, he does not persecute the object. Why doesn't the patient harm the object instead of vice versa? The fantasy of persecution is on some level a wish that the self rather than the object be harmed. Nightmares are a form of paranoid persecution. One patient, who dreamed that the analyst was choking him, asked plaintively: "Why can't I dream that I am choking you?"

The paranoid's suspicion of the object, often mixed with criticism and contempt, may be genetically linked to identification with a critical and contemptuous parent. The patient alternates feeling criticized with being critical himself. Relinquishing the critical attitude would mean giving up the critical mother. The paranoid is unable to do this because he would rather have an object that hates him than no object at all. The object is saved through what Kernberg (1975) calls projective identification. Kernberg also notes how the patient devalues the object. Apparently the patient can only maintain the relationship by regarding it as expendable and unimportant. The patient saves the analyst from his rage by making him insignificant. One patient confessed he would feel no sense of loss if the analyst died. His pattern with women was to leave them if they became too important to him because he feared being devastated by rage and self-hatred if they rejected him. He was able to sustain a relationship with a woman analyst only by not taking her too seriously.

The paranoid, by his defenses, is able to maintain some distance from his objects, which the depressive is unable to achieve. The depressive's object attacks him from inside the self, and he entertains killing himself in order to get rid of the critical introject. The paranoid's strategy allows him to disgorge the toxic introject by projecting it outside himself. In the alternation between paranoid and depressive defenses, patients who achieve some progress on the continuum from narcissism to object awareness begin to see the object, rather than themselves, as the cause of their distress. Paranoid patients achieve progress when they acknowledge that they want the object, rather than themselves, to suffer.

However, the aim of treatment is not merely to provide for discharge of aggressive feelings while in a regressed state of narcissistic transference. That is a first step in redirecting energy.

Eventually it is hoped that the patient will be capable of making constructive use of aggression without attacking either the self or the object. The goal of treatment is to permit the patient to feel and think everything and to accomplish what he wants to in life. The method the analyst uses to achieve this goal is to resolve the patient's resistance to saying everything.

The patient who repetitively attacks the analyst may be avoiding positive feelings. In such a case, the analyst works eventually on the resistance to loving.

Each transference is a resistance to the next higher-level form of transference. A narcissistic transference is ultimately a resistance to seeing the analyst as a separate person. Negative transference operates as a resistance to having positive feelings for the analyst. Aggressive feelings may be used to block libidinal ones.

Repetitive communications are one of the most common and frustrating treatment impasses. In 1920, Freud proposed that the compulsion to repeat was an instinct "beyond the pleasure principle." Patients in psychoanalysis used the treatment to recreate experiences from the past. They obliged the analyst to treat them as their early objects had done, apparently not for the purpose of gratification or pleasure, but because: "All instincts tend toward the restoration of an earlier state of things" (Freud, 1955, p. 37).

It is possible that the conservative nature of this instinct operates in the interest of maintaining an introjected object. Thus, new patterns of adaptation, although apparently desired, threaten the loss of an object. The analyst himself, once the relationship has become valuable, becomes an object to be preserved. Maintaining the status quo may then become a formidable obstacle to progress.

It is possible to use the feelings aroused by the countertransference to understand the patient and to provide the impetus for the kind of emotional communication the patient needs to progress in treatment. Patients in the status-quo phase may literally put the analyst to sleep by repetition and avoidance of feelings. The therapist needs to experience the feelings the patient induces in order to help the patient put them into words.

The analyst is called upon to make a range of emotional communications so that the patient will be able to experience the whole gamut of human emotions with him. The range of subjects discussed should include whatever can be talked about between two people. As the patient puts everything into words, he expands the domain of the ego until "where id was, there ego shall be" (Freud, 1964, p. 80). At that point, the patient may seek and profit from understanding. Eventually, both patient and the analyst should be able to say everything.

This chapter was originally published in 2013 in *Modern Psychoanalysis, 38*, 3–25.

References

Fairbairn, R. D. (1952). *An object relations theory of the personality.* New York: Basic Books.

Freud, S. (1955). Beyond the pleasure principle. In J. Strachey (Ed. & Trans.), *The standard edition of the complete psychological works of Sigmund Freud* (Vol. 18, pp. 7–64). London: Hogarth Press (Original work published 1920).

Freud, S. (1957a). On narcissism: An introduction. In J. Strachey (Ed. & Trans.), *The standard edition of the complete psychological works of Sigmund Freud* (Vol. 14, pp. 67–102). London: Hogarth Press (Original work published 1914).

Freud, S. (1957b). Instincts and their vicissitudes. In J. Strachey (Ed. & Trans.), *The standard edition of the complete psychological works of Sigmund Freud* (Vol. 14, pp. 117–140). London: Hogarth Press (Original work published 1915).

Freud, S. (1958). The dynamics of the transference. In J. Strachey (Ed. & Trans.), *The standard edition of the complete psychological works of Sigmund Freud* (Vol. 12, pp. 97–108). London: Hogarth Press (Original work published 1912).

Freud, S. (1964). The dissection of the psychical personality. In J. Strachey (Ed. & Trans.), *The standard edition of the complete psychological works of Sigmund Freud* (Vol. 20, p. 80). London: Hogarth Press (Original work published 1933).

Freud, A. (1965). *The psychoanalytical treatment of children* (Nancy Procter-Gregg, Trans.). London: Imago (Original work published 1946).

Freud, S. (1966). Project for a scientific psychology. In J. Strachey (Ed. & Trans.), *The standard edition of the complete psychological works of Sigmund Freud* (Vol. 1, pp. 283–387). London: Hogarth Press (Original work published 1950).

Kernberg, O. (1975). *Borderline conditions and pathological narcissism.* New York: Jason Aronson.

Kohut, H. (1971). *The analysis of the self: A systematic approach to the psychoanalytic treatment of narcissistic personality disorders.* New York: International Universities Press.

Kohut, H. (1972). Thoughts on narcissism and narcissistic rage. *Psychoanalytic Study of the Child*, 27, 360–399.

Margolis, B. D. (1978). Narcissistic countertransference: Emotional availability and case management. *Modern Psychoanalysis*, 3, 133–151.

Meadow, P. W. (1969). The relative effectiveness of two educational techniques used in the extinction of maladaptive responses which block learning. *Dissertation Abstracts International*, 21, 2.

Meadow, P. W. (1974). A research method for investigating the effectiveness of psychoanalytic techniques. *Psychoanalytic Review*, 61, 79–94.

Meadow, P. W. (1978). Theory of the technique. Unpublished lecture. New York: Center for Modern Psychoanalytic Studies.

Rosenfeld, H. (1971). A clinical approach to the psychoanalytic theory of the life and death instincts: An investigation into the aggressive aspects of narcissism. *International Journal of Psychoanalysis*, 52, 169–177.

Spotnitz, H. (1963–1964). The toxoid response. *Psychoanalytic Review*, 50, 81–94.

Spotnitz, H. (1967). The maturational interpretation. In E. Hammer (Ed.), *Use of interpretation in treatment* (pp. 107–109). New York: Grune & Stratton.

Spotnitz, H. (1969). *Modern psychoanalysis of the schizophrenic patient: Theory of the technique.* New York: Grune & Stratton.

Spotnitz, H. (1976). *Psychotherapy of preoedipal conditions: Schizophrenia and severe character disorders.* New York: Jason Aronson.

Spotnitz, H., & Nagelberg, L. (1960). A preanalytic technique for resolving the narcissistic defense. *Psychiatry: Journal for the Study of Interpersonal Processes*, 23, 193–197.

Spotnitz, H., & Meadow, P. (1976). *Treatment of the narcissistic neuroses.* New York: Manhattan Center for Advanced Psychoanalytic Studies.

Sterba, R. (1934). The fate of the ego in analytic therapy. *International Journal of Psychoanalysis*, 15, 117–126.

Strachey, J. (1934). The nature of the therapeutic action of psychoanalysis. *International Journal of Psychoanalysis*, 15, 127–159.

Chapter 10

Transference and the power of enactment

Obstacles and opportunities in psychoanalytic training programs

John Madonna

Michael Balint (1954) cautioned over 60 years ago that "The greatest mistake we could make would be to consider our present training system as a final, or even settled, solution of our many problems" (p. 157). We must remain conscious of Balint's warning today, insofar as the possibilities for replication and enactment of individual pathology, by all who engage in the analytic training enterprise, continue to be numerous and compelling. If improperly managed these challenges can compromise, if not destroy, the candidate's opportunity for personal growth, professional development, and successful entry into an analytic career. Consequently, the exact nature of the training analyst's role has been the focus of vigorous discussion throughout the past 60 years. Some, citing the risk to neutrality, objectivity, and transference of the training analyst serving in multiple roles within the milieu of the institute, have advocated various levels of separation and restriction of the training analyst's function to analysis only vis-à-vis the candidate. Others, arguing that extra-analytic contact is not only inevitable, but also perhaps clinically desirable, have advocated integration, albeit carefully so.

Training analyst as evaluator: early opposition

Grete Bibring (1954) and others discussed this issue at the 18th International Psychoanalytic Congress. Bibring cited the training analyst's potential loss of neutrality due to his function as evaluator, and the greater level of exposure which comes with teaching conference work, and the inevitable casual contact which is a part of institute life. The candidate's agenda to first become an analyst and only secondarily to be cured can result in the training analyst being perceived as a "dreaded judge." The analyst's "expected criticism is anxiously circumvented by the candidate and (the analyst) is constantly suspected of hostile reactions which may destroy the candidate's training opportunity" (p. 169). The situation was seen as a tense one in which a paranoid response, crusting over underlying pathology and obscuring it, would not be infrequent, obfuscating pathology in the guise of pseudo cooperation with the analytic process. Or perhaps the candidate simply does apparently diligent work on pathology, which is fabricated or tangential.

In her explication of the difference between a therapeutic and a training analysis, Paula Heimann (1954) furthered the discussion saying that "when the analyst acts as a representative of the training committee, the analytic situation essentially assumes the character of a triangular relationship with the analyst in the role of both parents, and often specifically of the combined parental figure" (p. 165). The extra-analytic contact can feed this perception, with the candidate at times feeling as though the analyst is allied with him, or in collusion with the authority structure, which will be judging him. The opportunity for splitting can be strong as Heimann indicated. Heimann also cautioned that the analyst's personal problems, exacerbated by the institutional milieu, can also enter in as potentially disruptive influences. She stated that, "personal conflicts with colleagues, friendships and animosities, may rouse anxieties about (the analyst's) reputation more than with the analysis of a patient, because the result of the training analysis is known to his colleagues" (p. 164).

In line with this, if ambitious, the analyst may be inclined to expect the analysand to be exemplary in order to demonstrate the analyst's professional efficacy. Heimann also warned that the analyst may use the analysand to illustrate/fulfill his or her own theoretical orientation. Or the analyst may transmit in one way or another doubt about the analytic process, or enact any number of other pathogenic projections.

Gitelson (1954), in his opposition to integration, expanded the discussion that took place 60 years ago by calling attention to an additional complicating issue. He cited the growing preponderance at that time in the application of "normal," or rather "pseudo-normal" candidates who enter training with culturally promoted ego-syntonic resistances (i.e. counter-phobic and denial mechanisms, as well as the intellectualization of symptoms). He asserted that there will be many whose pathologies would fit well within an ecological system of the analytic milieu. That is, "in a social setting in which aggressiveness, ambition, and hard work have a high premium attached, a gifted analysand can live through his analysis as he lived through his life, cleverly disguising his neurosis" (p. 179). Such candidates, he believed, would particularly use the classroom experience to their advantage and the analyst who also teaches would be particularly apt to be the focus of such defenses on the part of the candidate. Gitelson cited Lawrence Kubie's dramatization of the situation: "under such circumstances subtle neurotic mechanisms can be temporarily inactivated only to reappear in later years after the therapist has faced the stresses of his professional life" (p. 178).

Integration or separation: subsequent debate

Discussion of the dual role of the training analyst continued through the years immediately subsequent, and was well reviewed by Laquercia (1985). Notable discussions pertinent to the problems of the training analysis were those of Lewin and Ross (1960), Greenacre (1966), and Anna Freud (1966).

While acknowledging the value of the training analysis, some researchers (i.e. Nacht, Lebovici, & Diatkine, 1961) continued to cite the potential compromise in the transference, which can be the result of the analysand's dependence on the analyst for when and if she or he enters the profession. Bernfeld (1962) echoed Nacht, Lebovici, and Diatkine in this regard. Kairys (1964) proposed separating the training analysis from the rest of the student's experience as a remedy. Students would then be judged primarily on their academic and clinical work. McLaughlin (1967) agreed. Dorn (1969) likewise took this position but went even further, suggesting that the designation of "training analyst" be dropped entirely. Stone, as well as Van der Sterren and Seidenberg (1975) and Lifschutz (1976), advocated that training analysts not report to evaluation committees. Their argument for not doing so was that such reports were inherently susceptible to countertransferential abuses.

Conversely, some commentators advocated the position that the training analyst ought indeed to report to evaluation committees. Laquercia (1985) cites Calef and Weinshel (1973) as to the reasons: the synonymous goals of analysis and institute; a violation of confidentiality need not necessarily be inherent (i.e. rather being focused and limited); it is important for candidates to know that graduation into the profession is after all fundamentally contingent upon analyzability, and that the analyst is the primary judge of this. To not report could in fact encourage a mutual deceit "reinforcing the impression that all is well," when it may not be. Both Shapiro (1974) and Reich (1973) suggested that a mature and resolved analyst could handle such a report without compromising the analysis. The honesty and goodwill of such an analyst would be more apt to enable the candidate to "deal appropriately with the evaluative aspects of the analyst's dual role" (p. 299). The 1974 American Psychoanalytic Conference on Education and Research (Goodman, 1977) stated that the training analyst should not be sectioned off from an institute's total program, as it was a "prerequisite and preparatory experience," but that the more personal material need not be included in reporting.

Shapiro went on to make very definite recommendations to ensure this outcome. His plan stressed the notion of therapeutic alliance between analyst and candidate in which they would together analyze through to decisions upon such issues as when the candidate ought to commence classwork, supervised work with patients, and graduation. Stone (1974) according to Laquercia (1985) also advocated a second analysis after the more didactic training analysis was completed, and independent of curriculum requirements.

The former in this case would be in keeping, after all, with Freud's own early training method, which was circumscribed and didactic in nature.

Some current considerations

In more recent times, Casement (2005) echoed earlier concerns in his discussion of the difficulties managing the power differential between training analyst and candidate. He advocated the need for adequate checks to prevent the analyst from becoming inappropriately concerned about his/her theories regarding the candidate's communications and pathologizing candidates who disagree and challenge.

In line with this, at the institutional level limitation/constrictions on creative thinking can be imposed on both faculty and candidates as a consequence of an institute's need to define itself as the holder of the fundamental theoretical truth. This propensity becomes a distinguishing factor which provides defense against uncertainty, as well as justification for the sometimes excessive measures employed in evaluation and training. As holder of the truth, other institutes and schools can be marginalized, if not dismissed entirely. The effort necessary to engage in enlightening discourse, to reveal uncertainty, to acknowledge theoretical shortcomings can be avoided. This attitude can of course imbue the transferential susceptibilities of candidates with a special urgency toward conformity rather than honest theoretical inquiry. Candidates and some faculty become in this way victimized and do not advance their own unique and valuable ideas to their detriment and that of their patients and the field. Nor does such constraint make for good analytic ambassadors to the clinical community at large.

It is imperative that an institute's curriculum offers courses in comparative theory and technique by instructors who truly represent other views, as well as coursework and training in formal research. Too few of our institutes produce the scholar analyst's necessary to move the field forward. I think it is imperative that institutional leaders resist the repetition of the comfortable, compelling need to defend against the uncertainty and ambiguity inherent in the work, which we do. As explorers, we should feel challenged and uncertain.

Another dimension of the power differential can be seen in the institutes, which are guided by charismatic leaders. Such leaders are often responsible for the formation of institutes and are the driving forces in their growth and development. The energy and creativity that they bring is often essential. When such leadership is enlightened and benign, much can be accomplished. Such leaders who set the tone and pace can promote diversity of thought, theoretical inquiry, balanced administrative protocols, and sensible training formats. Conversely, some charismatic leaders may be inclined to luxuriate in the attention and adherence he or she receives from a transferentially charged membership. That leader can use this leverage to perpetuate agendas and/or enact unresolved transferential issues. Vibrant and healthy institutional life can be subverted into a pseudo cult-like state with damage being done to those training analysts and candidates who do not conform. That candidate is especially vulnerable if his analyst happens to be a charismatic leader. Leader worship and subjugation of the self, in order to avoid rejection, can result in a lack of forward progress.

The authority of charismatic leaders, even those who are benign, should be subject to the real authority of boards of advisement and regulation. The presidency or directorship of an institute or school should be an office elected by faculty and board vote. Nor should their tenure be unlimited.

Casement cited another issue of concern in his discussion of the potential for abuse of the candidate by assessment committees, which were unaware of the person of the candidate, and the issue of readiness in relation to that. In the absence of input from the training analyst, and without the presence of the candidate at evaluation meetings, there may be an inclination toward "wild analysis on the part of the committee."

Related to this is the stratification of the advancement process. Though it is necessary that our training of candidates be substantial in order to have a way to measure and support progress, the stages which some candidates are required to traverse can be so numerous and convoluted as to be disheartening. In some institutes, the standard expectation for a training analysis, supervised clinical work, and coursework can be dramatically exceeded. Candidates can, for example, be expected to engage in tiers of supervision, proliferation of coursework, and special advisements. This is in addition to functioning in a multitude of voluntary service capacities. Some would argue that such a volume of activity is necessary to ensure professional commitment and excellence. To some extent this may be so, though I think that there may be times when the proliferation of expectations may be more a reflection of the competitive urges of an institute attempting to overcome uncertainty regarding its credibility.

I think also that complex stratification of requirements may be more in the service of the financial interests of training analysts and institution. The predominant reliance upon candidates' analytic, supervisory, and coursework fees is a form of infeeding, which is the result of a failure to creatively subsidize institutional life by, for example, bringing analysis to the community in more practical applied forms, for example via grant writing for research and special projects. To not engage in such innovative application simply perpetuates the current cottage industry, which replicates a feudal society in which there are haves and have-nots. It is a society, which requires submission and subservience. One in which the rewards when they do come, after a long while, are more monetary in nature and with a likely surfeit of resentment. I believe this type of conduct to be a breach of trust, a violation of ethics and should be vigorously examined.

Sonnenberg and Myerson (2007) also discuss another type of breach, the educational boundary breach committed by senior analysts and administrators, as well as the perils of countertransferential inductions, which result in "intense identifications" and "regressions." These have the potential to leave training analyst, candidate, and evaluation committee members "more empathically involved and more psychologically vulnerable than in earlier periods in the history of psychoanalysis" (p. 212).

Kernberg (2006) has been a proponent for the position that the training analysis be "totally disconnected from all other educational processes affecting the candidates" and be conducted by all successful graduates who have been certified (and not appointed) five years after graduation (p. 1662). This would better enable the reduction of the adverse effects of "institutionally fostered idealization of the training analyst" and thus provide a better opportunity for the development of transference and its resolution. Better resolution of what he calls the "paranoiagenic" responses on the part of the candidate may also consequently become possible. Kernberg's (2006) review of the more current literature regarding this and other problems in psychoanalytic education is informative. Though the concern that everything ought to be done to prevent the impairment of the transference stands in support of Kernberg's assertion that the training analysis ought to be separated from the rest of the candidate's experience, concerns remain. It is my opinion that total separation is apt not to be feasible in smaller institutes where the need for teaching faculty is crucial. Second, I do not believe that a candidate should be deprived of the learning, which she or he may have if the training analyst happens to be a gifted teacher or expert in some important aspect of analytic theory. In addition, the analyst ought not be deprived (and perhaps be left resentful) of the opportunity for professional activity that would be fitting for a senior level professional, so long as the welfare of the candidate can be ensured.

It has been my experience, in the analytic school with which I am associated, that training analysts, even with the restrictions that Kernberg and others espouse, will be seen. They will be seen in various contexts, in larger institutes teaching other students, conducting other administrative and public functions, or simply interacting with colleagues in hallways and faculty rooms. To enforce pervasive restriction vis-à-vis the candidate runs the risk of casting the training analyst as a phantom, a shadowy clandestine figure who operates incognito. And this may well serve to promote the very paranoiagenic reaction about which Kernberg is concerned. Perhaps it would be more prudent to place trust in the realization that transference will be flexible in its adaptation to reality and persistent in repetitious manifestation, and wherever it appears it becomes grist for the mill in the analytic hour. In fact, transference may actually be accentuated, that is pushed to the foreground in such contexts as the classroom of a teaching analyst. Of course there must be a commitment on the part of the analyst, and candidate, to analyze all that presents itself whatever the institutional context.

In keeping with the spirit of Balint, that we strive toward solutions for the training problems which continue in our time, and given the visceral nature of the debate which has persisted, it is incumbent upon us in this era to strive to find ways to improve the analytic training process. Several innovations have been employed at the Boston Graduate School of Psychoanalysis (BGSP): these have included process teaching, the use of logs, and simultaneous dual analysis.

Innovations in training

Process teaching

The aim of further developing the training system for psychoanalytic candidates has been facilitated somewhat in one analytic school (BGSP, 2009). A three part training program is conducted, which includes a training analysis, clinical supervision, and class work. The training analyst does not report to an evaluation committee, but does engage in process teaching. The program maintains a focus on an integration of cognitive and emotional learning. Students are encouraged to study the emotional responses, which are stirred in them as a result of the material read and the comments of the instructor and classmates. Students understand beforehand that they are free, and in fact will be encouraged, to discuss these reactions in written weekly logs submitted to the analyst/instructor, as well as in class.

By the process of examining the interface of the student's emotional responses with that of the theory which is studied, students develop a felt understanding of their own intrapersonal and interpersonal dynamics as well as those of others. Observational skills become enhanced, as does the capacity for more effective analytically oriented exchange/intervention.

As classes are to some extent analytic group laboratory experiences, the student's capacity to tolerate the exposure inherent in this learning method is carefully assessed prior to acceptance into the program, as well as into particular classes.

Logs

In addition to other class requirements, students at the BGSP are expected to submit logs. Logs are brief, succinct commentaries completed by students, typed on five by eight note cards and submitted before each class recounting the student's impressions of the previous class. Logs are an important tool for students to communicate their cognitive understanding of the theory that they are studying. In addition, they serve as a vehicle for private personal communication to the instructor regarding the student's emotional reactions to the theory, as well as the emotional reactions to the instructor and fellow classmates. Though they are not graded, logs can be a valuable device for the instructor to monitor not only the level of cognitive learning achieved by the student, but the emotional well being and the unfolding dimensions of the transferential issues of all of the students in the class.

Logs, because their commentary does not rely on immediate and direct verbal expression to the analyst and because of their anonymity to classmates as well as their framing as reflective of but outside the perimeters of formal class discourse, can help to promote progressive communication. Transferential stirrings can be heightened as a consequence. For the same reasons, the power differential between student and teacher may actually be somewhat mediated insofar as the candidate may feel emboldened to express himself or herself regarding a number of issues including the analyst's teaching style, competence, etc.

In-class interventions

In a process-learning class taught by an analyst whose candidate is a student, it may happen that the candidate becomes transferentially stimulated by the analyst's presence, comments, or behavior, as well as that of classmates or the theoretical material studied. That candidate may make a tranferential communication to the analyst, in the form of a question or comment. The analyst ought to respond in a manner consistent with how he would respond to any of the other students in the class. That is, by tactful questioning aimed at facilitating progressive thought and understanding on the part of the candidate and always in reference to the theoretical readings for that class.

In those instances in which a candidate's remarks or behavior are perceived to represent some greater level of experience of, and perhaps difficulty or struggle with, transferential issues, the analyst may choose to make an in-class intervention in the interest of providing a sense of safety and containment, furtherance of the working alliance, cognitive clarification, or as a preliminary to the work to be done in the analytic hour. These interventions by the analyst should not be interpretations of the candidate's issues and ought to be framed in terms of the theory studied. I believe that such interventions are appropriate, given the inevitable transferential occurrence which takes place in such classroom contexts, and if done with deliberation and knowledge of the candidate's issues and the intent of the candidate's own remarks. More will be said about in-class interventions in the case illustrations presented which follow.

Dual analysis

Training analysts at the BGSP, as in most other institutes, do not participate in decisions with evaluation committees regarding the fate of a candidate. However, the issue of how information regarding a candidate's suitability for an analytic career has been a concern insofar as analyzability is a fundamental aspect of preparation. Many have proposed a second analysis after formal training. And while this would not necessarily provide important information about the candidate as she or he progresses through the formative stages of training, it could nevertheless provide opportunity to come at the transferential issues unhampered by the difficulties discussed, albeit later on. Many candidates at BGSP have continued in a subsequent analysis.

In the ongoing effort to grapple with the issue of analytic report, I am aware of one case in which a dual simultaneous analysis was conducted. This enabled a level of report (of a didactic and limited/non-confidential nature) to the evaluation committee by the first training analyst, but not by the second. Both analysts were senior level and skilled in the management of the issues involved, including, in particular, the obvious potential for competition and splitting. The arrangement seemed to work and was especially helpful in enabling the candidate to successfully work through a particular difficult resistance (which is described in a case example which follows).

In undertaking this variation, it was hoped that the positive effects of a less contaminated simultaneous analysis would be translated into observable effects seen not only in the first didactic analysis, but seen also in a more accentuated way in supervision, as well as the candidate's course work experiences. The utilization of such an approach assumes that a clear baseline of functioning has been ascertained at the outset by all who would be involved with the candidate, that is, that the candidate's dynamics are known well enough. While this was not done in the case about which I am referring, admissions impressions and other application criteria might even be supplemented by formal pre (and then post) psychological testing. The candidate successfully completed his analysis and graduated the program.

Case examples

The following cases are illustrative of some transference repetitions and efforts made to address them.

Enactments of envy, jealousy, and rivalry

This first case is an example of transference enactments of envy, jealousy, and rivalry between candidates and how they are heightened in the compelling theater of institute life, in particular how interaction with training analysts emerges within the business of the training institute. In the institute/school setting in which analysts are seen by candidates and talked about by candidates, the transferential acting out of early parent-child issues can become profound. One young woman in training analysis put it this way:

> Sometimes seeing my analyst interact with people who I may not be fond of, makes me feel protective over her ... sometimes I also wonder "why the hell is she talking to so and so?" I guess it can sometimes make me doubt my positive transference to her, because it makes me doubt her taste in people.

When I asked one bright young analysand in training what he thought the challenges were for young analysands, he said, "We have the opportunity to sleep with our siblings. In my case, I get to sleep with my sisters." His did not always manifest in the form of actual sexual encounters, though that was certainly the case at times. Often, it was apparent in heightened loyalties, confidence sharing, and gossip. Nevertheless, coming from a family in which he was favored by his mother and older sisters, much to the chagrin of his father and younger brothers, he was simply replicating and enacting an old transferential pattern. Nor was it coincidental that the analyst this candidate had chosen was a woman.

Of interest was this young man's recollection of an early life incident when he had been lost at a mall while shopping with his mother. She had momentarily turned her attention away from him. He remembered her minimizing the event, as well as his terror regarding having been traumatically separated from her. He said by repetitive eroticized, albeit unsatisfactory, relationships with women students "I get to pressure my analyst" by messaging, through my behavior: "Help me. Look! I am lost," in this sensual, and in many ways counterproductive, activity. In line with this, many of those women with whom he slept were analysands in training, and one of whom was so with his analyst. He seemed to be ensuring that when she did not see him, he would nevertheless be in his analyst's mind via the presentation of this young woman, no small portion of the sessions of which would, he assumed, be about him. The candidate admitted that the complexity of the situation he thought might have served to "complicate" the analyst's efforts. There may well have been a retaliatory intent in this.

In addition, the conquests/acquisitions of love objects not only fulfilled this candidate's male competitive urges in terms of the other male analysands, many of whom were his friends. In this case many of the women, and some of the young men, were working with other female analysts. The envy, jealousy, and need to compete with them all for the attention of the collective mother could be seen as, at least in part, an indication of the intensity and extensiveness of his transferential need. He was certainly in the minds of many if not all of those training analysts, to the extent that he was directly or indirectly the subject of their work as well.

This young man was certainly not alone in his exploits. His partners were, he said, willing. And his male friends and rivals were equally engaged in the intra-group sexual competition. The point is that the closed system of the particular psychoanalytic community enables opportunity for enactment at a level of immediacy and heightened intensity that is difficult for the young, and at times the not so young, to resist. Though such behavior can distract, complicate, impede, and be potentially destructive to the treatment(s) in process, well handled by the analyst, they can also provide opportunities for accelerating the treatment. This can occur in that the transference becomes emboldened, made more directly apparent in the analytic hour, as it is so obviously displayed in the broader context of the analytic community. The faculty, and analyst in particular, observing and being aware of those enactments come into possession of valuable reference points which can become grist for the analytic mill, leverage points for inquiry, clarification, and interpretation. Candidates also in their student group experience (separate from the classroom) and which is a part of their curriculum have the opportunity to have their behavior noted and analyzed by fellow students and group analyst.

The classroom as stage for transference

The next situation has specifically to do with how the classroom can serve as theater, an important venue for the potential expression of the transference heightened by the presence of the analyst as instructor in that setting. In that context the analyst may have the opportunity to exercise prudent interventions, which augment the analytic process.

In this setting the candidate may strive to be the gifted student, the exceptional scholar, only to be met with inevitable frustration when the analyst does not attend to him or her in a transferentially gratifying way. Or, disillusion and frustration may occur when the analysand collides with course reading material, which seems inscrutable. Narcissistic injury can result with the realization that one's chances for becoming a favorite have evaporated. One analysand of mine frequently complained after each class about his desire to be a positive contributor in this analytic field, and how depressed he was becoming that it did not seem to be happening. Seeking recognition and affirmation from the analyst, he continued to strive, despite the emotional toll, to produce exemplary performance and considerable written work, which only exacerbated his highly intellectualized approach to life in his classes, as well as in his interface with the world at large.

The difficulty with having the analyst as instructor cannot be overstated. Echoing the 1954 Conference, a young analysand recently commented on "an obvious disadvantage" of contact outside of the consulting room:

> The connection and relationship that is so hard earned in the consulting room runs the risk, if it is removed, of seeing the analyst in his natural, natural personality. These observations and impressions affect the transference. For example, when the analsand acknowledges limits or idiosyncrasies in the analyst's personality, it may lead to a loss of confidence in the analyst's capacities. Metaphorically, the blank page of the analyst's mind that should give the patient license to say everything, has the potential to be obscured.

This analysand also stated that by having the opportunity to observe the analyst's behavior/communications in class, the analysand may develop expectations for response in the analytic hour which do not meet expectations and are consequently disappointing.

Or it can lead to an inclination both in the analytic hour as well as in class to talk to the analyst in ways and about things to which the analyst is partial, rather than what is of import for a successful episode of treatment and learning.

However, though this was his stated concern, the opposite seemed to take place for him. In the analytic hour he was avid in voicing his skepticism of my abilities, interest level as well as equally aggressive investigating of his agenda, motives, and competitive transferential repetitions. It often happened in this case that the impressions generated in class provided the focus for the work done during the hour.

Much depends upon how well the analyst succeeds at achieving and maintaining a balanced response posture; that is, just enough of the right kind of contact with the candidate during the class. For example, should we as training analysts and classroom teachers avoid, or not, the inclination to address our analysand's pathology by using certain aspects of the reading material to indirectly reference issues with which our analysands struggle, knowing that, as one student put it, "having an analyst as an instructor could be a little awkward and uncomfortable because he or she would know more than your average professor would about you."

On the other hand, when a candidate in his discussion of class material presents opportunity in the form of a question or personal comment in class, it would be inappropriate and not therapeutic to ignore what may, on a deeper level, be an analytic communication by that student. A candidate of mine reminds me of a class discussion of the obsessional need for compulsive responsibility as a burdensome aspect of that disorder. He had been previously complaining vociferously to me in his sessions of the unfairness of his parents who had pressured him all of his life to work hard, while simultaneously ignoring every other aspect of his life. This of course was a disguised complaint to me about the hard work of analysis that he believed I expected him to do. I said jokingly, "There are no free rides in life Mr. A, are there?" His laughter suggested that his complaint was understood. But would such have been possible with someone less able to tolerate the attention, even in the somewhat insulated context of the class process? The issue of in-class interventions is not an easy one. All such efforts ought to be done prudently and based on the knowledge of the candidate's intrapsychic struggle and tolerance. Such interventions should also take into account the circumstances of the class context and the emotional communication to the analyst inherent in the candidate's question or comments. The analyst should proceed in a thoughtful, careful, yet natural manner in order that the intervention does not reflect subjective countertransferential stirrings. Once done, careful evaluation as to effects in class, logs, and in the analytic hour ought to be conducted.

The class process discussion experience can also facilitate motivation and focus by the indirect referencing of taboo issues against which the candidate is defending. Hearing "it" talked about in the literature, by classmates on a more personal basis, and didactically by the instructor demystifies and normalizes the consideration of "it" whatever that "it" may be for the particular individual. I am thinking of one young female analysand of mine who was emboldened to talk in her session about the suicide of her brother as a result of the class reading and discussion of guilt regarding sibling loss. The suicide of her brother had "changed (her) life forever." Prior to the class experience with her analyst present she had not been able to talk about this loss.

As indicated previously, it is also so that difficult revelations/displays of individual pathology can be precipitously stimulated by class readings, discussions, the analyst's comments, or mere presence. The transference never stops, nor is it always easily controlled. These reactions can take such common form as intractable silence, inability to think or learn, flooding exposition of personal experience, a demanding yet unsatisfiable need to know and actions of one sort or another, which replace progressive communication. Any of these have the potential to disrupt the class, and challenge or defeat the analyst in his/her instructional role. It is only through effective intervention by the leader that such challenges can be averted, and the stage set for the analytic work of the session.

The first case presents some of the problems in training analysis having to do with the training analyst functioning in multiple roles, how those problems were worked through, and the specific use of a dual analysis in the process of resolution.

The favorite child

In this case a candidate strove, at some cost, to attain the position of "favorite child" with his analyst. This bright man in his mid-thirties, a doctoral level psychologist, applied for an analysis as a part of his institute training. The analyst to whom he applied was senior level and the dynamic, indeed charismatic, founder and director of the institute. The attraction was heatedly transferential and compelling. The candidate was quickly lost in a sea of desire, yet insufficiently able to recognize the origins and dimensions of the experience, despite the training analyst's efforts. This candidate, determined to be on the fast track to graduation, set about to demonstrate his value to this reincarnation of his own erotic, impulsive, and at times dangerous mother. He saw his analyst everywhere, including in a group of which he was a member and which she was the leader. The group was a difficult experience insofar as he had to contend, up close and personal, with group members who also were attracted to his analyst. It was difficult enough having to compete with fellow students within the institute at large. In the group he was quiet, stifling his true feelings, muffling his resentment.

Feeling thwarted in the group context, the analysand seized the opportunity to distinguish himself and after only two years of study organized a noteworthy conference in which his analyst was a principal speaker with two other well-known theoreticians/practitioners in the field. The conference was important insofar as it provided a forum for the speakers of several institutes to come together to discuss important theoretical issues, which had divided them. More specifically, as the conference was sponsored by the analysand's institute, it lent a level of credibility in the geographical region at the time, and was consequently somewhat formative in the institute's development.

A significant point was that the analysand organized the conference by himself. He did not share, nor did he want to share, the effort. The undertaking was strenuous. This along with the partial gratification of his transferential aims (i.e. the vicarious yet poignant realization of early oedipal strivings) resulted in his becoming quite ill with a respiratory infection that greatly impeded his ability to speak. As a result, he was nearly voiceless in his role as conference moderator and was unable to effectively introduce or interact well with the quest speakers, but particularly with the object of his desires. It should be said that this candidate's analyst was quite ambitious, prolific in writing and committed to engaging in conference presentation, and project development. Whether for her own ends, or to crystallize the transference for more immediate access to analytic work, allowing this level of extra analytic contact was probably at that phase of the treatment premature, if not imprudent. The point is that the training analysis was not sufficiently effective at this juncture, certainly due to the candidate's own heightened elation with the prospect of this transferential enactment, as well as his analyst's insufficiency at that stage of the work.

Relentlessly, two years after that the analysand, in his continuing quest to be the favorite child, organized another conference, which again featured his analyst along with several internationally known luminaries in the field. By this point in the treatment, the analysand's transferential longings and competitive strivings, standing out as they so dramatically did, underwent a more thorough scrutiny and analysis. This time the analysand accepted help. The conference was a huge success. There were 400 people in attendance with a considerable amount of notoriety and money generated for the institute. He did not become sick. But he was still unable to easily interact with his analyst and was unable to participate with her and the other speakers at all at the social event following the conference. Although he was beginning to make progress, the dimensions of transference becoming known, he was far from resolution. This enactment of transference desires carried with it the preclusion of maturity, presence, and efficacy as a grown man and professional in a world of fellow professionals and colleagues. He had not, at that point, quite yet arrived.

The analysand seemed to gain much in reputation through his many continuing efforts at replication even after graduation, yet most, if not all, of these seemed to end in a sense of disappointment, as of course all enactments ultimately must. There is no substitute for a thorough analysis. Though often preoccupied with her own ambitions, agendas, and challenges, his analyst sought and ultimately, to some extent, succeeded in enabling this analysand to analyze his motives and work through the transferential imperatives of the case. Fortunately, also for this candidate, he, owing to the tolerance for innovative practices, which were allowed at his institute, had a simultaneous second analysis. His second analyst was a quieter, more reflective person. Their work together enabled him another perspective on his transferential process, which was quite helpful in enabling him to hold his desire, that is, to exercise restraint.

The candidate was eventually able to gain a greater level of mastery. No longer driven to be the favorite child, he was eventually able to participate with his first analyst outside the analysis on a more collegial level toward ends, which were more in keeping with his own mature personal and professional needs, his desire having become a manageable memory.

The perils of training analysis were recognized over 50 years ago to be many. They are familiar to us today, as is transference and the power of enactment in all phases of institute life. And today, as was the case then, insufficient analysis is the most profound challenge to a successful training analysis. This, as Bibring (1954) said, leaves the candidate without "an equilibrium and inner resilience" with which to "comprehend without inhibition the unconscious conflicts in others and remain undisturbed in a life long contact with acute neurotic (and psychotic) phantasies of their patients" (p. 169). Our training institutes remain imperfect despite our best intentions and efforts. Our analysts, teachers, and administrators continue to be subject to the foibles of human nature. The recourse, as always, must be analysis, in depth and unremitting, if the persistent challenges inherent in the preparation of candidates are to become opportunities in our search for excellence.

This chapter was based on a presentation to the Department of Psychiatry's Psychoanalytic Training Institute of Trinity College in Dublin, Ireland (March 1, 2008).

This chapter was originally published in 2010 in *Candidate, 4*, 20–34.

References

Balint, M. (1954). Analytic training and training analysis. *International Journal of Psychoanalysis*, 35, 157–162.

Bernfeld, S. (1962). On psychoanalytic training. *Psychoanalytic Quarterly*, 31, 453–483.

Bibring, G. (1954). The training analysis and its place in psychoanalytic training. *International Journal of Psychoanalysis*, 35, 169–173.

BGSP (2009). *Handbook*. Boston, MA: Boston Graduate School of Psychoanalysis.

Calef, V., & Weinshel, E. M. (1973). Reporting, non reporting and assessment in the training analysis. *Journal of the American Psychoanalytic Association*, 21, 714–726.

Casement, P. (2005). The emperor's new clothes: Some serious problems in psychoanalytic training. *International Journal of Psychoanalysis*, 86, 1143–1160.

Dorn, R. M. (1969). Psychoanalysis and psychoanalytic education: What kind of journey? *The Psychoanalytic Forum*, 3, 239–274.

Freud, A. (1966). *The problem of the training analysis. In the writings of Anna Freud*, 6, 410–420. New York: International Universities Press.

Gitelson, M. (1954). Therapeutic problems in the analysis of the 'normal' candidate. *International Journal of Psychoanalysis*, 35, 174–183.

Goodman, S. (Ed.). (1977) *Psychoanalytic education and research: The current situation and future possibilities.* American Psychoanalytic Conference on Education and Research, 16–23. New York: International Universities Press.

Greenacre, P. (1966). Problems of training analysis. *Psychoanalytic Quarterly*, 35, 540–567.

Heimann, P. (1954). Problems of the training analysis. *International Journal of Psychoanalysis*, 35, 163–168.

Kairys, D. (1964). The training analysis: A critical review of the literature and a controversial proposal. *Psychoanalytic Quarterly*, 33, 485–512.

Kernberg, O. (2006). The coming changes in psychoanalytic education: Part 1. *The International Journal of Psychoanalysis*, 87, 1649–1673.

Laquercia, T. (1985). *The training analysis in psychoanalytic training: A historical and contemporary examination and evaluation* (Dissertation). California Graduate Institute.

Lewin, B. D., & Ross, H. (1960). *Psychoanalytic education in the United States.* New York: Norton.

Lifschutz, J. E. (1976). A critique of reporting and assessment in the training analysis. *Journal of the American Psychoanalytic Association*, 24, 43–59.

McLaughlin, F. (1967). Addendum to a controversial proposal: Some observations on the training analysis. *Psychoanalytic Quarterly*, 36, 230–247.

Nacht, S., Lebovici, S. & Diatkine, R. (1961). Training for psychoanalysis. *International Journal of Psychoanalysis*, 42, 110–115.

Reich, A. (1973). Special types of resistance in training analysis. In *Annie Reich: Psychoanalytic contributions*, 337–343. New York: International Universities Press.

Shapiro, D. (1974). The training setting in training analysis: A retrospective view of the evaluative and reporting role and other "hampering" factors. *International Journal of Psychoanalysis*, 55, 297–306.

Sonnenberg, S., & Myerson, W. (2007). The educational boundary. *International Journal of Psychoanalysis*, 88, 203–217.

Stone, L. (1974). The assessment of students' progress. *Annuals of Psychoanalysis*, 2, 308–322.

Van der Sterren, H. A., & Seidenberg, H. (1975). The problem of the training analysis. *Journal of the American Psychoanalytic Association*, 3, 630–640.

Chapter 11

Bringing to mind

Research with patients on the primitive edge

Jane Snyder

Recently I was teaching my advanced research seminar at the end of the day on Friday. Two class members who each lived a long drive away were absent due to predictions of "torrential rains." The dangers of driving were discussed: the unpredictability of the weather; the inaccuracy of weather predictions; the difficulties in making it to class; the difficulties of doing research, of focusing the mind, of spending more time with patients who are already difficult to spend time with. The sessions bring up difficult feelings or a complete lack of feeling, in some cases feelings of fragmentation or a sense of losing oneself, and in other cases a sense of isolation and unbearable aloneness. I think it is safe to say that while all class members are working on their papers, none of them is enjoying the research process at this point. They complain: "It is difficult; it is the last thing I feel like doing. I would do anything else; clean the whole house before working on my paper. I cannot write more than one sentence at a time." Most are working on the data analysis. They are irritable; they feel inadequate; they do not want to go crazy. Almost all are researching patients on the "primitive edge," somatizing, pre-psychotic, narcissistic, perverse. As I left my office to go to my car, the torrential rains began and I stepped up my pace, misstepped on my slightly high-heeled sandal, turning my foot under and breaking it. Was this accident the result of feeling induced by the class?

Recontexualized

Recently I was teaching my advanced research seminar at the end of the day on Friday. Torrential rains were predicted. I had just assumed the presidency of the Boston Graduate School of Psychoanalysis (BGSP) and had finished the first month of the academic year. Everyone was asking me about my vision for the school. I was aware of new responsibilities and of being the one where the so-called buck stops. My class was concerned about the dangers of driving in unpredictable weather and the unpredictabilities of the research process. As I left my office to go to my car, the torrential rains began and I stepped up my pace, misstepped on my slightly high-heeled sandal, turning my foot under and breaking it. Was this accident related to my assuming the presidency? Did it symbolize my sense of taking on a huge burden, my concerns of being adequate to the job?

A third version

Recently I was teaching my advanced research seminar at the end of the day on Friday. Torrential rains were predicted. I had been dealing with the impending separation from a family member who was taking on a work assignment in what sounded like a dangerous place. I was concerned about her safety and my culpability in her agreeing to do such a thing. As I left my office to go to my car, the torrential rains began and I stepped up my pace, misstepped on my slightly high-heeled sandal, turning my foot under and breaking it. Was this accident a self-punishment for the impending separation? A plea for her to stay? Self-attack instead of anger at her for going? A self-sacrifice to keep her safe (Andresen, 1984)?

Or in light of the upcoming conference, was this accident symbolic of my somatizing tendencies of which I had previously been unaware? Was I bringing the conference to mind?

When I appeared at BGSP on crutches, everyone asked what had happened to me. I asked students and patients what they thought. Ideas included that I had dropped a knife on my foot; the presidency was too much for me; I was showing people I was vulnerable so they would be nice to me; I had dropped something on my foot while helping a daughter move; I was slowing myself down; I was twinning with a student who had a hurt leg; I was twinning with a student who had hurt her finger; and I had kicked someone. I had become re-embodied.

Case study research

How do we know how to explain such events? What associations are relevant? In *The New Psychoanalysis*, Meadow (2003) writes:

> The analytic session is the first research tool used to delve into the subjective life in a meaningful way in order to discover connections among emotion, physiological functioning, life strivings, and death. We must concern ourselves with early pathways for the discharge of emotional tension and impulses.
>
> (p. 43)

This is what Rothman (2011) has done in her study. She has discovered connections among these realms. As a researcher, she has inferred these connections based on clinical evidence.

As psychoanalysts engaged in clinical work with patients, we are always researching the operation of the unconscious. This is what we do. We listen to the symbolic communications of our analysands as they consciously report their experiences, thoughts, and wishes. We pay attention to the gaps between what is consciously expressed and desired and what is implied by actions and by contradictory communications and what is absent in the communications. We pay special attention to the feelings generated in us as we listen and sit with the patient, and we observe the nexus and sequence of associations of all sorts in the session, verbalized and unverbalized. From these observations we infer unconscious meaning, underlying motivation. As researchers we take one more step beyond the analytic hour, we record our observations in writing so that we can systematically examine the process from session to session. A lot can be said about what data we remember and what we omit and about how to record data. I advocate writing up the session right after it occurs rather than during it in order to be emotionally present and to avoid interfering with the session process. Over time, even though some material will be omitted or forgotten, the repetitions in the transference, the repetitive enactments, the usual ways of experiencing and handling affect, and repetitive communications will be recorded. The unusual will also be remembered: the occasional dream, the break from the typical, a different emotional experience, treatment-destructive behavior. Clinically we work from such observations and make ongoing inferences and hunches about what is going on with our patients. In doing research we are careful to be systematic in our observations and recording of data. We look at everything and in that way control for our biases. Rothman knew she wanted to study somatizing patients for a long time before I started working with her as a research chair. She had notes on these cases, but it was necessary to more systematically write up each session and examine the process over a period of time to control for any biases she may have had in data selection.

Meadow describes the single-case study as "the most powerful tool available to us for generating explanations that link unexplained observables" (1995, p. 12) and goes on to say, "This process of defining, tracking, and uncovering is, simply stated, our methodology" (1996, p. 366). She also notes the importance of letting the patient direct the "flow" of the session, not interfering with the patient's associations. In doing so, the session is directed by the patient's dynamics. The emphasis that modern psychoanalysts place on the contact function while working with narcissistic or preoedipal patients is very helpful in the research process, as Shepherd (2004) notes in her paper on the single-case study and the contact function.

Define, track, and uncover

How do we know what to define and track? How do we arrive at a research question? In a recent meeting of the Research Committee in Boston we discussed this question. Some faculty members said they work with the student to identify the primary resistance in the case and pose the question as a study of that resistance. This is what Rothman did in her study. I usually emphasize the transference-countertransference matrix and help the student formulate a question based on this particular manifestation of the resistance. For example, I am working with a student who has been treating a patient for many years who is constantly in a miserable, "aggrieved" state. Her grievance is that she is never understood or "seen" by the other, or if she is, it is very fleeting. The other is always too self-absorbed. She has gone through life without getting what she wants because she lost out early in life due to self-absorbed, unseeing parents. She has been cursed. The sense of grievance is manifest in the transference as well. The analyst is accused of not getting it, of having a good life and not "getting" her misery. Whatever the analyst says is wrong. The patient is hypervigilant about being wronged, ignored, misperceived. The analyst is hypervigilant about saying the right thing, having the right feeling, which is hopeless.

The research question we developed is: What is the function of this state of perpetual grievance? Over the last year the patient seems to be a bit more receptive and positive about letting in some of the analyst's occasional comments, expressing some feeling of being connected, and valuing the analysis. The analyst has also felt more sympathy for the patient, more connected. However, in recent months the patient has developed severe somatic symptoms (she always had some, migraines for instance) that have been diagnosed as a severe allergic reaction to toxins in the environment. Her body is inflamed. The sense of grievance is jacked up; her whole body is in revolt. "Has the analysis failed?" the analyst wonders. Should she have known about the physical vulnerabilities? She feels guilty, helpless, also surprisingly cold and angry in the face of the patient's accusations. The patient has attacked her for not knowing or for blaming her ailments on psychological causes. She needs to keep coming to get help with anxiety, she says; the neurologist can help her physiology. She is searching for something nontoxic outside; she is flooded with toxicity inside. She asks the analyst, "Is there hope?"

This case reminds me of Rothman's description of the body as "the last line of defense." In reporting on a panel on psychosomatics, Aisenstein (2010) notes that "primitive sensory traces" rooted in the body before the acquisition of language become "invested by excessive endosomatic excitation," and when repeated in the transference, "have the opportunity to gain meaning" (p. 1213). I think this is the current process with the patient and analyst I have described.

What will this student track in the data? She will study states of grievance and nongrievance, what affects precede and follow such states. She will study the symbolic communications regarding grievances and nongrievances, the changes in transference and countertransference states, and the question of what is the danger of giving up the grievance. What does it accomplish psychically for this patient? The student will make inferences regarding the unconscious motivation for maintaining this state, and back up her inferences with data.

Enactments

Enactments are also an important source of data and help in understanding the patient who is on the primitive edge. Early emotional experience is laid down in the body, in sensory memories and action patterns as well as in somatic processes. Later in development some experiences become mapped with language and can be thought about, verbalized, and retranscribed in language. Some experiences and fantasies, however, are never thought. They are enacted. They are re-experienced with the potential for enactment in the transference. These are never conscious (Meadow, 2003).

I see a patient who is engaged in a repetitive enactment in the transference. She originally came for treatment of suicidal depression, which she described as ongoing since young adulthood. She also reported nightmares and flashbacks of sexual abuse by a brother during childhood, a relationship she felt her mother knew about but did nothing to stop. A previous beloved therapist had died of cancer a year and a half into treatment, and she had not been able to find a replacement. This therapist had given her tea and hugged her at the end of sessions. She was ambivalent about me; I looked like her previous therapist but seemed "cold." We continued working together on a month-to-month basis leading up to my summer vacation, the announcement of which enraged her. I indicated I would be available by phone, and we did have a ten-minute phone conversation during the break.

When I returned, she was completely different. She wanted to be close to me, declared she loved me and wanted to hold my hand and be hugged by me. Thus began a repetitive cycle of her declarations of love, longings for physical contact, and her wish to be adopted by me and to have an extra-analytic relationship. But the fantasy of this mother-daughter relationship was not sufficient; she wanted the real thing. I dreaded the sessions. Inevitably after a brief discussion of her day-to-day concerns, she would express "her feelings" and insist we could have this relationship. She would be a good daughter; I would not get into trouble because she would not tell. We could have coffee, go shopping, have phone conversations, etc. I felt pressured and trapped; exploration did not abate her insistent demand for action. When I did not comply, she became critical and attacking, complaining that I was cold and unfeeling, I was only interested in her money, she was just another patient, I had no understanding of trauma. She threatened to leave and did leave for brief periods, usually calling a week or so later begging to return. She could not be with me without these intense and overwhelming longings (and rage at the lack of physical gratification), and she could not be away from me. On one occasion she got up and stood in front of my chair and would not move. I felt truly trapped, frightened, and enraged. In response to my order that she sit down, she refused to move. I told her if she did not sit, she could not return; she sat.

Despite her professions of great love for me, I do not feel loved. I feel hated and pressured, unable to move. She has wondered if her feelings might be misconstrued as sexual. She is presently on a break, a longer one than usual. She calls me occasionally to report on her life, usually around holidays including Mother's Day. She refuses to come in due to "her feelings" and at this point has achieved an extra-analytic relationship similar to that of a distant daughter keeping in touch with her mother.

A research question for this case would be focused on understanding the repetitive enactment in the transference: the demand to be held, to be adopted, to actualize a mother-daughter (possibly sexual and illegitimate) relationship, and the rejection and rage when this is not forthcoming. I am proven over and over again to be a cold unfeeling mother; she is the needy and deserving child. In the countertransference, I feel trapped in this cycle, and on one occasion was actually trapped in my chair. This may also be a reenactment of elements of the early sexual abuse she suffered as a child. The only way out is to comply: meeting the demands of someone who professes love, but feeling violated and trapped. I feel forced into the position of victimizer, ungiving and rejecting. This legitimizes her immense rage. She is less interested in talking and reflecting than in repeating this cycle over and over. Meanwhile her outside life has improved considerably. She is no longer suicidal, but the feeling of being stuck in this repetitive cycle in the transference-countertransference enactment has not changed.

Surface and depth

Back to my research class. I have taught this class for a number of years. In the beginning there was a great deal of energy and excitement as students presented their cases and searched for a research question. The class was very cooperative. The students were usually deeply affected by the emotional dynamics of a case and were able to verbalize their feelings and assist the student presenter in the process of formulating a question. This constructive process continued through several semesters as we discussed methodology in light of the process material and as we researched articles for the literature reviews. Now many of the students are in the data analysis phase, submerging themselves in process or avoiding doing so. There is often a feeling of torpor and resistance in the class. The feeling is one of irritability and avoidance. They are willing to talk about the process of writing or not writing, but not about the cases. They just want to get out. How will they find the threads in the data? How can they write about the unarticulated? If a patient has left, how can they try to get him back when the feelings of being with him are so difficult to endure: feelings of being rejected or of entering states of fragmentation, loss of a sense of time and space, or in some cases, nausea, somnolence, agitation?

In thinking about what we are doing as researchers with patients on the primitive edge, swimming comes to mind, swimming in the soup or in the muck, keeping afloat, swimming with sharks. These images are particularly apt for the data analysis phase when the student is submerged in process data from her work with a preoedipal patient. When resistance is broken through in the class, a lot of aggression is expressed. The preference is to stay on the surface. The class process parallels that of the operational thinker with the propensity to stay on the surface, to express daily life concerns and little else. What are they not saying? A patient who often talks about the day-to-day events of her life recently reported a dream. In the dream there was a question of illness, of consulting me as the doctor, then swimming in the dark, but "without fear." Suddenly she saw a light. As analyst-researchers we are swimming in the dark for quite a while with many of our patients.

The psychosomatic researcher Pierre Marty (2010) sums up the psycho-analytic research process: "We must know how to wait in what we believe to be indeterminate in order to find our position, and to accept what we believe to be imprecision in order to address better the precise nature of reality" (p. 360).

This chapter was originally published in 2011 in *Modern Psychoanalysis, 36,* 42–51.

References

Aisenstein, M. (2010). Panel report: Clinical treatment of psychosomatic symptoms. *International Journal of Psychoanalysis*, 91, 1213–1215.

Andresen, J. J. (1984). The motif of sacrifice and the sacrifice complex. *Contemporary Psychoanalysis*, 20, 526–559.

Marty, P. (2010). The narcissistic difficulties presented to the observer by the psychosomatic problem. *International Journal of Psychoanalysis*, 91, 347–363.

Meadow, P. W. (1995). Psychoanalysis: An open system of research. *Modern Psychoanalysis*, 20, 7–30.

Meadow, P. W. (1996). Psychoanalysis: An open system of research. *Modern Psychoanalysis*, 21, 359–380.

Meadow, P. W. (2003). *The new psychoanalysis.* New York: Rowman & Littlefield.

Rothman, R. (2011). When the body does the talking. *Modern Psychoanalysis*, 36, 4–28.

Shepherd, M. (2004). Single-case-study methodology and the contact function. *Modern Psychoanalysis*, 29, 163–170.

Chapter 12

Emotional communication and learning in university classrooms

Danielle Egan

My work as a university professor started long before my training as a psychoanalyst. Although the goals of clinical work clearly differ from those of the project of pedagogy (the working through of painful and/or traumatic life experiences versus the creation of various tools to engender better understanding of a particular academic subject), it is my belief that a psychoanalytically informed pedagogical approach helps cultivate a more conducive learning environment. However, it is important to note that this approach may be more appropriate in some educational settings than others. I am a professor at a small liberal arts college in upstate New York. Unlike other large state universities, liberal arts teaching revolves around small classes, close connections, and strong mentoring, as well as small seminar type classrooms. For example, I have had many students to my home for dinner and I often teach a seminar at my house; in other words, there is a depth of interaction that is far less common in large universities. For better and for worse, I am witness to dynamics, defenses, transference, and character structure in my classroom as well as to the ways in which these weave together to form group dynamics. I believe that this is punctuated all the more by the fact that I teach about gender, sexuality, race, class, and culture—topics that often hit close to the bone.

While the structure of interaction in my college classes differs significantly from my work as an analytic candidate, the development of transference and countertransference, resistance, symbolic communication, and group dynamics are similar. For example, Ogden's (1994) psychoanalytic and phenomenological "third," defined as the intersubjective phenomenon that develops within the analytic encounter, can also be seen in the hermeneutics of discussion based classrooms. Within the educational context, thoughtful and self-reflective dialogue produces growth, synthesis, and new ways of envisioning the world—a process that the philosopher Hans-Georg Gadamer (1989) calls the "fusion of horizons." This requires listening and attending to differences in perspective, life experience, and ways of being in the world. As analysts we are well aware that this is no easy task. I have found Jessica Benjamin's theory of the intersubjective or symbolic third particularly instructive for illuminating the conceptual intersection between the psychoanalytic session and Gadamer's pedagogical model.

For Benjamin (2004), attending to the other in a deep and meaningful way requires the resolution of our resistance to surrendering narcissistic grasping and thus splitting as a defense. For Benjamin (2004), responsibility, recognition, and mutuality are crucial. As she argues,

> Once we have deeply accepted our own contribution – and its inevitability – the fact of two-way participation becomes a vivid experience, something we can understand and use to feel less helpless and more effective. In this sense, we surrender to the principle of reciprocal influence in interaction, which makes possible both responsible action and freely given recognition.
>
> (p. 10)

In much the same way that a fertile analytic context requires attention to a particular set of affective, subjective, and technical considerations, an instructional environment needs this as well. This requires attention to the enactments and engagements taking place between professor and student as well as between the students to better understand the constantly evolving intersubjective sphere of the classroom.

Over the past several years, I have found myself paying more attention to the affective tenor of the classroom. I am more attuned to the ways in which affect can enhance or hamper student learning. Attending to the substantive comments as well as the symbolic communications (i.e. messages about the here and now dynamics of the room, reflections of a particular psychic state, or illuminations of individual and group transference) has fostered more fruitful dialogue and deeper learning. Noting my own countertransference feelings and the associations that come into my mind during a seminar has also helped render visible the emotional resistances to learning on the part of some students. Whereas intellectual discourse is part and parcel of every class, I also draw heavily from techniques developed by Spotnitz (2004) in his analytic work with patients to lessen the impediments to synthesis and growth. Most specifically, I employ emotional communication—that is, I draw on my own countertransference feelings to reflect the affective state of the individual or group so that they may feel understood. I do this in order to resolve emotional resistances to learning about difference, inequality, and privilege (Meadow, 2000; Spotnitz, 1985).

Joining emotion in the classroom

A recent experience drove home the benefits and complications of using emotional communication in the classroom. My co-professor and I were listening to the findings of a workshop I had created for our Dreams, Desire and Madness seminar on gender, sexuality, and mother/daughter relationships in the films *Black Swan* and *Heavenly Creatures*. Our goal was to have students think critically about gender formation, homoeroticism, and what happens when the mother/daughter relationship moves from containment to smothering. After about an hour of collaborating, students began presenting their psychoanalytically informed synopses. During the last group, Emma's anxiety became the presentation overtaking any of the points she and her collaborators were attempting to make. Although mild anxiety is common (after all, pre-senting publically is an anxiety provoking event), this was different—she could not get her words out, and ideas were replaced by self-attack (i.e. "This is stupid," "I have nothing to say," "I know this is probably all wrong," "We have nothing unique to say"). She was shaking and sweating and kept inter-rupting her group members as they tried to present. As Freud notes, anxiety is often a signal affect; while it is obviously deeply uncomfortable, it is often a feeling state that comes when other feelings are being defended against, con-sciously or unconsciously. Although she was outwardly nervous and self-deprecating to the point of denigration, my feeling was that frustration and anger were at the core of what was taking place. In addition, it was clear that Emma's classmates were getting more and more uncomfortable. Normally, I would not intervene like this, but Emma, her group, and the class were witness to and stuck within her anxiety and, as a result, the learning process had ground to a halt.

I decided to ask a question that might allow Emma to express her frustra-tions in a way that could alleviate her anxiety and not put her sense of self at greater risk. Going with the feeling underneath the anxiety, rather than the signal itself, I exclaimed, "What was I thinking subjecting you all to such a redundant and boring assignment for the past 90 minutes! What a crappy workshop I created." At base, I wanted to help Emma voice her anger in a way that was safe and would not cause further shame, self-attack, or embarrassment. The students seemed a bit stunned, but Emma let out a laugh. I continued, "Really, what is wrong with me?" She then laughed again and said, "It seems like the same thing is being said over and over." I agreed, "I should have crafted better questions." At this point, my co-professor was looking astonished and said, "Wait. This is not our fault." This threw me for a second because I was focused on the student and so I was not thinking about my colleague. I said, "You are right. But I should have been clearer." She looked flummoxed. "But that is not our fault." I said, "It is all me. I am falling down on the job." Turning my focus back on the student group, I asked, "What should I have asked?" Emma thought a minute and began to talk about how she viewed the film unlike others and that she did not think that Lily (the character played by Mila Kunis) was a figment or fragment of Nina's (Natalie Portman) psyche. My co-professor agreed with her and said that all of these things were a matter of interpretation. Emma calmed down and was able to talk more. She discussed scenes in the film that made her think this way and after that, she was able to support her group members as they presented. Basically, Emma's capacity to learn was revived and the class continued in a productive way. At the end of class, students write logs (confidential communications about whatever they are thinking or feeling about the class), and Emma's said, "I did not realize I was so frustrated. I did not feel like I could voice my opinion, but I felt better once I did."

What happened? I had made a definitive statement earlier in class that the character Nina was suffering from a psychotic break and that Lily was a split off part of herself. I believe that instead of being able to voice her difference of interpretation and her frustration at my definitive claim, Emma's feelings were transformed into anxiety and self-attack. It would be impossible for me to infer why Emma might do this, but it is my sense that my emotional communication helped her voice her frustration and thus it fostered a better learning environment.

Matching aggression

I have spent the better part of my career teaching highly provocative topics related to identity issues to undergraduates. Relationship violence and sexual assault are two topics that have been particularly emotive due to their gendered nature and due to the fact that they are such common parts of too many women's lives. Unlike topics such as physics or the history of World War I, resistance to learning about gendered violence is often palpable to the point of derailing discussion, particularly when acquaintance rape or date rape is the focus. Early in my career, I was less than clear on how to work with this and, at times, I found myself mired in the resistance rather than effectively working through it. On one occasion, I was teaching a group of 35 students using Peggy Sanday's book, *Fraternity Gang Rape*. In the book, Sanday (2007) chronicles the events surrounding the gang rape of an unconscious woman that took place at the University of Pennsylvania. Sanday argues that the unresponsive female body became the medium or object through which a group of men could have sex with one another. The corpse-like state of the victim and the disavowal of her subjectivity was the way in which the defense against homoeroticism could be surmounted without threat to their sense of identity or to their place within what the anthropologist Gayle Rubin (1994) calls the "charmed circle" of normative heterosexuality.

Looking back, there was one class that I wrote a great deal about in my teaching journal and have come to realize it was this class that catalyzed my desire to learn more about how to work with strong affect in the classroom. Discussing *Fraternity Gang Rape* had been painful because many of the men in the class felt that Sanday (2007) was indicting all men. They were hostile and frustrated and were crowding out discussion with their vociferous commentary. As they continued to voice their beliefs about women and proclivities toward false accusation, the women in the class got quieter and began shutting down. Jared was one of the most vocal students. In his proclamations about female complicity and feminist hatred toward men, he said, "Look, if I ask a woman to my room at midnight and she comes, the expectation is that she is going to have sex with me." I asked, "What if she is drunk?" He asserted how that should not be his concern, everyone drinks and that should not mean she does not want to have sex. Jared continued on about how it was not uncommon for people to have drunken sex on college campuses and sometimes people pass out. For Jared, consent was assumed when a girl agreed to come to his room even if the topic of sex was not broached when said invitation was offered.

Although initially I felt calm when Jared began voicing his opinion, his hyperbole, lack of reflexivity and, frankly, disturbing comments eventually made me increasingly frustrated. I feared that if I reacted to his claims, I would be viewed as too emotional and/or experienced by him and perhaps by others as a "feminist bitch." I was also increasingly and deeply concerned about my quieted female students and the emerging group dynamic where one student stifled the voices of so many others. Going back to the text to highlight the theoretical and empirical grounding of Sanday was proving useless. Quite simply, intellectual discussion was not gaining any traction, and ignoring Jared or telling him to keep his thoughts to himself would be equally problematic. Nevertheless, my growing feelings of frustration grew to the point where something had to be done so I asked, "Jared, do you have any guy friends that you trust? And, I mean really trust." He said, "Yeah, lots." I continued:

> So, let's say you are out with one of those guys and you two spend the night cracking jokes, having fun and getting hammered. You do not want to walk to your place because it is cold and you are too drunk and so you decide it is best to just spend the night. What if you drank some more and passed out? If you woke up the next morning and realized that you had been fucked up the ass, do you think you would feel violated?

Jared exploded, "What the hell! That is not the same thing. That is completely different. Are you fucking kidding me?" Another student, Jenna, interjected, "Actually it is the exact same thing. You never expect that someone you trust would take advantage of you, but sometimes they do in horrible ways." Women began to speak more about the corollaries and one man in the class, Trevor, said, "I have never thought about it that way." Jared remained silent throughout the rest of the class.

After class, I thought, "What the hell did I just do? If this comes out on the teaching evaluations, I will never get tenure." I made an appointment with my Chair and told him what happened. He thought it was completely understandable and even thought it was good for the students, but he also agreed that it could potentially harm me if Jared complained about me publicly. In my journal, I wrote and underlined—"What do I do with this kind of stuff in the classroom? I was not trained for this!"

I do believe that an emotionally evocative intervention that matched his aggression was correct, but as I look back on that intervention now, I might have done it somewhat differently. I might not have challenged him so directly, thereby reducing the risk of narcissistic injury, which his abruptly truncated communication seemed to suggest. If I had paid more attention to the management of my own countertransference feelings, I might have been better able to think about what defenses were operating in this young man (disavowal? denial? shame? envy? guilt? reaction formation?), and responded to his expressions in a less ego-oriented, more emotionally encompassing way.

When we match someone's emotion, we are acknowledging and joining the affect residing under the surface of the individual's public presentation. Such feelings can be outside the realm of consciousness, or they may be known but unspoken due to fear, shame, etc. In all of these contexts, it is the students' countertransference and symbolic communications that offer the teacher tools for understanding. Within the analytic encounter, an analyst arrives at a more complex understanding of the analysand's resistance to emotions, thoughts, or reflection over time. When an analyst has a clear vision of what may be happening, he or she may reflect the affective state, conscious or unconscious, back to an analysand. This creates a different kind of awareness, one that is felt in an affectively resonate rather than an intellectual way (Spotnitz, 2004). The goal is to help resolve psychic barriers that hamper developing a deeper constellation of feeling, thinking, and acting. The longitudinal nature of the analytic relationship and the cultivation of transference produce a space and relationship where this can be possible.

Emotional communication and diversity education

Teaching in the First Year Program (FYP) at my university is a unique experience—two professors co-teach an intensive seminar for four and a half hours each week with first year students who are "living and learning" together. This class is a particularly powerful one because of the emotional rollercoaster that comes, for many students, with being away from home for the first time, coupled with having to spend so much time doing residential programing and classroom exercises with a group of people they have just met. Students and faculty often joke that it is like the reality show, *Big Brother*. Compound this with a seminar theme, which asks students to think critically about their identity, history, and culture and it can be particularly intense, even explosive. Seminars in this program are driven by faculty interest and can range in focus from *Film Noir in Cold War America* to *Mud* (exploring fertility and soil in Northern New York). A colleague and I decided we would teach a comparative class on gender, sexuality, and the body. In both iterations of the seminar we faced emotional upheaval of epic proportions and, both times, it hit completely unexpectedly.

Our first year teaching the course, more often than not, students were onboard. At times, it felt like there was some anger or frustration, but that was rare. We had just finished teaching a series of short stories about coming out as gay, lesbian, or bisexual in rural America. The discussion was stilted but nothing out of the ordinary and students seemed excited about an upcoming break. However, the day before folks were to leave campus, we received an email that overnight students had spray-painted in the main hallway of the dorm that my co-professor and I were "cunts, whores and fucking dykes." Horrified upon receiving the email, we decided it was best to bring a mediator to class to discuss the event. Unfortunately, the mediator did less mediating and more lecturing on why those terms were problematic. The students never spoke, the room was tense and uncomfortable, and afterward everyone left. I was confident that the mediator's chastisement was not going to solve anything and that it might actually make things worse. After all, we had been teaching about gender and language for the better part of ten weeks. Because the emotional tenor of the seminar was never fully explored in process, we decided that the time had come to do so.

At the beginning of the next class, we asked people what they thought was happening in the class. After about five minutes of silence, a student raised her hand and said "I think people are angry because you grade too hard!" Hand after hand shot up with complaints about workload and grading practices. One somewhat sympathetic student calmly said, "I think we are working harder than most other FYPs, but I do not think people should call you two names, especially not those names." She was the only one who mentioned the wall, but her comment was ignored by the next student who believed that she should not have to read a whole novel in one week. Not all of the students were angry, but we found out later they were afraid of facing the ire of the students who were.

At the time, I had a strong sense that the complaints about work and grades were not really the issue (our workload was in direct proportion to every other FYP and our grades were at the program mean), but I never thought of them as symbolic communications. I got mired in the material, or what psychoanalysts might term the manifest complaints, rather than seeing their complaints as emotional metaphors (i.e. the materials in the class are hard on me, they are creating narcissistic injuries, this is too much, and you are making me feel horrible). Since there was only one week of seminar left after this class, we were never able to repair the damage. We found out that a male and female student spray-painted the walls and I convinced my colleague that punishing them with a suspension was going to do more harm than good. I wanted to understand what drove them to that place. I wanted to know how I could encourage them coming to me instead of having to go to a blank wall. Those students did come and talked about workload and grades and left. The course evaluations were split: half of our students said they loved the seminar; the other half said it was horrible and that we were horrible. While I was less concerned about the evaluations, I could not help but feel we missed an important opportunity.

The next Fall, a similar thing happened right around the same time of the semester. We revised the syllabus to include more essays about heterosexuality and white masculinity in an attempt to be more inclusive and students seemed more open. Upon arriving in another country for a weeklong conference, I received an email titled "Urgent!" Opening it, I read that anonymous students from our course had created an on campus web post, which ranked female students from the class on a numeric scale and used various sexist, homophobic, and racist comments. Reading it, my heart sank. Women were being described as "Asian cum dumpsters," "A crippled dyke," "Dog meat," and "Blow job worthy" (this last one was considered a compliment). Exasperated, I called my co-professor and said, "What in the hell is wrong with our class? I thought it was going well? It seems so much better than last year and clearly it is far worse." She responded, "What are you talking about? Last year they called us whores, dykes and cunts." I thought for a minute and then said, "Better us than the other students." She agreed. Over the course of the week, we received email after email from female students who were angry, hurt, and at times, ashamed. Upon investigation we found out that nothing else like this existed in other FYPs. Our information technology staff figured out which students did it, and we were gob smacked when we found out that it was created by two young white men who more often than not presented themselves as sensitive and reflective participants.

When we brought up the post in class, we were met with stony silence, much like the year before. Unlike the year before, however, I did not allow the discussion to be derailed by expressed frustrations about dorm life directed toward the women in the class. Using questions such as, "How should we make sense of this?", "Should we let this happen in our class?", "Should we have done a better job letting you all vent frustrations earlier?", and finally, "How should the women in the class feel about this?" made the conversations more productive. Nevertheless, I left feeling unsatisfied because like the year before, the semester ended soon thereafter and reparation never occurred. The class remained split and because of that a progressive learning environment was only partially realized.

My experiences in the FYP amplified the frustrations I have felt in other courses I teach which also meet a diversity requirement. Such courses often have a specific kind of emotional tenor and group dynamics. This includes a mix of students who are moved by the fact that their cultures, histories, and experiences that have always been absent in their educational experience are finally being addressed through sociological and artistic mediums to those who feel they are being blamed and/or ignored as a result. I have come to understand that the main resistance to diversity education, for some white students, is not learning about cultural difference, but rather is in coming to terms with the concept of privilege. In other words, I want them to see how societal inequality is a historically trenchant and systemic feature of various social institutions, which results in the privileging of some groups at the expense of others (Egan, 2013). While such texts often focus on history and macro level analysis, they nevertheless often produce a defensive response. It is my sense that some white students experience these seminars as narcissistically injurious and, as a result, the class is often stymied by defenses such as splitting, projection, and disavowal. It would be inaccurate to say that the cause of this response is uniform. For some, particularly white students who grew up poor or feeling deprived, the injury may be due to a feeling of lack of recognition. For others, it may be due to a lack of empathy, and/or unconscious racism. What is certainly the case is that these responses can hamper a productive learning environment for all of the students in a class. It is my strong belief that the purpose of such courses is not to inculcate students into a particular worldview, but resolving resistances to a direct and honest processing of emotional information.

Educational research has shown, in fact, that for white students, views of diversity and difference often regress after their first class experience (Hostager & Meuse, 2008; Hytten & Adkins, 2001; Kimmel & Simone, 2012; Ladson-Billings, 1996; Lawrence & Tatum, 1997; Lesko & Bloom, 1998; Mildred & Zúñiga, 2004). Instead of having a more reflective view of history, culture, and identity, they express more concrete concepts about race, gender, and class—what researchers have found is that cognitive dissonance is more protracted, but that it does give way too much more of a cosmopolitan view of the world in the long run (Keith, 2012). This is clearly good news, but it does not make teaching these classes easy and it can have painful consequences for untenured or adjunct members of a faculty whose contracts depend on strong teaching evaluations. Others have argued that this is a problem of maturation—namely, that students who take these classes have cognitive styles that are primarily concrete and binary and, thus, are too immature to be other oriented in their thinking. While I can see the value of this explanatory frame, I depart from it because similar findings are shown in graduate diversity courses in paraprofessional programs such as counseling and education. It is my supposition that if we want to understand the impediments to learning about highly charged issues, thinking about and dealing with the affective realm is crucial. As psychoanalysts have long shown, our thinking is interwoven within the dense thicket of our defenses.

Cultivating a working group

My program is lucky enough to have an endowed annual residency for a scholar/activist who offers lectures and workshops for the university and the community at large. During my tenure as chair of my department, I changed the name and focus of our department from a focus on gender studies to a more inclusive and representative approach, gender and sexuality studies. This shift better represented the areas of research as well as the expertise of several faculty and it also symbolized a commitment to offering courses which would speak to the diverse lives of LGBTQ students on our campus. Recently, I created a human sexuality seminar for people working in or getting ready to work in mental health, medical, or education settings. The class was created as a response to LGBTQ student concerns regarding mental health services, or lack thereof, on campus and in the broader community. My vision for the seminar was to have advanced undergraduate minors, graduate students in counseling and education, and practicing professionals take a course together in order to learn information and foster fertile dialogues that could translate into their work in the world.

While conceptualizing the course, I knew it would be challenging given the history behind its development (students voicing dissent and criticism of counseling in public forums) as well as the level of affective complexity attached to sexuality in the lives of individuals. Freud's (1905, 1908) insights in *Three Essays on the Theory of Sexuality* as well as in his essay on "Civilized Sexuality and 'Modern' Nervousness" illuminate the dense thicket of shame, desire, attraction, repulsion, and cruelty in the production of our sexual biographies and our cultural responses. Our idiosyncratic erotic constellation and the unconscious fantasies underpinning them often form the lens through which we view the sexual practices of others. Because our sexuality feels so ingrained and natural, it often makes deciphering the difference between benign sexual variation and self-destructive behaviors far more difficult (Rubin, 1994).

In this project, too, I decided that I would draw heavily on psychoanalytic technique. To this end, I decided to attend to ever evolving transference communications of the group by making use of the associations that emerged during the class period, being mindful of the associations and images that came to my mind during their discussions, and asking for student logs at the end of every class. As I noted earlier, logs are confidential communications written to me during the last ten minutes of class. Students are encouraged to communicate all they are thinking and feeling about the class. Because sexuality arouses so many feelings in individuals, working with the feelings aroused within the group was most salient. To this end, my main pedagogical goal was resolving resistance and cultivating a broader set of thinking and feeling around sexual diversity. It was my belief that once that happened, particularly for those individuals who felt discomfort, disconnection, and possibly even disgust, the integration of substantive material would take place as a natural byproduct.

Within the first two weeks of the seminar, log cards gave me more insight into the following: why the counseling staff felt under attack from students; how some straight and cisgendered students were worried about saying the wrong thing and offending their queer colleagues; how the graduate students were interested and wanted to learn more, but also feared hurting feelings; and more about the divisions amongst queer students particularly around experiences of race and class. Over the course of the semester, I have used my countertransference feelings to respond to student logs. I have also used themes apparent in the logs in class. When I used these communications as well as the associations emerging in the class it helped students talk about their thoughts and feelings regarding the reading(s) in a more focused and poignant way. It was not always easy but it was, by far, the most powerful pedagogical experience of my career. All of the participants felt heard. This should not translate into the idea that all of them felt happy. In fact, most students felt frustration and even rage at one point or another in the class, but they brought those feelings to the group. Class material was integrated and the materials produced for the community were beneficial and important. Every student said they would take the class again and that they would recommend it to their colleagues and friends. Many expressed that it was the best class they had taken in college.

I have found that offering students a way to voice all of their thoughts and feelings about class materials is the most useful way to surmount resistances to materials. By offering students the opportunity to express all of their confusion, rage, curiosity, empathy, and everything in between, they are better able to work through their resistances and listen to their peers. It also helps me understand all of my students and their reactions in my seminar. In essence, it helps foster what Bion (1961) calls a "working group" dynamic where deep and collaborative thinking and learning can take place. Currently, several of my colleagues use log cards in their classes. These have proved to be highly effective in terms of better conversations and they have translated into more positive teaching evaluations. It is important to note that the class material has not changed. We are still teaching difficult material; we have simply shifted toward taking emotional communications regarding the materials more seriously. Log cards are not for the faint of heart; one must be able to tolerate a range of feelings from students and not take action. Sometimes this is anything but easy. We have found that processing our feelings about the log cards is most useful. We are still at the beginning of this experiment, but so far it seems to be making a significant difference. While it is undoubtedly the case that emotional communication and various psychoanalytically informed techniques have improved my classrooms, it is also important to emphasize the difference between analysis and the classroom.

Conclusion: psychoanalysis and pedagogy

Although there are clear ways in which analytic training can amplify one's pedagogical practice, it is deeply important to highlight the complexities, which make practicing an analytic approach a different kind of project. As I hope the examples discussed thus far have highlighted, classrooms are filled with the complex dynamics and profound sensitivities, the evolving nature of group dynamics, and the ways in which transference and countertransference emerge between and among students, as well as between students and professor. The history, defense, character, and culture of every individual comes into the room and shapes the preference for certain people, ideas, topics, themes, and a rejection or discomfort for others. Jane Gallop (1997) long ago pointed out that the classroom is a site of passionate exchange of ideas and that the production of new thoughts is an incredibly libidinal and passionate practice. This is undoubtedly the case, however, as Freud noted in his discussion of ambivalence—affective experience is rarely singular and as such classrooms are also places in which passion, lust, anger, guilt, shame, projection, disavowal, care, contempt, love, and guilt abound. It is my belief that these things are far more present in classrooms where diversity and gender are the focus of critical examination. Understanding that the classroom is never simply a space of learning in the abstract is important, particularly for those of us who teach controversial topics. This can help us better negotiate the dynamics of the class and in the best of circumstances create pedagogical exercises (like log cards) to have a better gauge of the landscape of feelings and thoughts. Doing so effectively ensures that the learning process is not held hostage to splitting, projection, disavowal, subversion, or rage reactions. Nevertheless, as we adjust our pedagogical practices to achieve this outcome, we as teachers should proceed carefully, keeping the sensitivities and tolerance of our students in mind.

Although it seems obvious, the basic assumption of university teaching is providing a context where students can learn, integrate, and critically evaluate the claims of a particular set of disciplinary and/or interdisciplinary arguments about a particular phenomenon. They do not come to us with a problem, crisis, or even existential quandary to work through and as such, we must be particularly wary of blurring the boundaries of the couch and the classroom. Moreover, we do not come to know them in the same way we understand our analysands. I think the more aware one is of transference and countertransference, and the ways in which defenses function within dynamics, the harder it is not to slip into analytic mode. The intellectual context within which this all takes place makes it harder not to offer one's interpretation. However, the context of interaction (the classroom) and the potential for narcissistic injury illuminates why we should refrain. The judicious acknowledgment and allowance of students' feelings as presented in logs and classroom discussion, combined with the analytically informed and focused emotional communication of the professor, can greatly enhance the learning environment. When those learning environments are dedicated to being laboratories for the examination of such close to the bone issues as diversity and gender, a pedagogy, which attends to the powerful emotions that are stirred, is crucial.

References

Benjamin, J. (2004). Beyond doer and done to: An intersubjective view of thirdness. *Psychoanalysis Quarterly*, 73, 5–46.

Bion, W. R. (1961). *Experiences in groups.* London: Tavistock.

Egan, R. D. (2013). *Becoming sexual: a critical appraisal of girls and sexuality* Cambridge, UK: Polity Press.

Freud, S. (1905). *Three essays on the theory of sexuality.* New York: Basic Books.

Freud, S. (1908). 'Civilized' sexual morality and modern nervous illness. *The Standard Edition of the Complete Works of Sigmund Freud, Volume IX (1906–1908): Jensen's 'Gradiva' and Other Works.* London: Hogarth, 1–96; 177–204.

Gadamer, H. G. (1989). *Truth and method.* London: Sheed and Ward.

Gallop, J. (1997). *Feminist accused of sexual harassment.* Durham, NC: Duke University Press.

Hostager, T., & Meuse, K. (2008). The effects of diversity learning experience on positive and negative diversity perceptions. *Journal of Business & Psychology,* 23 (4), 127–139.

Hytten, K., & Adkins, A. (2001). Thinking through a pedagogy of whiteness. *Educational Theory,* 51, 433–450.

Keith, N. (2012). Getting beyond anaemic love: From the pedagogy of cordial relations to a pedagogy for difference. *Journal of Curriculum Studies,* 42, 539–572.

Kimmel, K., & Simone, V. (2012). University students' perceptions of and attitudes towards culturally diverse group work: Does context matter? *Journal of Studies in International Education,* 16 (2), 157–181.

Ladson-Billings, G. (1996). Silences as weapons: Challenges of a black professor teaching white students. *Theory into Practice,* 35, 79–85.

Lawrence, S. M., & Tatum, B. D. (1997). Teachers in transition: The impact of antiracist professional development on classroom practice. *Teachers College Record,* 99, 162–178.

Lesko, N., & Bloom, L. R. (1998). Close encounters: Truth, experience and interpretation in multicultural teacher education. *Journal of Curriculum Studies,* 30, 375–395.

Meadow , P. W. (2000). How we aim to be with patients. *Modern Psychoanalysis,* 14, 145–162.

Mildred, J., & Zúñiga, X. (2004). Working with resistance to diversity issues in the classroom: Lessons from teacher training and multicultural education. *Smith College Studies in Social Work,* 74, 359–375.

Ogden, T. H. (1994). The analytic third: Working with intersubjective clinical facts. *International Journal of Psychoanalysis,* 75, 3–19.

Rubin, G. (1994). Thinking sex: Notes for a radical theory of the politics of sexuality. In C. S. Vance (Ed.), *Pleasure and danger.* New York: Routledge & Kegan Paul, 12–48.

Sanday, P. (2007). *Fraternity gang rape: Sex, brotherhood and privilege on campus* (2nd ed.). New York: New York University Press.

Spotnitz, H. (1985). Large group analysis: Regression, progression, creativity. *Modern Psychoanalysis,* 10, 119–136.

Spotnitz, H. (2004). *Modern psychoanalysis of the schizophrenic patient: Theory of the technique.* New York: YBK Publishers.

Chapter 13

The darkness of night

John Madonna

Extraneous occurrences that impact the life of the analyst can complicate and obstruct her capacity to be emotionally present. Principal among these is the analyst's own illness, accident and injury; the decline through illness or accident of a loved one, or loss of that person through maturation, alienation, divorce or death; and that inevitable nemesis, the aging process. When these things happen, in addition to the physical pain and discomfort that can be pre-occupying, there is the worry and psychological distress related to the loss of function, the prospects of recovery or not, the existential issue of mortality, grief, and the loss of meaning. Focus on the self can be so absorbing that even if the analyst is able to work, his perception, judgment and usually sufficient capacity are apt to be impaired.

My father died suddenly at age 75 on a cool and sunny late October morning after his usual brisk walk around the park near the Greek Church where aged men defiantly luxuriated in the smoke of cigarettes as they waited outside for wives who prayed with Olympian determination for their souls. He simply sat on a park bench and fell into that long unending sleep. That was 15 years ago when I was 53. He was heartbroken, I think, of grief for my mother who died several years earlier after nearly 50 years of marriage. And though I did not grieve as much for my mother—she had been painfully ill for a long time with a terminal cancer and her death included an element of relief—I did so for my father. It seemed I cried for him every day. Everything reminded me of him. Italian songs, so much of what we ate, the physical resemblance to him in my sister and certain of my children, the old pictures and places, his voice in my own voice ... and in the silence itself, as he had been much of the time a quiet man. Though we were different in many ways the love and dedication was there on both sides.

My grief was perhaps also fueled by a sense of failed responsibility. He had a way of inducing that in me. Not through direct expectation so much as by my witnessing his own failure to achieve interactional salience with my mother, who fluctuated between being passionately loving and loudly dis-appointed. He had big dreams and sought to realize them, and while he was skilled with his hands and well-liked by people, he lacked business acumen, and so he did not. Then there was his unremitting longing to return to his family of origin with us, a tribe of wonderful Neapolitan singers who knew how to enjoy each other and life. Among whom he was truly happy. It never happened, and for all of this, and more, I felt sorry for my father and responsible. I could not attend to him the way my mother had all of their lives. I could not keep him alive.

Truth be told, on some deeper level, like every son who longs to be independent of parental influence and thus finally grown up, though I did not wish his demise, I was perhaps relieved by it as well. Though given the choice I would have him back, I had no longer to be emotionally responsible, nor worry as I observed him alone, lonely and grieving. Nor to be reminded of the guilt I carried, having been a spectator to, and thus in a sense a participant in, my mother's early marital infidelity. A life-long secret released only in my middle years in analysis. I grieved then out of the remnants of my guilt for that. And to the extent that I was in ways identified with my father, I was the first-born and only son, I was grieving for myself. I knew he held me in his mind and heart; he displayed his love in many ways, and that was gone. I was left, closer to death now, with no shield.

Work was both a refuge and an impediment. Early on I did not want my sorrow interrupted, as it was the final real-life emotional connection I had with my father and that past life, so I think to some extent I resented going to sessions and finding myself interested in the lives and stories of my patients. And though my acuity was not optimal, I managed to be present enough; being in the living of others was compelling and healing. Colson (1995) spoke of how he had, with the help of objective others, continued to work through his wife's illness and eventual death. He was able to do so, he said, because "the analytic situation, its relative degree of structure, predictability, regularity, safety and commitment facilitated in various ways a degree of dissociation between the turmoil outside the hours and my experience of myself as an analyst within the hours" (p. 7).

I think that my capacity to be more emotionally present and resonant was advanced by my father's death. My egocentrism, the reinforcement of which was one of my mother's principal contributions to my psychic development, was made permeable by that loss. The pain was so palpable and enduring that it altered my core indifference. It enlivened my awareness of the suffering of others and my empathy was moved from being more of an intellectual experience to becoming emotionally felt. That was the innovation brought about by this natural, albeit profound loss.

It was near, I think, to what Shapiro (1985) indicated in her poignant account of the effect of her mother's illness and death on her and her work. She said "the analyst's self-absorption while coping with loss helps to create an atmosphere parallel to the patient's early life." This can provide an opportunity to work through fundamental difficulties with "closeness and distance" as such exist in both analyst and patient (p. 45).

I met my father again some years after his death in the visage of a patient who had applied to me for treatment. He was a strongly paranoid older man who looked startlingly like my father. He showed up for his first meeting at the wrong time. When I made him aware of that he became disgruntled, accusatory and began to walk out. My usual tenacity was further informed by a strong countertransferential desire to not let him go, not let him out of my sight. My capacity for solicitousness, well developed by my many years of being so with my father, managed to keep him there and so commenced seven years of treatment, which had its moments of triumph for us both.

The great challenge in this treatment was managing the paranoid projections, and keeping objective and subjective countertransference sorted. I was aided in the latter by the fact that though he looked a lot like my father, he did not sound like him, nor were his issues similar to those my father struggled with. I was able to tolerate and manage the paranoia for as long as I did because I had experience with my mother's paranoid sensitivity. But it wasn't only this. I looked forward to the sight of this patient, the image of my father. My positive feelings for my father, and my mother also, judiciously infused treatment interactions with tolerance, empathy and humor, and enabled containment of this man's paranoia, as well as the emotional resonance with those aspects of his personality that were unobstructed.

I was ultimately, however, to suffer a second loss when after seven years this patient left treatment, having been overtaken by his suspiciousness. I felt a sadness that I could not have been of more help to him. And that I would not see his face again.

The stranger in the mirror

And so time passes and makes its inexorable claims. When I turned 60 I began to notice that the face looking back at me in the mirror as I shaved was looking a bit world-worn. The wrinkles, age spots and graying dried hair seemed unkind reminders. On occasion, in a surge of frustrated masculine vanity, and half awake, I would hear myself saying to that reflection in the mirror, "Who the hell are you?" Or "what are you doing in my house?" Thankfully, I was not answered. "Old age is not for sissies," said Bette Davis. It is particularly difficult for some people. I was brought up a minor Italian prince with love, inordinate at times, and with a measure of adoration, from my parents. I entered my young adulthood lean, sensual, hungrily ambitious and quietly competitive. I did not begin to emerge from my narcissism until I was well into my middle years after much accrued life experience informed by considerable analysis. Through my sixties, and now that I approach 70, it is difficult indeed to experience slowly diminishing function ... and appearance. In the darkness of night the worry about decline and death creeps in, joins with a relentless ache or pain, and disturbs an already restless sleep.

I write this on the day before I am scheduled for the first and only surgery I have ever had. It is an elective and routinely done resection of a benign enlarged prostate. Marlon Brando immortalized this condition, which is the bane of the older man, in the movie he starred in entitled *Last Tango in Paris*. It is a small consolation.

However, sometimes, fortuitously or through divine intervention, something happens that is restorative. Not long ago while at my office in Boston, I decided to take a walk. I had several hours between appointments. It was one of those beautiful warm autumn New England days. I had gone as far as Coolidge Corner and had begun the return. I noticed a shiny gray van. Behind the wheel was a young woman in her forties, stylishly groomed and fashionably attired. In the back seat was an older woman and approaching the vehicle was yet another. As I came nearer I glanced again at the driver and noticed that she was smiling. Suddenly she lowered the passenger window and said in a very animated way: "I just want to tell you, you are a very, very handsome man. You look terrific." Startled, I looked quickly over my shoulder to see the other man that she was obviously addressing. There was no one there. "No, I am talking to you," she said. Simultaneously the two older women enthusiastically chimed in, "Yes, yes, it is true."

My composure regained, I leaned toward the van and said,

> Thank you so much. Do you realize that I am a senior citizen, and that it has been about 30 years since an attractive woman has said anything like that to me on the street? You have made my day. Thank you so much, ladies. You have a wonderful afternoon.

To which they all in chorus said, "It is true, it is true." We made our departure laughing. Flushed with my narcissism reignited, though I did not skip up the street, my step was clearly lighter. Then an errant thought intruded: gray van, young woman driving older women, one of whom was using a cane and probably coming out of a doctor's office. That young woman probably works for an elder-care program and her mission in life is to make senior citizens like me feel good. Remaining stalwartly undeterred, I nevertheless accepted her perceptions as accurate. Whatever the case, she had succeeded in inducing a sense of joy in me. The power of words!

Inspired to reach for even more, I called my wife to share what had happened. Patiently supportive, as only a wife of many years could be, she commented somewhat anticlimactically on how nice that was. I interjected, however, that I had to cut the conversation we were having short, as it seemed another van had just pulled up and all the young women in it were waving at me. We both knew I had gone too far. The point is that life does at times provide some comic relief. We should take the time to embrace it. That said, I know I will be taking that walk down to Coolidge Corner again in the spring, and like Hedda Bolgar (2002) in a state of optimism and anticipatory gratitude, I will be on the lookout for a shiny gray van.

One positive ramification, however, of the aging process is that I love my work now even more than when I was younger. There is a gritty vibrancy to being an analyst, allowed to participate in the great struggles of individual lives for health versus pathology, life versus death. The stakes are often high, requiring great effort, emotional as well as intellectual engagement, meeting resistances, managing inductions, working through, making a difference. There is the need for the aging analyst to be ever vigilant that the "changes in narcissism" not lead to "increased cathexis of the superego and the ego ideal," thus resulting in "rigidity, compulsiveness, intolerance and involutional depression." To be avoided is "impatience with patients," an inability to flexibly respond to the "ever changing demands of the clinical situation," and a determined expectation for unconditional surrender to the analytic technique. Not doing so can lead to intimidation of and passivity in the patient, which can obstruct treatment (Eissler, 1993, p. 320).

On the other hand, if the analyst's narcissism engulfs the analyst's ego, he may be at risk of "tacitly encouraging" the patient/analysand "to feel and convey awe and respect." In such a circumstance the analyst may be inclined to accept admiring remarks as veritable truth and to attribute "inimical ones to hostile transference" (p. 320). All of this challenges and excites.

And yet I can find myself feeling impatient in the company of those preoccupied with what I see to be minor irrelevancies given the larger issues of their lives and the treatment. Or if I encounter myself in the other presenting issues, which I had thought I long ago mastered, only to be stirred and blindsided yet again, I can become impatient with myself. And I can feel throttled by the awareness of the limitation of time, knowing how long this work takes. Patience is required, as is the extra effort of diligence, which ensures careful listening and prudent intervention.

In the face of this, Eissler's (1993) conclusion is a wise one, and though some measure of motivating ambition remains within me, I have attempted to be guided by him in this regard. In acknowledgment of "inevitable limitations ambitious goals of earlier life periods are replaced by goals which harmonize with reality and (one's) own potentialities ... anxiety about failure (can) be reduced and consequently, also, therapeutic ambition – the archenemy of the psychoanalytic process" (p. 321).

> The analyst is able to come face to face with the patient's illness with greater tolerance. No longer will the patient's illness represent the enemy whose conquest is generally the analyst's primary goal, instead the disease's right to exist, so to speak, will be conceded in full, even taken for granted.
>
> (pp. 321–322)

In line with this, I have had the good fortune of knowing a number of people senior to myself. I have learned and was inspired by the grace and courage they showed in confronting the difficulty of their aging.

While the commitment to persevere can steel us in the face of time's ravages and the rigors of pathology, which we confront in others and in ourselves, courage and laughter are not always so easy to come by. When a child struggles with addiction, or becomes seriously ill, or dies, the analyst can be rendered by grief and cast adrift. Though we know it happens, children are not supposed to suffer, not supposed to die before parents.

Barbara Chasen's (2009) account of the tragic and sudden death of her 12-year-old son was heart wrenching. He was struck by a 16-year-old driver while mother and son were walking together on a road in the Berkshires. Emotionally devastated and uncertain of her capacity to do so, she "escaped" three weeks later to her office. She did so with the support of her family, friends and colleagues, as well as her own therapy and involvement in support groups for parents who have lost a child.

Chasen describes the reactions of those of her patients who had discovered what had happened and how she responded to their inquiries with tempered disclosure and heartfelt emotion. The sensitivity and affirmation of patients was apparent. Working against the backdrop of emotional discomfort and pain seemed to result in the deepening of the analytic alliance. Her patients expressed relief that she was again working. She stated, "their need for me has given me strength" (p. 10). Chasen was able to tolerate the "constant presence of an absence" to manage her own suicidal wishes. She was ultimately able to carry on as an adoptive mother to a child in need, a tribute to patients and the son who had given her so much joy (p. 20).

Mendelson (2009) also found relief in work after the death of his infant daughter from a congenital heart condition. He too acknowledged that he enjoyed the comfort and affirmation of patients who knew of his loss, and to whom he had disclosed. Because of his inclination to "inquire about patients' observations and interpretations of (his) subjective experience" he found that a "deepen(ed) analytic collaboration" became possible (p. 38). He describes, for example, how the experience of his daughter's illness and her eventual death resulted in a depression, which was detected by a patient. Mendelson's ability and willingness to discuss this with the patient enabled the clarification and working through of that patient's own depression. In another instance, his disclosure moved one woman to a more unreserved emotional commitment to the treatment. An outsider all of her life, she felt convincingly "included." Another patient provoked by Mendelson's preoccupation protested his resulting inability to grieve for the appropriate termination, which was scheduled to take place. Both were then able to do so in a way that was more fully focused and felt.

One colleague I know had to absent himself from work for a number of months after his son died suddenly in a tragic accident. Another colleague fled into her work after her daughter died from a rapidly destructive cancer. So rent with grief and anxiety, work, she said, was the only thing that grounded her.

Then there is one therapist's account of a 13-year marriage to a Vietnam veteran suffering PTSD. Mary Hanson Carter's (2002) husband carried the macabre images of comrades killed, miscalculations that may have contributed to some of those losses, bodies burnt and heaped in a shamble of body parts for disposal. The thousand-mile stare that began on the killing fields and in the jungles invaded the marriage and sucked the life out of it. A therapist and an optimist inclined to "finesse a decent outcome from a lousy hand," Carter comes to a stark realization that she has become so consumed by his reality ... so mastered by her empathic identification with her husband, that she has no nightmares of her own – only his (p. 246).

She saves herself by doing what spouses and therapists must sometimes do—strike a distance; she and her husband divorced. In the end she was left with the humility that comes when the battle is lost despite one's best effort:

> I am just another mortal struggling to make sense of contextless factoids that erupt out of the past, struggling to make them mean something, knowing that in the end that you play the hand you are dealt and wrestle with meaning in the darkness before dawn.
>
> (p. 246)

Though she does not discuss the effects of this unhappiness on her work with patients we can imagine that those effects were there.

In the face of irreparable loss of function, status or death, Elizabeth Kübler-Ross' (1969) stages of grieving are usually experienced. In Jozefowski's (1999) discussion of this process, based on her research with a number of survivors of traumatic loss, she acknowledges how disruptive, though necessary, the grieving process is. During the first, or impact, phase, shock and denial are intense. One feels violently torn from one's "assumptive world," that is, from the fundamental sense of security enabled by the rules and beliefs to which we subscribe to ensure constancy and safety. So massive is the rupture that we become emotionally numb, fall into a state of disbelief and disorientation. We can feel alienated from others, ourselves and life in general. During the next phase, the chaos phase, when the numbness wears off, vulnerability to damaging emotional and physical repercussions often results. A feeling of powerlessness, anxiety and fear, anger, guilt, depression can crescendo into disturbed perceptions, inordinate behavior and a pervasive sense of disequilibrium (pp. 57–67). When it is the analyst who is overtaken by this, there may be an added complexity, which is the erroneous belief that because of our training and professional experience we ought to be able to handle such challenges flawlessly. The shame associated with not being able to do so can make matters worse.

Recovery from traumatic loss, according to Jozefowski, requires spiritual alchemy. That is, "creating meaning from the death of their loved ones and at the same time honoring their lives" (p. 67). This is achieved by:

> Creat(ing) something tangibly beneficial for others from the loved one's death (organ donation and financial contribution); creat(ing) something symbolically beneficial for the intrapersonal self (for the expression of feelings about the deceased and to distinguish the transition of death); creating something altruistically beneficial from the transformed self to help others (presence through teaching and sharing).
>
> (pp. 68, 204)

Because of the nature of our work, analysts are in the unique position of being able to be instrumental in creating something beneficial to others. Having experienced the pain of loss, which in one way or another is at the root of all pathology, and having a sensitivity actualized and refined by the many dimensions of grief, the analyst can offer an attentive resonating presence, at times manifested without words. Transformed by suffering, the analyst is able to more precisely see and transcend the countertransferential issues, which formerly might have been obstacles to understanding, and provide interventions based on being in the moment. Perhaps the last frontier in the journey to full personal and professional maturation is in successfully confronting the prospect of our own personal losses.

I have had more than a few. Among the most challenging were the loss of my parents, especially my father, and the event that took place toward the end of the year, 2001. Several days after that Christmas, I was awakened in the dead of night by a sharp and crushing pain in my chest. The intensity of it was stunning. I immediately sat up, whereupon the pain abated only to resume when I again lay down. Sweating and fearful, I took several doses of aspirin and went off to the hospital. So began an odyssey of cardiovascular testing, as well as tests for gastro-intestinal anomalies, as I had also begun to experience a plethora of gastric symptoms. Though the tests all came back negative, I continued to experience discomfort in both areas. I forced myself to walk. And though I felt some small sense of achievement, I frequently had to stop due to the chest and arm pain. I was in regular contact with my doctor who made himself quite available during and after office hours. I lost a tremendous amount of weight, frequently vomited and could not easily sleep. My wife and children were worried. My own worry eventuated into full-scale panic. I just could not lift myself from the agony I was in the grips of. My doctors were unable to give me answers despite their experience, wisdom and technology. My wife, children, sister, friends and analysts, despite their support and encouragement, were unable to allay my fears. I knew something was seriously wrong and I felt alone and with no way to wrap my mind around what was happening to me. Anti-anxiety medication was prescribed, but I gave it up in three days. I was not going to allow myself to be lulled into a false tranquility without knowing what the problem was and what I could do about it.

My anxiety became so heightened that, though I continued to work, I began canceling appointments so I could get home. In between appointments I would gulp antacids and call my wife for reassurance. I could see that I was driving her crazy but could not stop. I had regressed. Though a 56-year-old man, I had become like a frightened child, obsessional and desperate for his mother's reassurance. There was a force in the room, a monster that I needed to be protected from. I remember in one conversation with my primary care physician saying, "I cannot do this alone ... I feel like I am at the threshold of the door but I cannot get through." I went into a full blown anxious depression. Thoughts of the relief that death would bring frightened me further. This was startling for family members who had always seen me as "a rock." On top of everything else, I was mortified that with all of my education, training and clinical skill, I could not raise myself; I was just like everyone else.

Though never very far from it, I returned to my faith and to prayer, which is so essential within it. Raised a Roman Catholic by my devout family, I was taught to believe that there was an interested God and he did answer prayers. My grandfather on my father's side was actually in the seminary as a boy in Italy at the turn of the twentieth century. My mother's mother was from a devout French Canadian family; two of her sisters became missionary nuns in the Order of St. Ann. Growing up I always knew I was in somebody's prayers, and I prayed for many. My dedication as a young child to Mary, also my mother's name, was noteworthy. I remember feeling that it was she who had heard the desperate prayers of the seven-year-old boy who was afraid that his parent's marital discord would result in their leaving one another. It was to her plastic statue that glowed in the dark that I prayed for my cousin Richard's recovery from an accidental shotgun wound to the chest. My parents stayed together and Richard did recover. I felt heard. Though I went to a parochial school my zeal diminished considerably and was barely alive as I entered early adulthood. However, I never stopped praying. Especially in tough times, and it always seemed to help. It was natural then for me to turn again to what had given me hope as a child. And I did not, nor do I now, find that belief contrary to my scientific inclinations. There is a lot that we do not know, despite the obvious.

As the summer proceeded, my gastric symptoms appeared to diminish; it was determined that I had Acid Reflux and began treatment for that. However, I was still not feeling well. Toward the end of a long series of medical tests, I had urged my primary care physician to schedule a nuclear stress test, which he did. I had early on had a standard stress test, which was negative. But I felt the symptoms in my chest and shoulders had to be cardiac in nature. A month passed and my gastric symptoms seemed to lessen. I wondered whether I should follow through with the nuclear stress test. I did so upon my wife's urging. It was fortunate that I did, and it is to her that I owe a debt of gratitude. A 90 percent blockage was found in the left anterior coronary artery. This is known as the widow maker by cardiologists, as heart attacks that occur in this region are usually fatal.

Two adjoining coronary stents were inserted in early December, almost a year after my symptoms first began. And so commenced my recovery. I was emotionally and physically worn out from the harrowing year I had had. And though depressed, I was also somewhat encouraged. I finally knew what was wrong and it had been fixed. More than this, however, with the guidance of coronary rehabilitation specialists, I knew that I could improve my cardiovascular system to an even better level than before. I became motivated.

I attended to a heart-healthy diet, regular exercise at a gym, a more sensible scheduling of appointments, better management of the inevitable stresses, and rest. My family supported me in very tangible, as well as emotional, ways. Eleven years later my coronary health and lifestyle is better than when I was much younger.

My memory of that time nearly a dozen years ago was that I did not disclose to my patients that I was ill, or the nature of that illness. That may have been for several reasons. First, I did not know the exact nature of that illness for nine months, after six of which I began to feel a bit better. For a while, I was under the impression that my problem was gastric and treatable, which treatable eventually it was. Nevertheless, my anxiety was appreciable and I am sure my ability for "reverie, holding, mirroring, role responsiveness … all functions that emphasize the substantial relational-participatory value of the analyst" must have been diminished (Torrigiani & Marzi, 2005, p. 1375). I did, however, without reservation talk about my distress with family members, friends and colleagues, as well as in my analysis and supervision. I felt like I was always talking about it, and though my anxiety was unremitting, the need to bring this issue up in sessions with my patients seemed to be precluded. In fact, I think I experienced those sessions as a respite; I was doing what I had always done to bind anxiety—work. And when I was working, I felt a sense of normalcy, if only briefly. Listening to the trials, tribulations and suffering of others was distracting and took some of the edge off my own worry. Nevertheless, I think now, with the benefit of hindsight, in that situation I would be more acute in my perception of indications in the transference of referents and more ready to bring appropriate discussion to bear.

I think I was also motivated at the time by a commitment to not intrude upon the experience of my patients. If they were aware of my illness, they did not inquire, except for one person. To his inquiry, I simply said that I was "alright." Perhaps, they were in unconscious collusion with my effort to contain the desperate gravity of the situation, joining me in a defense that I then needed. Had I been more transparent, it might have been, as Silver (2001) suggested, that certain of my patients might have "looked after" me in ways that could even have been treatment-enhancing for them and beneficial for us both. And it is true, and I felt it as Silver described it, that "illness makes the analyst no longer simply the observer of life's shifting patterns but an integral part, an emotional player, in clinical work ... different, lonely, in an individual struggle for survival," (p. 53) and consequently, there may be a benefit to judicious disclosure.

Fajardo (2001) certainly has no doubts about the utility of doing so. She made deliberate disclosure to most of her patients when she became ill. Her rationale was, as she stated: "my anxiety was palpable and disruptive, at least to me, and probably for each of them ... so I judged disclosure to be inescapable." She adds that:

> the patient's awareness of and response to the analyst's inner states will enable the analyst to both attend to the patient's needs in the collaborative relatedness with the analyst and hear references to the illness as metaphor and as the basis for transference relatedness.
>
> (p. 584)

That said, opinions vary and "how, when and what to tell a patient is acknowledged by Arlow and others as a difficult matter of technique ... determined by conscious and unconscious motives, reflecting defensive and instinctual needs" (Usher, 2005, p. 364). Usher refers to Dewald's caution about using interventions to fulfill a sense of having been missed, once the analyst returns to work, as well as "guilt and shame" regarding having become ill, and working nevertheless. Usher cites also the relief Abend experienced in not telling analysands about his illness, "rationalizing that when an analyst does disclose, he is inviting patients to be caring and sympathetic," thus precluding the experience and expression of anger out of consideration for the analyst (p. 365).

Dewald (1982) recognized the risk of contaminating the transference by the analyst saying too much on the one hand, and "overburdening the patient's adaptive capacity" by saying too little on the other hand. He advised that the analyst, to the best of his abilities, should:

> explore the full gamut of patients' responses, affects, and associations to the illness, and to do this in the face of countertransference temptations either defensively to promote premature closure and evasion of more threatening affects, or to use the experience for exhibitionistic, masochistic, narcissistic or other neurotic satisfactions.
>
> (p. 361)

Agreeing with Dewald regarding the complexity of the countertransference reactions in times of illness, Sandor Abend (1982) is, however, not a proponent of the analyst revealing factual information about his/her illness. Abend's position is based on his conviction that "what is real for every patient is what the patient observes, feels, thinks, wishes, fears, wonders about, and decides by means of a mental apparatus of which the unconscious component is invariably a significant part" (p. 368). Moreover, he questions those who propose that analysts are even capable of deciding to whom and when to disclose, saying, "At no other time is the analyst's judgment about this technical problem less likely to be objective and reliable" (p. 370). In fact, during his own illness Abend chose not to reveal. This is a position supported by Van Dam (1987), who cautioned about the inclination to act on countertransference when in a regressed state, asserting "we must suspect ourselves when we make revelations to our patients" (p. 654).

Nor is Rita Clark (1995) an advocate for the analyst disclosing the fact of illness to his/her patients. In her own case she cited "a well-entrenched ego ideal of avoiding self-disclosure to patients" (p. 146). She did, however, urge that, when seriously ill, the analyst should engage the services of a neutral analytic consultant, the equivalent of the Pope's confessor, to help maintain clinical and personal perspective.

My need for control was, in all likelihood, at play in my not disclosing. To admit the precariousness of my situation would entail acknowledging a vulnerability that at that time in my life was contrary to my view of what my professional demeanor should be. And though I think differently of it now, it would also have been contrary to my view of myself as a man. I had always been the caretaker, the "rock," particularly to my parents. As such, I had always been reluctant to seek help, although many people helped me in my life.

In line with this, there was in my case a definite shame in becoming ill. At 56 years of age, none of my colleagues, against whom I measured myself, seemed to be vulnerable in the way I had become—although this would change. Since that time I have watched as several colleagues have become ill. Two are very vivacious women who heroically returned to work after suffering heart attacks. Their intellectual acumen and professional dedication intact, they nevertheless were noticeably more subdued in their demeanor. One to my knowledge did not reveal her condition.

My own analyst was to become quite ill with a gastric blockage, which eventuated into a fatal cancer three years after I had gone through my ordeal. She was the charismatic president of the analytic school at which I was a faculty member; most of her patients were faculty members and advanced students, and everyone knew she was ill. I think, though this impression may well not be accurate, that we were all in denial—or maybe it was just me—for a long time as to the seriousness of her illness, as she herself may have been.

Irrepressible, she continued not only her individual and group analyses, but the many activities she was involved in administratively and with all of her usual gregariousness. Nor did her physical attractiveness seem compromised. Also during this time, several colleagues and I accompanied her to Scotland for a meeting of an international forensic society. We drank a Scotch or two and avoided the haggis. Though slightly tired, she seemed jovial enough. At one point, however, while walking together with my son, a student at the school who had come with us, he had asked her a question regarding how one tempers ambition and still enjoys life. She paused and then replied, "Well, your father and I know we are going to die." I remember feeling disheartened by her admission.

In analytic sessions with her subsequently, though she seemed fatigued, I felt she was attentive. She commented after one episode in which she was hospitalized that she had been so cold when the ambulance came for her that she was bundled in a number of blankets. She said that she was tired but comfortable such that in that moment she felt that it would be okay if she simply closed her eyes and died.

In another session when I had expressed how much she had meant to me and she had spoken about the need to carry on, she expressed the belief that there was only sleep after life ends. She added, I think knowing of my own religious sentiment that I could pray for her. That I believe was for my benefit. That is, something that would ease my anticipated grief over the loss of her—or so I like to think of it. Though I did not feel overwhelmed by it, nor that her interest in me either personally or clinically seriously altered, nor my own need to talk diminished, death was clearly in the room at that point.

As a way of summing up, the most sensible course regarding the issue of disclosure seems to me to lie in Torrigiani and Marzi's (2005) prescription:

> The analyst's illness can have innumerable and unique consequences for analysis... . It seems worthwhile emphasizing once again that analysis must be adapted and shaped on a case by case basis, according to the individual patient, the stage and circumstance of the analysis, and of course the seriousness of the analyst's illness itself, without trying to follow preset rules (whether they involve an impossible-to-achieve total neutrality, or its "backlash" opposite), but by exploiting the analyst's talent, training, personal resources and capacity for recovery, although they may at times be tested to their limit.
>
> (p. 1386)

What does all of this mean in terms of emotional presence? It is not always easy for the analyst to achieve and maintain emotional presence with patients when he or she is beset with events that distract and deplete internal resources. The challenge of illness and/or loss can be at times traumatic. The inclination can be to withdraw, to attempt to hide distress which is nevertheless often all too apparent to our patients. Conversely, we may feel compelled to disclose, to a greater or lesser degree. Participants at the 30th Annual Boston Graduate School for Psychoanalytic Studies Summer Conference (2014) were divided on this. The prevailing sentiment was as one participant stated:

> I believe it depends on the type of interaction/relationship the patient has with the analyst. I think truth is a healing power and opens the door to

deeper relations. It can be healing on a whole new level. I think the therapist has to decide when and with whom. They have to want to be open, be able to be present in the situation.

The sense of isolation and aloneness that decline, illness and loss evoke can in the darkness of night catapult us into annihilation anxiety. Those night terrors can linger into the day. It is important to afford ourselves the same advantage that we give our patients—the opportunity to talk about it. This should be done with those we love and who love us, our colleagues, or analyst and supervisors. And, if we are so inclined, with our higher power.

It is important also to realize, to the extent that we are able to do so, that suffering can bring heightened sensitivity, enlightenment and transcendence. Anyone who has lost someone loved is acutely aware of the preciousness of life, the fragility of relationships and the need to protect and nurture. The analyst who has this appreciation approaches the work of analysis much more attuned to the suffering of others and the flux of the life force and its opposite in the mind of the individual and in the relationships in which people engage. Emotional presence is more than technique guided by theory. It is the shared moment unencumbered by agenda, unfettered by expectation and ambition. This freeing of oneself is the innovation, which enables the analyst to achieve true encounter. Humbled by decline, illness and loss, we become more fully able to experience the other on the journey to authentic human relatedness. This enhanced capacity for empathy enables the existential transcendent encounter of one person with another, the I–Thou moment (Buber, 1958) and "in each becoming that is present to us we look toward the fringe of the eternal Thou" (p. 6). It is in this, I believe, that both analyst and patient emerge from the darkness of night.

This chapter was originally published in 2014 in *Modern Analysis*, 39, 166–185.

References

Abend, S. M. (1982). Serious illness in the analyst: Countertransference considerations. *Journal of the American Psychoanalytic Association*, 30, 365–379.

Bolgar, H. (2002). When the glass is full. *Psychoanalytic Inquiry*, 22, 640–650.

Boston Graduate School for Psychoanalytic Studies Summer Conference (2014). *Analyst transparency during times of illness and demise*. Wellfleet, MA.

Buber, M. (1958). *I and thou*. New York: Scribner.

Carter, M. (2002). Through the woods darkly. In J. Heriot & E. Polinger (Eds.), *The use of personal narratives in the helping professions: A teaching casebook* (pp. 239–246). New York: The Haworth Social Work Practice Press.

Chasen, B. (2009). Death of a psychoanalyst's child. In B. Gerson (Ed.), *The therapist as a person* (pp. 3–20). New York: Routledge.

Clark, R. W. (1995). The Pope's confessor: A metaphor relating to illness in the analyst. *Journal of the American Psychoanalytic Association*, 43, 37–149.

Colson, D. (1995). An analyst's multiple losses: Countertransference and other reactions. *Contemporary Psychoanalysis*, 31, 1–16.

Dewald, P. A. (1982). Serious illness in the analyst: Transference, countertransference, and reality responses. *Journal of the American Psychoanalytic Association*, 30, 347–363.

Eissler, K. (1993). On possible effects of aging on the practice of psychoanalysis: An essay. *Psychoanalytic Inquiry*, 13, 316–332.

Fajardo, B. (2001). Life-threatening illness in the analyst. *Journal of the American Psychoanalytic Association*, 49, 569–586.

Jozefowski, J. (1999). *The phoenix phenomenon: Rising from the ashes of grief*. Northvale, NJ: Jason Aronson, Inc.

Kübler-Ross, E. (1969). *On death and dying*. Toronto: McMillan.

Mendelson, E. (2009). More human than otherwise: Working through a time of preoccupation and mourning. In B. Gerson (Ed.), *The therapist as a person* (pp. 21–40). New York: Routledge.

Shapiro, R. (1985). A case study: The terminal illness and death of the analyst's mother – its effects on her treatment of a severely regressed patient. *Modern Psychoanalysis*, 10, 31–46.

Silver, A. (2001). Facing mortality while treating patients: A plea for a measure of authenticity. *The Journal of the American Academy of Psychoanalysis and Dynamic Psychiatry*, 29, 43–56.

Torrigiani, M., & Marzi, A. (2005). When the analyst is physically ill: Vicissitudes in the analytic relationship. *The International Journal of Psychoanalysis*, 86, 1373–1389.

Usher, S. (2005). Illness in the analyst: Implications for the treatment relationship. *Canadian Journal of Psychoanalysis*, 13, 363–368.

Van Dam, H. (1987). Countertransference during the analyst's brief illness. *Journal of the American Psychoanalytic Association*, 35, 647–655.

Chapter 14

Conclusion

John Madonna

The relational intersubjective and modern psychoanalytic theories of treatment, though different in their consideration of the influence of the drives and the use of transparency in treatment intervention, share the belief in the power of emotional presence, mutually attained, as a core necessity for cure. Moreover, the psychic health of the analyst as well as that of the patient is advanced when this effort is successful. Achieving emotional presence as the cases presented illustrate is often a complex, arduous, and perilous undertaking. The paranoid man about whom I wrote in Chapter 6 in which I became encapsulated in what felt like a deathly psychic chrysalis is illustrative.

Emotional presence is attained in ways that are multidimensional. It begins by the analyst making good initial connection, connection that responds to the maturational level that the patient has reached. It is a contact that pays attention to the degree of object relatedness the patient is capable of, providing just enough contact in the form of questions, empathic communication, including mirroring and joining comments, as well as a calibrated and judicious silence. Done well enough, the patient experiences the therapeutic environment as controlled and stimulus safe.

Once under way the analyst needs to study the form and flow of the transference, countertransference, and countertransference resistance learning as he goes; what the experience of the person has been, and is, in the perpetration of dysfunction and unhappiness. By identifying, holding, and metabolizing in constructive ways his own treatment destructive inclinations, the analyst becomes more receptive to the inner world of the patient. This inner world becomes known through the verbal report of the patient, and behavioral enactments that reflect transferential phenomena. Feelings, sometimes incongruous, which the analyst has, unsought thoughts, errant behavior, images, and dreams occurring through processes of projection and projective identification which the analyst experiences all have the potential to inform the analyst at conscious and unconscious levels.

Laquercia's discussion in Chapter 5 of symbolic imagery as an aspect of unverbalized communication emerging from the vast unconscious terrain of "unformulated experience" is an example of the salience of seemingly irrelevant unsought thoughts/images and how they can reflect a shared psychic experience which leads to memory, lost emotion, and progressive communication.

In a state of "depersonalized ... poised attention" while with a very "gentle" patient, Laquercia finds himself with the image of a rifle in mind, which elaborates into many such thoughts. Perplexed, and after pondering this for some time, Laquercia takes the risk to ask the patient if he knows of any reason why he should be thinking of a gun. The introduction of this new material into the session, a form of calculated transparency, results in an emotional response by the patient who says he is in a state of dread. He is about to visit a brother whom he has not seen in a long time. This brother had thrown him out of a car when they were children and Laquercia's patient was seriously injured, a fact not previously discussed in the analysis. This revelation resulted in the analyst becoming "awake and connected" to his patient "in a keen way."

As the analyst repeatedly accepts and holds these communications, the construction of shared psychic states develops. Differentiation ultimately occurs as the patient develops a felt confidence in the holding capacity of the treatment situation. The movement into object relationships is facilitated and enhanced by the recognition of the myriad of feelings the patient comes to express.

Judiciously guided by theory without succumbing to the tyranny of rigidly applied technique, the analyst is free to conceptualize and implement interventions in the context of the mutually constructed moment in ways that work rather than in ways that are dogmatically prescribed. In the context of this, the analyst may choose to answer questions that seem at first to be unrelated as I did in Chapter 1 with the young woman who was struggling for a sense of connection. Seeing a patient's penchant for irony, the analyst may utilize humor to foster a relaxation of defense and emotional communion. Or the analyst may simply follow the lead of the patient's talk about innocuous, seemingly irrelevant subjects. In more allowable reflective moments, the analyst may also wonder out loud about the internal experience he is having while with the patient. At those times when the analyst comes into focus as a target of the patient's rage, the analyst may respond with a communication which conveys sincerely felt emotion guided by the patient's induction and the analyst's understanding of the dynamics at play. On other occasions when the patient directs his hostility inwardly, the analyst resorts to joining and mirroring interventions whose aim is to redirect hostility. In Chapter 7, it was my ability to accept the patient's hostility and even be as crude as she was, which was restitutive. She was not alone in the world as a vicious person; I was there too and this felt good to her. As did her joy in attacking me rather than herself.

The analyst may find himself locked or mesmerized in a countertransference resistance which when fathomed provides a feeling, sensation, or insight which shared, enables progressive communication and the visceralness of authentic encounter. This is in keeping with the intersubjectivist notion of transparency and of therapeutic action facilitated by emotional presence in the form of empathy. Structural transformation takes place as the "analysis thus introduces a new other into the patient's experience, an other unique in the capacity to invoke past images and yet also to demonstrate an essential difference from these early points of reference" (Atwood & Stolorow, 2014, pp. 48–49). And of vital importance, the "analyst's newness as an other is insured by the constancy of his or her observational stance – the dedication to the use of introspection and empathy to gain and provide understanding of the meaning of the patient's experiences." The analyst through this "crystallizes in the patient's awareness as a transitional empathic presence" (p. 49), which leads, through identification, to the capacity in the patient for empathic self-observation, what Kohut (1984) referred to as transmuting identifications and the mutative power of empathy.

Gilhooley's discussion of the third in Chapter 3 well conveys this. His stirred emotion regarding his father's suicide many years previous prompted Gilhooley to continually reach out to his patient, Frank, who upon the death of his son had become suicidal. Gilhooley was filled with the induction of his patient's feeling, as "isolated, lost, disoriented and frightened as he was; completely adrift with no shore in sight."

"I was angry with Frank. I was angry with him filling me with these awful feelings of desperation, for his part in spilling out this shadow from my past and forcing me to see his humiliating shape of myself."

Provoked by Frank's induction and his countertransferential response, Gilhooley encountered his patient with an emotional communication, transparently delivered. He told Frank that he "could not stand this." The discussion that was able to then ensue revealed the mutual emotional dependency they shared as a result of the "magnetism of loss."

What ultimately occurred was the same but separately dreamed dream of waking up dead. This seemed to reflect the state of emotional symbiosis they had attained, a one-mind state, a "co-created third" realm of experience. This sharing enabled Gilhooley's patient to bear the fragmenting emotions, which were prompting his suicidal impulses. That man was able to transform that grief into a story of redemption, a dead son transfigured, a father and an analyst emotionally resonant and transcendent.

The analyst may also find himself, as did Jarreau in Chapter 8, in his discussion about intuiting the unknown, struggling with the inclination to have meaning, memory, or desire in attempting to defend oneself against the emotional pressures affected by the patient. That is, listening with the unconscious mind. In the two cases he mentions, it was only after he was able to let himself have the feeling that things were falling apart and sit quietly in the face of it that he was able to intuit an understanding of the feelings that his patients were struggling with, as he was himself feeling those feelings. In one case it was the fear of falling asleep signaling the patient's absence of emotion, in the other the fear of loss of the case signaling the patient's fear of loss of connection. His ability to remain quiet and to have faith in the eventual return of psychic equilibrium enabled the patients to also attain composure and understanding in the face of the emotional turbulence that was experienced.

Modern analysts, less concerned with the salience of the object, emphasize the recognition of the struggle of the drives as apparent in the transference and in life, and enabling their appropriate expression ultimately through language. Eschewing interpretation as a primary tool for intervention early in treatment, they also caution against employing a narrative approach, due to its emphasis on consciousness in attempting to create meaning. Meadow (2005) attributes psychic change to bearing in mind that we are "biological creatures responding to an environment with a unique balance between tension reducing and the conservative life seeking drive" (p. 89). She adds that "defining the content of each individual's unconscious in its own particular uniqueness" in how the patient presents himself in the session is the fundamental aim of modern analysis. The patient may be moved from "pathological defenses as in projection and denial" by the analyst:

> accepting the patient's perception of his situation, using emotional induction to enter the patient's fantasy, the patient who feels trapped will learn that the pain comes from inside. When these feelings are structured in language in the presence of the analyst, more sophisticated fantasies develop out of the creative processes within the patient.
>
> (pp. 95–96)

In these closely related orientations the acceptance of the state of the other, the ability to allow without attempting to change—the sitting quietly at the gate, the receptiveness to communication when it comes regardless of the form, the ability to discern the patient within ourselves in the myriad of ways that occurs, the sensitive attunement to the feelings—the pain and pleasures of it all, the capacity to respond in ways which are relevant, facilitative, and emotionally authentic (be it with the transparent directness or with the poignancy of joining and mirroring emotion) are what create the condition for cure. They also create the optimal conditions for learning in other important settings: training institutes, supervisory contexts, and academic classrooms at all levels.

We move then through the experience with patients, students, and those we supervise and train, guided and steadied by our theoretical compasses, attending to the emotional residues in their various forms and disguises that signify the possibility for a coming together, for emotional presence in the moment. Noting the resistances emanating from the other and from within ourselves, we move, at times slouchingly, toward what is an existential encounter, Martin Buber's (1958) I–Thou moment which transcends theory and technique, the capacity for which is the ultimate reflection of learning and cure. This is the truly human encounter that releases and enhances, taking us further, as Sartre (1981) says, beyond the irreducible realities.

References

Atwood, G. E., & Stolorow, R. D. (2014). *Structures of subjectivity: Explorations in psychoanalytic phenomenology and contextualism*. New York: Routledge.

Buber, M. (1958). *I and thou*. New York: Charles Scribner's Sons.

Kohut, H. (1984). *How does analysis cure?* Chicago, IL: The University of Chicago Press.

Meadow, P. (2005). *The new psychoanalysis*. Lanham, MD: Rowman & Littlefield Publishers, Inc.

Sartre, J. P. (1981). *Existential psychoanalysis*. New York: The Philosophical Library, Inc.

Index

Abend, Sandor 185–6
accidental injury 155–6
active technique 65
Adler, Gerald 21–4, 26, 28–33, 32, 39, 40, 43, 45, 102; borderline patients described by 22; countertransference defined by 21–2, 25; on holding relationship 30–1; on stalemates in therapy 29–30
aggression 86, 93, 127; frustration 99–100, 103; and students 165–7
aging process 175, 177–80
Aisenstein, M. 158
alcohol abuse 16
aloneness 22, 23
analyst: and aging process 175, 177–80; attacks on/anger towards 53, 66–7, 72, 136; attitude of 9; death and 50, 51–2, 54–5, 56, 59; defenses of 34, 49, 58, 59–60; ego identity of 25, 26–7; emotional impact of sessions on 109; family of 182, 183, 184; fantasies of 27–8, 31, 44; fear of change of 30; fees of 67, 69, 70–1, 72, 89–90; gaze of 62–3, 64, 65; illness of *see* illness, of analyst; and intuition 109, 111–12, 114; as parent 3, 4–5, 28, 33, 34, 37, 43, 77; pathology of 36; as patient 24, 28, 31, 32–3, 38–9, 40, 102; patient as 40; personal problems of 140; prohibitions issued by 64–5; self-awareness of 7; true self of 34–5; unconscious of *see* unconscious, analyst's
analyst–patient relationship: analyst's dependency in 53–4; anger in *see* anger/rage; and co-construction 13, 15, 65; and contact function 6, 9, 84,
126, 130, 157; and countertransference *see* countertransference; and frequency of therapy sessions 41–3; as holding relationship 9, 22, 23, 28, 29, 30; humor in 18; infantile features of 25, 26; and intersubjectivity 11–13, 15; love in 9–11; as marriage 105, 106; with paranoid patient 84–7; and poised attention *see* poised attention; and projective identification *see* projective identification; resistance in *see* resistance; and self-disclosure of analyst 12–15, 16–17; and sexual attraction 41–2; and sexual encounters 4; and sitting-up/couch sessions 41–2, 43; symbiosis in 38–9, 54, 56–7, 58, 59
analytic hour 144, 146, 148, 149, 150, 157
anger/rage 14, 22, 35, 39, 49–50, 53, 91, 97, 115–16, 160; of analysts 24, 25, 26–8, 68, 80–1, 102, 192; in dreams 80–1; and projective identification 35
anxiety 10, 15, 25, 28, 41, 62, 65; and illness/loss 63, 182–3, 188; as signal affect 164
apologies: by analyst 13, 14; by patient 16
Aron, Lewis 12–13, 14–15
astronaut image 79, 80
Atwood, G. E. 192
authority, analyst as 4
autistic defense 34, 127

Balint, Michael 139, 144
Benjamin, Jessica 162–3
Bernfeld, S. 141
Bernstein, J. 94, 102